MIMESIS
INTERNATIONAL

PHILOSOPHY

n. 28

Snježana Prijić-Samaržija

DEMOCRACY AND TRUTH

The Conflict Between Political and Epistemic Virtues

This book is published with the subsidy of University of Rijeka, UNIRI project NO. 13.04.1.3.06

www.mimesisinternational.com
E-mail: info@mimesisinternational.com

Isbn: 9788869771255
Book series: *Philosophy*, n. 28

P.I. C.F. 02419370305

TABLE OF CONTENTS

To Hana

INTRODUCTION

The most violent element in society is ignorance.[1] Recognition of the fact that no kind of societal violence can be held acceptable is a sentiment shared by all remotely sensible policies and theories. This awareness usually pertains to physical, psychological and verbal violence, as well as to other behaviours that can prove detrimental to individuals or to society at large. Yet, while violence is consistently faced with undivided condemnation, the ignorance from which it stems has remained exempt from any kind of direct scientific scrutiny. Reliance on stereotypes and prejudices, evident disregard for rational and responsible decision-making – be it on an individual, collective or institutional levels – and an obvious lack of knowledge/awareness

1 This was stated by Emma Goldman, a political activist and writer with whom I share many views, but who – in the virtue of her more radically anarchist beliefs – I am generally more inclined to disagree with. However, no one has ever come close to Emma Goldman's distinct and unambiguous articulation of what I consider to be the essence of this book. While ignorance is often criticized as a theoretical and academic deficit, and usually as the failure of individuals, it is seldom recognized as a serious, real-world social issue. It is disregarded as a mere lack of some old-fashioned virtue (such as the concept of *old knowledge*) and consciously ignored as an unfortunate, but inevitable component of realistic social circumstances. What is more, ignorance is often justified as socially inevitable or defended by dubious calls for personal opinions. Even when declaratively promoting epistemic virtues, many fail or refuse to acknowledge the real consequences of ignorance, instead choosing to struggle for ethical and political values. I am in no way trying to dismiss the importance of forming fair communities on ethical and political bases or question each person's freedom to think for themselves, nor am I attempting to oppose the stance that epistemic deficits can often stem from unjust social positions (a view further elaborated in the book). However, choosing to ignore the importance of knowledge in its diverse manifestations (from curiosity, intellectual responsibility, conscientiousness, caution and courage to truth, problem solving capacities, understanding and openness) and thus dismiss any epistemic assessment of social entities is an equally grave theoretical (epistemic, philosophical-political) and social deficit.

about the importance of a pluralistic, free, participatory, tolerant and inclusive society are often the most violent element of society.

Contemporary discussions about democracy exhibit a growing awareness about the necessity of justifying it – in addition to traditional political justification –from an epistemological perspective, on the basis of its potential to produce epistemically valuable decisions. Recent debates about the social desirability of particular social practices and institutions, increasingly present in social epistemology, philosophy of politics and philosophy of science, have proven eager to treat their epistemic features and contributions as inherently valuable – akin to the value ascribed to ethical and just social practices and institutions.

As an analysis of the epistemic properties of the democratic system or the potential of democratic deliberation to produce epistemically valuable decisions, this book can be considered pertinent to such an expansionist approach to social epistemology. My general aim is to justify the application of epistemology to real situations by exemplifying how such topics both pertain to and directly contribute to improving societal epistemic processes and the assessments of socially held beliefs. As I repeatedly emphasize throughout the book, social epistemology – given that it is concerned with the social aspect of knowing – is unprecedentedly connected to epistemic situations in the real world. It can therefore also be referred to as applied epistemology or real-world epistemology.

Keeping this in mind, we ought to admit that social epistemology (in its expansionist version) departs from traditional epistemological approaches that rarely tackled practical real world issues, instead focusing on the acquisition of knowledge in extremely idealized circumstances. Individual epistemic agents were imagined as persons of almost unlimited logical capacities, devoid of any constrains to their cognitive resources. Traditional epistemology usually implicitly presupposed that truth and rationality are entirely unrelated to social power dynamics or the social and political identities of knowers – a view that has come under fire since the advent of new trends in social epistemology. The epistemic subject was perceived as an asocial being, and socio-political circumstances as irrelevant to epistemic inquiries. Even when topics happened to pertain to other knowers, such as in debates about scientific practices or conversational norms of argumentation, they were articulated in a manner that preserved the existing *status quo* of epistemological debates. One could, at best, expect a preservative approach to (social) epistemology. And while traditional epistemology has more or less consciously refused to explicitly examine the interpersonal character and social aspects of cognition, movements such as postmodernism, sociology of knowledge and cultural studies have used these assumptions as the foundation of their theories and, consequentially, their popularity in continuously expanding intellectual circles. Particularly popular was their disregard for abstract conceptual and normative discussions about cognition in favour of theories that portrayed the relationships between power and identity as the underlying determinants of the formation of beliefs, thus obviously unsuitable for any attempt of objective evaluation.

In addition to my basic intention to emphasize the importance of epistemically assessing social practices, institutions and systems, this book prominently features the key dilemma between democracy and truth – the alleged tension between democracy as a system that aims to maximally secure ethical or political values, and truth as the central epistemic value. Although I use the notion of 'truth' as a generic epistemic value for the sake of simplicity, I actually endorse a far more comprehensive understanding of epistemic quality and value that encompasses a broad range of possible epistemic achievements – ranging from successfully resolving problems and exhibiting epistemic responsibility to ensuring empirical adequacy and striving for understanding, and like. The most recent expansion of epistemology related to the epistemic evaluation of social practices and institutions urged philosophers to reconsider the relationship between epistemic and political virtues. Just like epistemic sub-optimality can be motivated by politically justified initiatives (deliberative democracy, affirmative action programs) political injustice can be generated by the epistemic regard for truth (epistemic paternalism, epistocracy). Although much has been said about instances of injustice caused by epistemic reasons, epistemic errors stemming from the desire to be fair have remained largely undiscussed in spite of their obvious philosophical pertinence. Given the relentless tension between democratic and epistemic values, it seems necessary to investigate a hybrid platform of evaluation wherein assessments are motivated by the desire to harmonize epistemic and political virtues: a social practice, process or procedure should only be justified if it simultaneously satisfies political requirements and produces beliefs/judgments/decisions of high epistemic quality. I will argue in favour of a hybrid perspective – a concept particularly essential for the project of applied epistemology – that is reluctant to ignore epistemic assessments in favour of the political and instead caters to both. However, this introductory defence of a hybrid perspective cannot automatically provide a satisfactory formula for harmonizing epistemic and political virtues in particular circumstances of their conflict. It has been shown that situations of serious conflict – such as epistemic paternalism, expertism, epistemic justification of democracy or programs of affirmative action – are often resolved by sacrificing one value to the other, depending on whether the debate had taken place within the philosophy of politics or within epistemology. It is crucial to note that the hybrid perspective doesn't accept the reduction of epistemic values to the political (political instrumentalism characteristic of epistemic proceduralism) nor the reduction of the political to the epistemic virtues (epistemic instrumentalism inherent to veritism and reliability democracy).

I will attempt to show that the hybrid position's situational model – which is sensitive to the local and highly contextual properties of each situation – has the highest likelihood of producing evaluations equally respectful of both values. The point is that, for instance, we can neither decisively dismiss affirmative action and social practices that support fairness due to their epistemic questionability, nor automatically reject epistemic paternalism and the inclusion of experts in decision-making procedures because of their political opacity. On the contrary, the best available calibrating approach to such cases of 'negotiating' or 'trading' between values can be found in the Aristotelian epistemic virtue of *phronesis* – practical *knowledge* about what is good or bad for people.

We must remain aware of the situational and contextual nature of hybrid evaluations, as well as the inadequacy of ideal-theoretical approaches that neglect the non-unitary character of real-world situations and the usage of contextually sensitive epistemic standards. However, my defence of the hybrid model and its situationist version as best suited to real social dynamics still provides only a partial solution: I am merely arguing that it is comparatively more capable of resolving conflicts between epistemic and political virtues.

***

The first chapter, *Social epistemology*, is a certain introduction to social epistemology as a relatively new area of research that has recently witnessed a rapid surge of popularity. Whilst its legitimacy within the wider area of epistemology was initially met by a certain scepticism, social epistemology is now recognized as a fruitful expansion of traditional epistemological topics to new loci: groups, institutions, social practices and social systems. Although social epistemology, including the sub-discipline of collective epistemology, extends epistemological research far beyond the scope of traditional epistemology, it retains the essential presuppositions of traditional individual epistemology: the normative character of the discipline and the intrinsic and objective epistemic quality of doxastic states (regardless of whether this quality is defined as the feature of a proposition or as a virtue, whether it bears monist ties to truth or is understood as a broader plural value). This extension of traditional epistemology is congruent with the view that epistemology can and should be interdisciplinary and practically applicable. Its role is not exhausted in mere explanations and theoretical assessments of the beliefs held by individuals, groups, institutions, social practices and systems, but in active suggestions about their improvement.

In the second chapter, *Extended epistemology and hybrid virtue*, I register that epistemology has significantly expanded the initial scope its interests and topics. The first expansion, both the oldest and the most seldom questioned, encompassed discussions about cognitive processes such as perception, reasoning, memory, and so on, thus moving away from the traditional epistemic preoccupation with defining knowledge and providing a normative framework for assessing the justifiedness of beliefs. The second was related to a value shift that substituted the rigid monism of truth as the only real epistemic value with a pluralist account of values that can be considered an epistemic success or a guarantee of high epistemic quality – values such as, among many others, understanding, empirical adequacy and the reliable usage of available evidence. This type of expansion was most directly articulated in virtue epistemology and its efforts to shift the target of epistemic evaluations. Instead of evaluating the truth or justifiedness of a particular proposition, virtue epistemologists shift their focus to epistemic virtues – such as epistemic responsibility, courage, curiosity, impartiality, conscientiousness, and the like – exhibited by epistemic agents. The third expansion of epistemic topics pertained to the legitimization of social epistemology, the notion of the social situatedness of doxastic states and the substantial expansion of research onto social entities and practices. It is important to note that, although each mentioned expansion of epistemology had substantially broadened the traditional scope of research, they have still retained the traditional epistemological belief in the objective validity of epistemic values and virtues. The final extension of epistemology – one pertaining to the epistemic evaluation of social processes, practices and institutions – necessarily brought attention to the relationship between epistemic and political/ethical virtues. It was revealed as necessary to introduce a hybrid perspective or an assessment platform that would ground evaluations on attempts to harmonize epistemic and ethical/political virtues: a social practice or entity can and should be justified only if it fulfils ethical/political requirements while respecting or generating the epistemic quality of beliefs/judgments/decisions. However, the introduction of the hybrid perspective raised the issue of harmonizing epistemic and ethical/political criteria and virtues in circumstances of their divergence. I have tried to show that the situational model within the hybrid position – which is sensitive to the local and highly contextual properties of each situation – seems like the most promising method of generating evaluations equally respectful of both values.

In the third chapter, *Epistemic justification of democracy*, I start to develop my account of the hybrid approach as the most promising method of justifying (deliberative) democracy. I assumed that the epistemic justification of democracy is necessary for its final and comprehensive legitimacy. It is insufficient for a system to be merely ethically and politically justified as it must also be recognized as capable of generating epistemically high quality decisions. Likewise, I have assumed that deliberative democracy – given that it exhibits, along other democratic features, a heightened awareness of the importance of public participation and civic debates – is the best form of a democratic system. It was immediately evident that insistence on the epistemic justification of democracy introduced certain tensions into debates about justifying democracy. Although these tensions had originated from abstract principles, they soon manifested in realistic circumstances of having to choose between epistemic and democratic values. This finally articulated the dilemma between democracy and truth. Tensions derived from this conflict of values can, of course, be solved by arguing in favour of only one group of values and dismissing the other, as was often comfortably done by epistemologists and philosophers of politics. Instead of choosing to remain entrenched in either the epistemological or the ethical/political camp, I will opt for the hybrid perspective – a unified model that assess social systems by balancing both values. The extended domain of social epistemology provides us with conceptual tools and an excellent theoretical framework for giving a carefully deliberated answer to the dilemma between democracy and experts (truth).

In the fourth chapter, *Democracy and procedures: do democratic procedures insure epistemic quality?*, I begin to investigate epistemic proceduralism's – an essentially hybrid perspective – capacity to insure the epistemic justification of democracy. Epistemic proceduralists have definitely breathed new life into discussions about the epistemic justification of democracy by explicitly questioning the balance between epistemic and political justification. Since this debate was initiated in the domain of philosophy of politics, they contributed by boldly pointing out the insufficiencies of the existing discussions. However, both the strong and the moderate approach share the stance that standard epistemic values not only mustn't be given primacy when justifying democracy, but that they also can be legitimately sacrificed to democratic goals. In attempting to prove that a fair democratic procedure has an intrinsic epistemic value completely independent of the epistemic value of the final result – truthfulness/problem-solving capacity or like – pure epistemic proceduralism effectively reduced epistemic value to democratic fairness. Likewise, its moderate version was proven to be a certain epistemic dualism that postulates two independent intrinsic epistemic values – the value of truth and the epistemic value of democratic fairness. However, the exact intrinsic epistemic value of fair procedures –independent of the value of truth – was left highly ambiguous, as well as the relation between the epistemic and the political intrinsic values of democratic procedures. This chapter also begins our discussion about the role of experts in democratic societies, a staple problem of epistemological proceduralism closely bound to their rejection of the standard approach to epistemic justification and the significance of epistemic results. By rejecting truth as a criterion of epistemically justifying of democracy, they also reject any inclusion of experts in decision-making processes. I have tried to argue – in contrast to the proceduralist standpoint and within the situational hybrid perspective – that involving experts does not automatically give rise to anti-democratic epistocratic practices, and that it is possible to divide epistemic work in a manner that preserves both standard epistemic and ethical/political values.

In the fifth chapter, *Democracy and the epistemic value of consensus*, I discuss another hybrid approach that I baptised as consensualim. Consensualism is characterized by the stance that conciliation is a necessary precondition of any correct decision and that establishing consensus in public discussions among interested citizens is the best way of harmonizing epistemic values and the values of deliberative democracy. This approach differs from proceduralism because it acknowledges the independent epistemic value of the epistemic result, either in the form of the epistemic value of truth/correctness or its problem solving capacity. In this sense, consensualism is a more genuine attempt to devise a hybrid perspective that harmonizes epistemic and ethical/political values. While proceduralists reduce or sacrifice epistemic virtues to the ethical and political by refusing to acknowledge the epistemic value of decisions independent from fair procedures, consensualists clearly postulate the importance of the epistemic virtues of truth, correctness and problem-solving capacity. Nevertheless, they have still retained the proceduralists' declarative and permanent fear that any attempt to involve experts – as a possible epistemic requirement – necessarily undermines not only the consensus itself, but also the democratic aim. That is why consensualists exclusively seek the epistemic quality of decisions in the qualities of public debates, exchanges of reasons and civic conciliations. However, we have seen that any consensus attained in decision-making processes in our sub-ideal epistemic reality – which is far from the ideal of rational consensus in ideal conversational circumstances – simply cannot automatically generate epistemic quality in the virtue of a fair method. Methods of consensus and public debate inherent to deliberative democracy simply fail to justify epistemic optimism and instead give rise to unacceptable vices – such as epistemic conservatism, resistance to innovation, narrowness and conventionality – that cannot generate epistemically valuable decisions.

In the sixth and final chapter, *Reliability democracy and the role of experts in a democratic society*, I investigate the last hybrid approach to the epistemic justification of democracy, a stance which I am inclined to promote. Reliability democracy is a position wherein it is claimed that that institutions, social practices and systems are justified if they involve reliable procedures – methods or mechanisms that produce epistemically valuable beliefs and decisions. Reliability democracy is the stance that deliberative democracy, in order to be epistemically justified, must generate beliefs, judgments and decisions that are true, truth-sensitive or truth-conductive. Advocates of this approach argue that no inherent feature of democratic decision-making methods – regardless of whether we're speaking about majority vote or democratic deliberation – automatically guarantees the epistemic quality of beliefs and decisions. Should they aim to deserve their epistemic justifiedness, democratic procedures must include additional mechanisms for ensuring truthfulness. In other words, neither the mere fact of procedures or consensus nor the sheer inclusion of experts can guarantee epistemic quality. We need to develop reliable democratic mechanisms or truth-sensitive procedures. It has been shown that these reliable procedures presuppose the division of epistemic labour between citizens and experts: just like the establishment of a rational consensus, experts are an indispensable component of epistemically justified reliable democratic procedures. I then proceed to prove that the introduction of experts, despite of numerous previous suspicions, ensures higher epistemic quality without automatically entailing epistocracy. According to my opinion, this ensures a proper hybrid perspective – one wherein we have managed to epistemically justify democracy while fully preserving its ethical/political justification.

I conclude the book with the stance that the dilemma between democracy and truth is nothing but a false dilemma. Neither truth nor experts pose a threat to democracy. It is entirely possible to concurrently ensure both values and thus resolve the conflict between epistemic and ethical/political virtues. The false impression that a conflict actually does exist can be largely blamed on the traditional approach — while original discussions about the justification of democracy in philosophy of politics were blind to central epistemic values, epistemology neglected the fruitfulness of appraising social entities and practices from an epistemic perspective. Our solution assumes the hybrid approach to evaluating democracy (democratic institutions and belief/judgment/decision-making practices) borrowed from extended real-world social epistemology. This approach is unique in simultaneously evaluating social entities and practices from both perspectives. Values can be balanced and harmonized in a manner that does not entail the reduction or instrumentalization of one virtue in favour of the other, nor a merely declarative respect towards the other discipline. We must always remain aware of the situational and contextual nature of hybrid evaluations, as well as the inadequacy of ideal-theoretical approaches that neglect the non-unitary character of real-world situations and the usage of contextually sensitive epistemic standards.

***

This book is the final outcome of years of research and countless debates that I have had the opportunity to lead with my colleagues at the Department of Philosophy, as well as with colleagues at conferences. Although this work has provided me with the opportunity to unite many of my beliefs into a single, compressive attitude, subjective accounts can be still found in several published articles for which I ought to thank my reviewers. I am particularly grateful to the colleagues whose stances I am discussing about, and whom I have had the luck to debate with and learn from. It is beyond doubt that their comments and constructive criticism have enabled me to write a book with fewer mistakes – my gratitude thus goes to Fabienne Peter, Phillip Kitcher, Thomas Christiano, Johnathan Wolff and Miranda Fricker. I am equally grateful to may dear colleagues and friends who has helped me with their advice and suggestions, including Andrea Mešanović, Elvio Baccarini, Luca Malatesti, Nebojša Zelić, Petar Bojanić, Sanja Bojanić and Ivan Cerovac, as well as my PhD students, whose zeal introduced me to new ideas and enriched my knowledge of this topic. Special thanks goes to my daughter Hana Samaržija for our conversations and her immeasurable help in preparing this book.

1.
SOCIAL EPISTEMOLOGY

1.1. *Is social epistemology 'real' epistemology?*[1]

Social epistemology extends traditional epistemological enquiries onto the doxastic attitudes of individuals in contact with other epistemic agents, as well as to the epistemic properties of groups, institutions and social systems. Narrowly understood, traditional epistemology put emphasis on the conceptual and normative questions of defining knowledge, truth, justification and the necessary conditions for asserting that someone is in possession of knowledge. In the wider sense, it evaluated the processes of belief formation (perception, inference, memory, intuition, testimony or like) and inquired about the sources, processes and scope of acquiring and maintaining knowledge. Keeping in mind this wider account of epistemology, social epistemology is a sub-discipline of epistemology that has shifted its interest to examining and critically evaluating doxastic attitudes within social environments – namely, critically evaluating the processes through which beliefs, decisions and opinions are formed, maintained and revised by individuals, groups, institutions and, in the widest sense, social practices and social systems.[2]

---

1 This question was first raised in the title of Alvin I. Goldman's eponymous article about the nature and aims of social epistemology. From our current perspective, Goldman can credibly be considered the founder and one of the most prominent advocates of social epistemology as an autonomous branch of epistemology. In a series of articles and books published since the 1980s, he has defined and elaborated numerous topics related to cognition and society in adherence to the traditional methods of analytic philosophy. The aforementioned article attempted to reflect on the status of social epistemology by responding to common critiques and discussing its possible future developments.

2 Alvin I. Goldman. 2010a. 'Why Social Epistemology is Real Epistemology?', in Haddock, Adrian, A. Millar and D. Pritchard (eds.), *Social Epistemology* (Oxford: Oxford University Press), pp. 1–29, Alvin I. Goldman and

While standard analytic philosophy generally avoided discussing the interpersonal character or social aspects of knowledge, movements such as postmodernism, sociology of knowledge and cultural studies have based most of their stances on knowledge and cognition on this assumption. This is why the questions of doxastic attitudes in social environments, or the topics of social epistemology, are still often associated with the aforementioned movements. However, it should be kept in mind that these theoretical approaches rejected traditional epistemology, proclaimed its death and either challenged, reconfigured or entirely negated the conventional epistemic concepts of truth, objectivity, rationality, or like. Similarly, the normative complexity of forming and revising beliefs in a social context – as well as the influence of social relationships on forming both the beliefs that result in epistemic success, and those that amount to epistemic failures – were entirely exempt from any sort of inquiry. The legacy of such an approach to traditional epistemology has rendered standard analytical epistemology somewhat indignant to the very concept of social epistemology and its interest in examining doxastic attitudes in social environments. This aversion came to its expected consequence in the insistence that social epistemology cannot be considered a proper epistemological branch, but is rather something akin to social psychology or another topic of research within social sciences – at any rate, something completely unsuitable for philosophical scrutiny.[3] By failing to clearly distinguish between different approaches to doxastic attitudes in social circumstances, analytic philosophy and epistemology did not just callously renounce an extensive and significant topic fully deserving of philosophical analysis, but contributed to prejudices about the deep and unsurmountable rift between analytic (Anglo–Saxon) and postmodern (continental) philosophy. That is precisely why we will begin this introduction to social epistemology and its topics by stressing the differences between several different approaches to the topic of doxastic attitudes in social contexts or the topics social epistemology at large. This approach has two main aims: firstly, I will argue for the legitimacy of critically researching doxastic attitudes in society within analytic philosophy. My second aim will be to

---

Thomas Blanchard. 2015. 'Social Epistemology', in *Stanford Encyclopedia of Philosophy* <https://plato.stanford.edu/entries/epistemology-social/> [accesed 19 June 2017]

3 William Alston. 2005. *Beyond 'Justification': Dimensions of Epistemic Evaluation* (Ithaca: Cornell Universiti Press).

defend a certain intersectional attitude, the thesis that contemporary analytical and continental philosophies have more to gain from mutual communication and reasonable debates on philosophical issues, than from accentuating their methodological or conceptual differences.

1.2. *Three models of social epistemology*

Given the aforementioned complaints about social epistemology not being 'real' epistemology, it seems crucial to define the criteria for recognizing 'real' epistemology. Namely, the fundamental properties which have constituted 'real' epistemology throughout its historic development. I will list its central and basic characteristics, as seen by Alvin I. Goldman: (1) an epistemic agent is an individual in the sense that all doxastic attitudes begin and end with the individual who is – within a group, a collective, an institution or a community – the final bearer of beliefs; (2) epistemology is primarily a normative discipline because it is concerned with the epistemic evaluation of beliefs – are they justified, rational and true – or the questions about how we acquire and retain knowledge; (3) the aforementioned epistemic criteria for ascertaining the justifiedness or rationality of a belief are not plainly conventional, but are rather assumed to have a certain objectivity or objective validity (when we evaluate a belief as justified, we are implying that there are certain objective circumstances that make the belief – unlike its negation – justifiable); (4) the concepts of 'knowledge', 'justification' and like either imply some kind of connection with truth – truth being understood as an objective or mind-independent property – rather than as something that we subjectively ascribe to a belief; (5) the central task of epistemology is critical evaluation of the ways we 'make decisions' about adopting, maintaining or revising beliefs or other doxastic states.[4] Given the aforementioned characteristics, different approaches to social epistemology can be qualified as either 'real' or revisionist.

1.2.1 *Revisionism*

In contrast to traditional epistemology, the revisionist approach derives many of its properties from the aforementioned theoretical approaches of postmodernism, deconstruction, social constructivism, the so-called 'strong program' of the Edinburgh school of thought,

4 Goldman, 2010a.

and like. 'Revisionists' share the common notion of declaratively and explicitly debunking many, if not all, settings characteristic of traditional epistemology. Richard Rorty, the most notorious convert from analytic to postmodern philosophy, proclaimed the 'death' of epistemology, deeming that knowledge cannot be perceived as a reflection of nature and that beliefs aren't objective representations of the external world. Instead, he proposed that epistemology should be replaced with the study of conversational practices.[5] The understanding of 'truth' as a property that presumes a connection between beliefs and the external world (which we describe, characterize, reflect, imagine and represent in our beliefs, or like) thus loses any kind of metaphysical foundations. It is reduced to a mere social construction or fabrication which is attributed to beliefs due to certain social reasons external to doxastic attitudes themselves. Truth thus becomes a mere convention or social artifice, and knowledge (including scientific knowledge) becomes something that society simply opted to believe is knowledge – a sheer institutionalized belief (in the sense that any other belief/theory could have become equally institutionally defended and promoted).[6] Similarly scorned is the stance that the rationality of a belief can be objectively evaluated, given that the social and cultural context are claimed to define the very norms of rationality, as well as all other norms.[7] These approaches commonly reject the concept of individuals as the bearers of epistemic agency or doxastic attitudes, instead positing groups, collectives or communities as the basic creators and bearers of beliefs.[8] Within these approaches, epistemology thus ceases to be a space for critically exploring the nature or the objective properties of our beliefs – any attempt to examine doxastic attitudes is reduced to inquiring about the manner in which social relationships, conventions and power dynamics form and promote certain beliefs rather than others, or to investigating the underlying institutional norms which promote a certain belief as rational or true. All inquiries about doxastic

---

5 Richard Rorty. 1979. *Philosophy and the Mirror of Nature* (Princeton: Princeton University Press).

6 Latour, Bruno, and Steve Woolgar. 1986. *Laboratory Life: The Construction of Scientific Facts* (Princeton: Princeton University Press); Steven Shapin. 1994. *A Social History of Truth* (Chicago: University of Chicago Press).

7 Barry Barnes and David Bloor. 1982. 'Relativism, Rationalism, and the Sociology of Knowledge', in Hollis Martin and Steven Lukes (eds.), *Rationality and Relativism* (Cambridge, MA: MIT Press), pp. 21–44.

8 Lynn Hankinson–Nelson. 1990. *Who Knows: From Quine to Feminist Empiricism* (Philadelphia: Temple University Press).

attitudes are thus aimed at unmasking or deconstructing existing epistemological constructs (regarding the perception of something as knowledge, as true, or like).

It is more than evident how such an approach to the relationship between cognition and society can be considered a deviation or a revision of epistemology's traditional interests.[9] In that sense, it could be said that social epistemology is not 'real' epistemology.

1.2.2. *Conservativism*

The second approach to the topics of social epistemology can be deemed 'conservative' inasmuch as it selects those historically elaborated epistemological topics that are related to society or interpersonal relationships in order to 'transfer' them to a separate, yet legitimate, sub-discipline known as social epistemology, continuing to discuss them in a contemporary context. That is why we can treat this approach to social epistemology as a certain attempt to 'preserve' traditional topics within the new umbrella of social epistemology. Goldman claims that this is a case of 'preservationism' in understanding social epistemology. It is important to point out, however, that this approach assumes that epistemology is legitimate discipline with all of its basic properties, and that social epistemology is a mere cluster

---

9 However, it is important to emphasize that this isn't an attempt to portray all instances of epistemological relativism as revisionism. Namely, relativism is neither an unknown nor an unpopular stance in analytic philosophy. Recent debates are becoming increasingly aware of the relativity of epistemic evaluations and judgments to certain systems of standards (contextualism) or underlying evidential systems (Alvin I. Goldman. 2010b.'Epistemic Relativism and Reasonable Disagreement', in Feldman Richard and Ted A. Warfield (eds.), *Disagreement* (Oxford: Oxford University Press), pp. 187–215; Ernest Sosa. 2010. 'The Epistemology of Disagreement', in Haddock Adrian, A. Millar and D. Pritchard (eds.), *Social Epistemology* (Oxford: Oxford University Press), pp. 278–297). The so-called 'new age' relativism precisely presupposes the existence of many epistemic systems and claims that justifications can vary in accordance with the relevant underlying epistemic system. However, this form of relativism ought to be differentiated from revisionist nihilism – a stance that explicitly negates the existence of any facts/objective properties on the basis of which these systems could be compared or evaluated. (Crispin Wright. 2007. 'The Perils of Dogmatism', in Nuccetelli Susana and Gary Seay, (eds.), *Themes from G.E. Moore* (Oxford: Oxford University Press), pp. 25–48; Crispin Wright. 2009. 'Fear of Relativism', *Philosophical Studies*, 141: 379–390).

of topics within the history of epistemology that evaluates cognition in the context of social phenomena.

It cannot be denied that there are epistemological purists such as Plato, Rene Descartes, or the more recent William Alston, who have continuously argued against the philosophical relevance of the influence of society on our beliefs (supporting their by stating, among other arguments, that philosophical speculations about anything other one's individual beliefs are inevitably vulnerable to uncertainty and ambiguity). They are, however, in the minority. It is highly probable that we could all, after a brief discussion, find common ground within this conservative approach to social epistemology, as it preserves the legitimacy of topics less or more related to other epistemic agents. Throughout the history of epistemology, as well as in contemporary epistemology, most philosophers have not challenged topics related to other epistemic agents. For example, the question of acquiring knowledge by communicating with other people, or the epistemological problem of testimony, first attained legitimacy through John Locke, David Hume and Thomas Reid – today, it is certainly one of the key topics of contemporary (social) epistemology. It's almost unimaginable that any epistemological conservative, their personal research preferences notwithstanding, would agree to eliminate the problems of forming beliefs on the basis of testimony, the justification and conditions of accepting the accounts of others, the justification of trust as a particular doxastic state, or like, from the domain of 'real' epistemology. Likewise, many distinguished epistemologists who consider their work entirely external to the sphere of social epistemology are engaged in intense debates about having stances and beliefs different from those of others, the properties of disagreements between epistemic peers in possession of the same evidential bases, as well as about the possible resolutions of such disagreements.[10] In other words, the conservative approach or 'preservationism' is characteristically respectful of epistemological topics that consider society a legitimate, traditional and 'real' topic of epistemological inquiry, but forgoes any incentive to regard itself as a special epistemological sub-discipline such as social epistemology, or like.

10 See, for instance, Kieth Lehrer and Carl Wagner. 1981. *Rational Consensus in Science and Society* (Dordrecht, Reidel); Jennifer Lackey and Ernest Sosa. (eds.). 2006. *The Epistemology of Testimony* (Oxford: Oxford University Press); Richard Feldman and Ted A. Warfield (eds.). 2010. *Disagreement* (Oxford: Oxford University Press) or like.

It would be wise to mention additional topics of traditional epistemology related to the problems of society and cognition which were introduced prior to the formation of social epistemology as an autonomous branch, and which are now formally classified as social and belonging to social epistemology. The majority of the epistemology of science, a field particularly promoted by Karl Popper – understood as an inquiry about the epistemic processes inherent to scientific research – is nothing but a good example of social epistemology that focuses on evaluating the relations between individual cognition and the scientific context of inquiry.[11] After Popper, many other debates have tackled the issues of cognition within the scientific community. For example, are there any experts on a particular topic? If so, who are they and can laymen reliably recognize them? Should laymen blindly trust experts/scientists? Are laymen in the position to accurately assess the stances of experts/scientists? Should we, in the context of scientific research, encourage the epistemic diversity of expert attitudes or just the most promising scientific position? And so forth. The aforementioned problem of testimony can also be found within the epistemology of science – it reflects upon the relationships of trust between experts/scientists whose teamwork necessarily depends on relying on the opinions of other scientists. In the context of these debates about conflicts between experts, we might wonder whether it is rational to demand that someone changes their belief (or the degree of their belief) if a peer in possession of the same evidential grounds maintains a different opinion. Is it even possible – and if so, on what grounds – for peers (individuals of comparable cognitive abilities in possession of the same evidence) to maintain different beliefs in a justified and rational way? In addition to these, there is the question of whether peer disagreement between experts somehow compromises their (value neutral) status, as well as the timeless problem of resolving existing disagreements between experts. In the end, it ought to be explored how laymen should interpret disagreements between experts.[12] Another important and legitimate topic of social epistemology is the issue of whether the social desirability of scientific beliefs should be evaluated in purely epistemic terms (by, for example, assessing the levels of

---

11 Karl Popper. 1962. *Conjectures and Refutations: The Growth of Scientific Knowlwdge* (New York, Basic Books).

12 See more in Feldman and Warfield (eds.), 2010; Sosa, 2010. Alo see David Christensen and Jeniffer Lackey. (eds.). 2012. *The Epistemology of Disagreement*, (Oxford: Oxford University Press).

cognitive excellence or the used evidence) or it should additionally take into account the 'use value' of beliefs, understood as the practical (moral, prudential, social and political) interests of the community.[13]

Furthermore, extensive discussions about the norms of conversational practices and the rules of argumentation clearly belong to social epistemology. Differently articulates, this is the question of what makes a certain belief, social practice or intuition deserving of justification from the perspective of social epistemology.[14] In the context of these discussions about argumentation, the norms of justifying or accepting beliefs cease to be intrapersonal in order to become interpersonal: the justification of a belief extends to the question of whether the proposed belief is acceptable to others, or whether someone can successfully justify their belief when confronted by (actual or potential) opponents.[15] There is also the question of the nature of argumentation and its legitimacy, in the light of the fact that the genuine validity of an argument isn't necessarily equivalent to its ability to successfully persuade an interlocutor: the illustrative example of the *enthymeme* (a conclusion with a missing premise) as a profoundly interesting phenomenon within oratorical practices and everyday communication, in which this invalid argument is frequently used without being dismissed as problematic.

In short, the contemporary manifestation of social epistemology interested in these topics is definitely 'real' epistemology. These numerous topics pertaining to the phenomenon of cognition in social environments were the subject of extensive philosophical discussions prior to any incentives to delegate them to a particular epistemological sub-discipline, let alone the polemics about whether social epistemology is 'real' epistemology. Developments within discussions

---

13 Jason Stanly. 2005. *Knowledge and Practical Interests* (Oxford and New York: Clarendon Press): Snježana Prijić–Samaržija. 2007. 'Trust and Contextualism', *Acta Analytica*, 22(2): 125–38; Fantl, Jeremy and Matt McGrath. 2002. 'Evidence, Pragmatics and Justification', *The Philosophical Review*, 111: 67–94.

14 Alvin I. Goldman. 1987. 'Foundations of Social Epistemics', *Synthese*, 73(1): 109–144.

15 Ludwig Wittgenstein. 1969. *On Certainty*, ed. by Anscombe G. E. M. and G. H. von Wright (Oxford: Basil Blackwell); Annis, David. B. 1978. 'A Contextualist Theory of Epistemic Justification', *American Philosophical Quarterly*, 15(3): 213–219; Lehrer, K., (1990), *Theory of Knowledge* (Boulder, Westview); Michael Williams. 2001a. *Problems of Knowledge* (Oxford: Oxford University Press).

about these topics naturally led to the formation of social epistemology as a specific domain of epistemology.

1.2.3. *Expansionism*

However, it is indubitable that there are topics which have not been discussed systematically within traditional epistemology, which require philosophical and epistemological elaboration, and which pertain to the questions of cognition and society. In that sense, it is sensible to speak about a third approach to social epistemology, 'expansionism', which extends the traditional scope of epistemological discussions about cognition and society. Goldman argues that 'expansionism' is, in spite of its new topics, another form of 'real' epistemology as it is fully respectful of all the fundamental settings of traditional epistemology.

For example, let's focus on two major new topics: (i) evaluation of the epistemic properties of group or collective doxastic agents and (ii) evaluation of the epistemic properties and consequences of social practices, social systems and their policies. Firstly, many epistemologists, their presuppositions about individuals being the basic units of cognition notwithstanding, believe that groups or collectives (commissions, juries, courts, scientific panels, governments, and like) can be the bearers of doxastic states, judgments or beliefs[16] and claim that such states ought to be evaluated from an epistemic perspective as justified, rational, true or like, according to the same standards commonly applied to individual ones. Likewise, epistemic virtues and vices can be ascribed to both collective or plural, and individual agents.[17] It is interesting to note that

16 For instance, Margaret Gilbert. 1989. *On Social Facts* (New York. Routledge); Margaret Gilbert. 2004. 'Collective epistemology', *Episteme,* 1(2): 95-107; Bratman, Michael. 1993. 'Shared Intention', *Ethics*, 104: 97–113; Frederick Schmitt. 1994. *Socializing Epistemology* (Lanham, Maryland: Rowman & Littlefield); Philip Pettit. 2003. 'Groups with Minds of Their Own', in Schmitt Frederick (ed.) *Socializing Metaphysics* (Lanham, MD: Rowman and Littlefield), pp. 167–193; Miranda Fricker. 2010. 'Can There Be Institutional Virtues?', in Gendler Tamar S. and John Hawthorne (eds.), *Oxford Studies in Epistemology,* 3: 235-252.; Alvin I. Goldman. 2014. 'Social Process Reliabilism: Solving Justification Problems in Collective Epistemology', in Lackey Jennifer (ed.), *Essays in Collective Epistemology* (Oxford University Press), pp. 11–41.

17 Fricker, 2010.. See also Sarah Wright. 2014. 'The Stoic Epistemic Virtues of Groups', in Lackey Jennifer (ed.), *Essays in Collective Epistemology* (Oxford University Press), pp. 122–141.

these discussions have given rise to the concept of collective epistemology as a new field focused on the doxastic states of groups – understood as a basic form of collective entities. The second new topic is concerned with the epistemic analysis of social systems – the judicial, educational, scientific, political system, the media and like – by critically exploring whether their practices and procedures, as well as the consequential decisions and judgments, are epistemically valuable (rational, justified or like), and whether they are conducive to efficient resolutions of problems, truth and knowledge. This inquiry can be extended onto entire systems in order to explore the epistemic justification of democracy as a comprehensive decision-making system within a society.[18]

These new topics stray from traditional inquiries inasmuch as they cater to the possibility of applying epistemology to everyday life. For example, showing that certain social decision-making processes lead to decisions of better epistemic quality (more rational and justified) clearly belongs to the idea of so-called applied epistemology. This suggests that social epistemology can contribute to the ameliorative project of seeking common good by improving the epistemic practices (the processes of making decisions, judgments and appropriate policies) of a society. It is beyond argument that we ought to distinguish epistemological theories from epistemological applications that pertain to the 'real world'. Should we refrain from delving into an extensive debate about the primacy of either theoretical or pragmatic approaches, it can be argued that applied epistemology is 'real' epistemology in the same sense that applied ethics has long been legitimized as 'real' ethics. The fact that social epistemology can entertain features of applicability does not affect its adherence to the basic settings of traditional epistemology. On the contrary, social epistemology emphasises the prospects of reviving certain epistemological topics which have, for various reasons, remained cybernated and isolated from wider philosophical and scientific developments.

It ought to be also acknowledged that social epistemology indeed shares some of its new topics with sociology, social psychology, political theory and other social sciences. However, the interdisciplinary

18 See, for instance, Alvin I. Goldman, 1999. *Knowledge in a Social World* (Oxford: Oxford University Press); Philip Kitcher. 2001. *Science, truth, and democracy* (Oxford and New York: Oxford University Press); Philip Kitcher. 2011a. *Science in a Democratic Society* (Amherst, New York: Prometheus Books); Kevin Zollman. 2007. 'The Communication Structure of Epistemic Communities', *Philosophy of Science*, 74(5): 574–587.

character of these new topics does no harm to their philosophical and epistemic content inasmuch as the introduction of mathematics didn't jeopardize the philosophical relevance of logic, as political theory didn't jeopardize political philosophy and as neuroscience did not call into question the authenticity of philosophy of mind.

***

Thematically, this book belongs to the expansionist approach to social epistemology – an analysis of the epistemic properties of the democratic system or the potential of democratic deliberation to produce decisions of high epistemic quality. My primary aim is to directly promote the justification of applying epistemology to real situations in order to accentuate the manner in which these topics contribute to improving the epistemic processes and evaluations of beliefs in society. However, before proceeding, I find it important to further discuss the relationship between the revisionist and the expansionist approach to social epistemology. Namely, the dynamics of these two approaches is far more complex than the existing conclusion that revisionism isn't, while expansionism is, 'real' epistemology. In spite of their nihilist attitude towards epistemology, revisionists have introduced certain topics that social epistemology shouldn't ignore. This particularly pertains to the influence of (social) power on forming and revising beliefs, judgments or decisions, and the susceptibility of 'institutional beliefs' to the value systems (including interests) of those capable of promoting them. An epistemological approach obviously requires us to tackle these questions by respecting a fact which is scorned by revisionists, and which we hold in deep regard – the fact that epistemology is still alive, and that social epistemology is more vital and relevant than ever before.

1.3. *Lectures from Foucault's revisionism*

As a paradigmatic and charismatic representative of postmodernism and social constructivism, Michel Foucault is often and extensively criticized by many proponents of analytic (social) epistemology.[19] However, in assessing the philosophical phenomenon of Michel Foucault, which is

19 Critiques of Foucault, among others, prominently feature in Goldman. See, for instance, Goldman, 1999.

usually unilaterally associated with a revisionist approach to epistemology, one should not miss the duality inherent to his attitude to knowledge and truth.[20] On the one hand, he is personally extremely attached to the traditional epistemological attitude which presumes a value inherent to the acquisition and accumulation of knowledge. He treats curiosity and understanding as genuine epistemic virtues, and is equally fond of researching by collecting new information about different topics. Throughout his opus, Foucault clearly promotes the ideal of an intellectual erudite, a person positively passionate about knowledge – understood as the accumulation and conscientious absorption of information. Foucault's works *History of Madness* and *Discipline and Punish*, as well as his careful analysis of historical documents, testify about their author's search for valuable truths that ought to be unearthed and learned from. Moreover, Foucault's evident understanding of the importance of collecting evidence and arranging them into precise arguments implies a stark awareness of the fact that his reader desires the rational security (justification) that can only be attained though adequate evidential proof and lucid reasoning. All of this seems to suggest that Foucault believes that the traditionally understood, 'old' concept of knowledge is a valid epistemic aim, and that one can attain some sort of objective truth about the world through conscientious intellectual scrutiny. On the other hand, Foucault is vocal about his stance that knowledge is necessarily socially constructed in a way that abolishes any notion of its objective value, either as a true or as a justified belief. Truth is neither sought/explored nor revealed – instead, it is constructed in accordance with numerous limitations imposed by economic and political systems. Foucault's account exhibits a purposefully subversive and revisionist attitude towards the idea of objective truth. The neutrality of observers and readers are reduced to a mere myth as everyone has their own 'regime' of truth. From such a starting point, all knowledge needs to be deconstructed in order to unearth the power relations that underlie a certain construct. As this 'new' understanding of knowledge stands in clear opposition to the basic settings of traditional epistemology, Foucault's account can legitimately be described as belonging to revisionism or epistemological nihilism.

---

20 This is excellently noticed and elaborated by Nenad Miščević. 'After Foucault – Social Epistemology facing new and old knowledges', <http://www.transeuropeennes.eu/en/articles/282> [accesed 19 June 2017]

Foucault is, to a certain extent, aware of this duality. He tries to reconcile these two passions in the theory of 'the good knowledge of the oppressed' – the notion that the concept of knowledge/truth as constructs determined by social power relationships is not necessarily conflicted with the idea of an objective truth. The perspective of an erudite casts light on the wider historical context and thus provides a foundation for subjecting systems of power and their truths to further criticism: one can simultaneously nurture a subversive attitude towards the bad knowledge derived from power and accumulate the good knowledge of the oppressed. Furthermore, the morally superior position of marginalized or oppressed groups enables them to understand how power deceives – coupled with the erudition of intellectuals, it provides insights into injustice and makes it susceptible to effective criticism.

We can wonder whether Foucault's stances can be incorporated into real social epistemology without anatemizing him as an 'enemy'. Is social epistemology ready to cater to revisionism without compromising its traditional settings? I will attempt to argue in favour of two theses: (i) the attempts to subvert knowledge or postulate the impossibility of objective knowledge/truth/justification cannot be a legitimate epistemological stance, and is a revision or negation of the traditional epistemic enterprise which cannot be appended to 'old' knowledge; (ii) it is both possible and desirable to introduce Foucault's account of the influence of power dynamics and the different perspectives of the 'oppressed' and the 'ruling' on cognition and knowledge to the existing paradigm of 'old' knowledge.[21]

1.3.1. *Dualism of 'old' and 'new' knowledge*

We have already mentioned that the 'old' school of twentieth century Anglo–Saxon epistemology primarily linked epistemological discussions to formulating criteria of defining knowledge, the necessary and sufficient conditions for knowledge, theories of truth and justification, and like. While some authors who belonged to the 'old' school, such as Alston, even tended to admit that justification, in spite of widespread acceptance, does not correspond to any objective property of a belief, this traditional approach is directly tied to the

21 Snježana Prijić–Samaržija and Petar Bojanić. 2014. 'Social Epistemology Between Revisionism and Expansionism', *European Journal for Analytic Philosophy*, 10(2): 31– 48.

notion of objective truth and knowledge. For example, Alston claims that there is no 'objective' property of a belief that corresponds to the notion of being 'justified'[22] because there is neither a theoretically neutral way of defining the notion of justification that would resolve existing discussions between opposing theories[23], nor a robust set of paradigmatic examples of legitimate beliefs which would help us resolve these debates.[24] This is, however, not applicable to truth: "(...) to the greatest measure, the fundamental and central goal is to acquire, retain, and use true beliefs about matters of interest/importance."[25] Only those epistemic properties of beliefs that promote the goal of truth can be considered epistemic desiderata, such as: possessing adequate evidence and founding beliefs on adequate evidence; forming beliefs through reliable processes or generating beliefs in accordance with a properly functioning cognitive sequence; forming beliefs in accordance with intellectual virtues; possessing evidence about the adequacy of used evidence; the ability to defend one's beliefs; responsible acquisition and retention of beliefs; coherence and orderliness, and like.[26] As we can see, Alston's stances not only excellently illustrate the nature of epistemology, but also undoubtedly correlate with Foucault's historian passion for acquiring and accumulating the knowledge necessary for postulating convincing arguments.

Nevertheless, Alston is simultaneously a paradigmatic representative of the same 'old' school of thought that is notoriously conservative towards new topics: the influence of social power relations of the formation/construction of beliefs and attempts to deconstruct beliefs through exhaustive analysis of the underlying power dynamics are topics incongruent with 'real' epistemology. Social epistemology, in so far as it explores society's influence on the formation and acquisition of beliefs, is not 'real' epistemology: according to Alston, these and similar issues ought to be delegated to sociology, social psychology or other social sciences. In other words, the purist perspective of those who defend the accumulation of knowledge (objective truth and knowledge) renders Foucault's epistemic duality unacceptable as it simply isn't a distinctly *epistemic* duality. At best, his thesis merely rests on two standpoints – while the stance on the accumulation of

22 Alston, 2005., p. 21.
23 Alston, 2005., pp. 23–25.
24 Alston, 2005., pp. 25–26.
25 Alston, 2005., p. 30.
26 Alston, 2005., p. 93.

knowledge can belong to the domain of epistemology, his theories about the subversion of knowledge have their place in some other disciplines, such as social theory or political action. Intellectual circles fond of the standard analytic approach more commonly tend to characterize Foucault's duality as mere postmodernist inconsistency, epistemic irresponsibility or a contradiction.

We have seen, however, that most contemporary philosophers have rejected Alston's purist approach to social epistemology in favour of a more balanced view, arguing that inquiries about the epistemic properties of beliefs derived from relationships with others, as well as the epistemic properties of groups and social systems (interpersonal epistemic relations) can be considered 'real' epistemology. Foucault's concept of 'new' knowledge isn't expansionist – we cannot treat it as an expansion of old topics – inasmuch as he had abandoned the framework (of 'real' epistemology) within which such an expansion would be legitimate. However, it is still crucial to note that expansionism is little else but the sensible and reasonable extension of 'real' epistemology to Foucault's topics. Characterizing Foucault's theory as revisionist mustn't be equated with rejecting his relevant and exciting subject matter, which epistemology shouldn't renounce. Such thinking leads us to Miranda Fricker and Lorainne Code's excellent arguments about the fruitfulness of a less rigid approach to epistemology.

1.3.2. *Social situatedness of knowledge: expansion of 'real' epistemology to Foucault's topics*

Contemporary discussions about social epistemology have given rise to new voices that are not only prepared to subject Foucault's theories to serious consideration – as a certain methodological nihilism that encourages the revision of existing 'old' stances – but support the expansion of existing epistemological discussions to unambiguously foucaultian topics. As an example, Miranda Fricker[27] emphasises the philosophical benefits of extending traditional epistemological topics to Focault's account of the dynamics between power and knowledge. In dealing with the ethical-epistemological issues of trust and testimony and defining the social criteria for gaining the status of a reliable/ virtuous epistemic agent, Fricker has developed a rich conceptual

27 Miranda Fricker. 2007. *Epistemic Injustice* (Oxford: Oxford University Press).

framework for reflecting upon topics previously either marginalized or entirely exempt from traditional Anglo–Saxon epistemology. Much like Foucault, she is particularly interested in the influence of social power on beliefs. Fricker defines social power as a social agent's (indviduals, groups or institutions) *ability*, in relation to other social agents, to influence things in the social world.[28] In accordance with this notion of social power, Fricker is particularly interested in the issue of power derived from one's identity (identity power) – the question of practicing social power determined by a collective concept of social identity. In this vein, Fricker provides convincing arguments in favour of the stance that collective imagination contains numerous prejudices and stereotypes related to gender identities, which result in a certain distrust towards the testimonies and opinions of women. Fricker puts particular emphasis on the epistemic injustice thus performed upon women (members of religious and racial minorities, the poor, or other marginalized groups) in circumstances when their testimonies aren't considered as reliable/relevant as they could have been outside the given system of social power. For Fricker, there is no epistemological issue more important than the ways in which social power (most closely associated with collective stereotypes of identity) can produce epistemic injustice within a communicational practice, thus undermining the goal of the epistemic process – the acquisition of knowledge.[29] Communicational practice reflects social power

28 Social power is the practically socially situated ability to control the actions of others, and it can either be actively or passively performed by individual agents or appear on a purely structural level. Fricker is aware of the validity of the stance that social power is/should be the object of protest and emphasizes the necessity of critically modulating the question of power, but tends to use the concept of power as a neutral term (exercising power/control isn't necessarily aimed at hindering someone's interests). This is probably the most evident difference between Fricker's consistent epistemological approach and Foucault's treatise that somehow melds an epistemological perspective with political activism.

29 Using the example of testimony, the listener utilizes social stereotypes as a strategy for assessing the credibility and reliability of their informant, primarily perceiving them as a member of a certain social group (educational, gender, age, class, racial, religious, regional or like). The subsequently ascribed reliability is derived from this identification, and prejudices generally either lower or increase the speaker's perceived credibility. The epistemic injustice performed upon 'the oppressed' appears in to principal modalities: testimonial and hermeneutic injustice, both of which epistemically harm the knowing subject.

inasmuch as it produces various forms of dysfunction: for example, a speaker can either be attributed less credibility (credibility deficit) or more credibility (credibility excess) than what would be reasonably justified. While deficits tend to remain the detriment of Foucault's 'the opressed', excess credibility is usually attributed to elite groups with privileged education, or like.[30]

Although Fricker is explicitly aware of the separate issue that epistemic injustices tend to imperil 'the oppressed' to subsequent economic and political mistreatment, she distinctively separates the epistemic dimension from other damages. Furthermore, Fricker can in no way be accused of relativism, epistemic nihilism or any notions about the general subversion of knowledge. On the contrary, she firmly locates her position within the domain of the epistemology of virtue – the 'old' presuppositions of justifying truth and rationality serve as the framework for a critical analysis of the epistemic dimension of the social practice of ascribing trust.

A similar, yet possibly more radical, approach to expanding epistemology to Foucault's topics can be found in the works of Lorainne Code.[31] By distinguishing 'general' and 'real' knowledge, she faults twentieth century Anglo–Saxon epistemology (the aforementioned 'old' epistemology) with damagingly limiting their focus to the apriorily necessary and sufficitient conditions for knowledge in general. Code remarks that social epistemology ought to emcompass the chaotic incoherence of real epistemic relationships, observing them from critical, descriptive and normative perspectives. She further approaches Foucault's attitude by stating that any inquiry into knowledge is bound to generate numerous new topics that often blur the boundaries between traditional epistemology and ethical-

---

30 Both varieties of dysfunction can lead to further deterioration of epistemic character and hinder successful cognition. For example, as members of an elite often grow accustomed to being given excess attention and credibility, they develop the vice of epistemic arrogance (they become dogmatic, insensitive or hypersensitive to criticism, or unwilling to sensibly assess opinions that differ from their own) which hinders their ability to acquire true knowledge. This topic will be further discussed in the remainder of the book.

31 Lorraine Code. 1995. *Rhetorical Spaces – essays on gendered locations* (London/NY: Routledge); Lorraine Code. 2006. *Ecological Thinking: The Politics of Epistemic Location* (New York, Oxford University Press); Lorraine Code. 2010. 'Testimony, Advocacy, Ignorance: Thinking Ecologically about Social Knowledge', in Haddock A., A. Millar and D. Pritchard (eds.), *Social Epistemology* (Oxford: Oxford University Press), pp. 29–50.

political debates. Unlike purist philosophers such as Alston and many others, Code purports that 'real' (social) epistemology shouldn't focus on propositions themselves, but on belief-forming processes.[32]

Like Fricker, Code divulges the main topics of social epistemology from the issues of trust, power, representation and negotiation in epistemic communities, and explores models of epistemic dependence, epistemic vulnerability, epistemic risks, and like. Just like Fricker emphasised the real dimension of a socially situated knower, Code is visibly critical of the 'neutrality principle' which overlooks the specific social positions of the agents who partake in an epistemic process. In contrast to the reductivist abstraction and formal analysis of orthodox Anglo–American epistemology, Code puts emphasis on the scope of real-world knowledge, argues in favour of epistemic advocacy and supports the inclusion of previously marginalized/silenced sources of evidence (for example, assessments of the efficiency of Tanzanian medical procedures should be sought from actual Tanzanians, rather than only from experts).[33] These stances indubitably render Code the contemporary social epistemologist most closely associated with Foucault's account of the epistemic relevance of the perspective of the oppressed.

In the form of ecological naturalism, as Code dubs her standpoint, social epistemology can scrutinize the structures and implications of political, economic and social systems without unjustifiably presuming the neutrality, impersonality and social ambiguity of the knower (who is devoid of race, class, ethnicity, gender or similar features). It can emphasise the importance of the particular place or situation in which knowledge is produced and disseminated – as such, it calls for acute understanding of all details which may encourage or hinder knowledge acquisition. This description makes it somewhat difficult to differentiate Code from Foucault at all. However, it is essential to note that Code, similarly to Fricker and entirely unlike Foucault, remains within the framework of 'real' epistemology. She unambiguously grounds her standpoint by arguing that knowledge is indeed possible, and that it is desirable to evaluate both the real-world and the natural conditions for attaining knowledge. Code is equally critical of the ideas that 'real-world knowledge' isn't knowledge and that beliefs shouldn't be assessed in terms of justification, rationality and truth.

32 The same stance is excellently defended by Richard Moran. 2006. 'Getting Told and Being Believed', in Lackey Jennifer and Ernest Sosa (eds.), *The Epistemology of Testimony* (Oxford: Oxford University Press), pp. 272–306.

33 Code, 2010.

Thus, Fricker and Code have successfully demonstrated that it is possible to step out of Goldman's eliminative criticism of revisionism and entertain Foucault's account of the specific epistemic position of the oppressed without undesirably succumbing to his nihilism or subversion of knowledge. Namely, both Code and Fricker show that epistemological topics can undergo significant expansion and that analytic and postmodern perspectives are far less irreconcilable than what was commonly assumed.

1.4. *Social epistemology between traditionalism and reductionism*

We have repeatedly emphasized that social epistemology – given that it is concerned with the social aspect of knowing – is unprecedentedly connected to epistemic situations in the real world. Thus, it can also be referred to as applied epistemology or real-world epistemology.[34] Having this in mind, we ought to admit that social epistemology (in its expansionist version) is a departure from the traditional epistemological approach that rarely tackled practical real world issues – instead choosing to focus on the acquisition of knowledge in extremely idealized circumstances: individual epistemic agents were imagined as persons of almost unlimited logical abilities and without any constrains to their cognitive resources. Moreover, traditional epistemology usually implicitly presupposed that truth and rationality are entirely unrelated to the questions of social power or the social and political identities of knowers – a view that has come under fire since the advent of new trends in social epistemology. The epistemic subject was perceived as an asocial being, and socio-political circumstances as irrelevant to epistemic inquiries. Even when topics related to other knowers, scientific practices or conversational norms of argumentation

---

34 I use the term 'real-world epistemology' as a homage to Jonathan Wolff's 'real-word philosophy of politics', which differs from traditional or dominant theories in advocating an approach that is not based on attempting to apply abstract ideal principles of justice to particular situations, but instead studies real circumstances existing social relationships in order to assess their justness. Although it may seem as if the philosophy of politics was necessarily linked to the real world (as opposed to epistemology), what Wolff is attempting to emphasize is that the ideal-theoretical approach to the phenomenon of justice is often blind to the perspective of specific social relations, which further hinders correct evaluations of just practices. Jonathan Wolff, 2015c. 'Political Philosophy and the Real World of the Welfare State', *Journal of Applied Philosophy* 32(4): 360–272.

did arise, they were articulated in a manner that preserved the existing *status quo* of epistemological debates. One could, at best, expect a conservative approach to (social) epistemology.

And while traditional epistemology has more or less consciously avoided to explicitly examine the interpersonal character or the social aspects of cognition, movements such as postmodernism, sociology of knowledge and cultural studies have used these assumptions as the foundation of their theories and their immense popularity in continuously expanding intellectual circles. Particularly popular was their disregard for abstract conceptual and normative discussions on cognition in favour of theories that portrayed the relationships between power and identity as underlying determinants of the formation of beliefs unsuitable for objective evaluation. It is worth repeating that orthodox postmodernist claims about 'the end of epistemology' don't stop at emphasizing the importance of the social dimension of knowing. This initial thesis is actually their original contribution to the discussion. Problems arise when theories about the social character of knowledge start to imply that the epistemic agent is a mere function of power relationships, which, consequentially, renders all norms of truth and rationality obsolete. Epistemic subjects are thus completely reduced to their social political role and their beliefs on socio-cultural constructions, while the analysis of the beliefs becomes deconstruction – the disclosure of the socio-cultural influences behind these particular beliefs.

In short, it is crucial not to overlook the differences between *traditionalism* and *reductionism*, or the modernist and the postmodernist worldview, with regard to the dynamics between knowing and society: while the first tried to explain cognition without discussing the issues of power and the social dimension of beliefs, the second attempted to reduce the epistemic subject to their place within societal power relationships. True or 'real' social epistemology tries to position itself between traditionalists and reductionists[35]: the social dimension of cognition is accepted without compromising the central values of traditional epistemology – epistemic values such as rationality, justification, truth, truth-conductivness, problem-solving and like. Epistemic agents (individuals, social groups, institutions and systems) form, retain and revise their beliefs/judgments/ decisions under the

35 This distinction between traditionalism and reductionism was first made by Miranda Fricker. 1998. 'Rational authority and social power: Towards a truly social epistemology', *Proceedings of the Aristotelian Society,* 98(2): 159–177.

influence of society. However, their beliefs/judgments /decisions cannot be reduced to mere social constructions, but should instead be assessed as rational, justified or truthful, evaluated in accordance with their epistemic quality or their ability to efficiently resolve problems.

1.5. *Individual, collective and social epistemology: in(ter)dependence*

This short overview of the justifications of the legitimacy and the status of social epistemology between two opposing tendencies to either deny or radicalize the social aspects of cognition, as well as its positive influence on understanding the phenomena of cognition and belief formation/revision, and improving the epistemic properties of social entities and practices still hasn't resolved all potential reservations. It is possible to describe social and collective epistemology as mere expansions of individual epistemology. Should we accept the autonomy of social epistemology, it is possible to wonder about the differences between collective and social epistemology. It is equally sensible to question the trend of introducing multiple new disciplines within a field so vocal about its eagerness to preserve the traditional settings of (individual) epistemology and oppose the revisionist demand to comprehensively reconceptualise the acquisition of knowledge. These dilemmas can be rendered even more complicated by taking into account other initiatives which have demanded the methodological separation of collective epistemology: it is widely accepted that individual epistemology, since it focuses on the individual knower, contains outdated theories and distinctions which cannot be automatically applied to corresponding phenomena related to group beliefs without limiting or even hindering discussions about collective epistemic agents.[36]

Without delving deeper into debates about classifications and terminology, it is important to distinguish between three types of targets in epistemological research: (i) individuals and individual beliefs, (ii) groups and group beliefs, and (iii) general social practices, social institutions and systems. Of course, inquires about these three targets often intertwine and overlap: for example, research about the epistemic status of institution has clearly shown that instituions are

36 Gilbert, Margaret and Daniel Pilchman. 2014. 'Belief, Acceptance and What Happens in Groups: Some Methodological Considerations', in Lackey Jennifer (ed.), *Essays in Collective Epistemology* (Oxford: Oxford University Press), pp. 189–212.

a specific collective entity which differs from other groups (such as clubs, committees, juries and like) only in the degree of their structural complexity, rather than in nature. It is equally impossible to avoid tackling the influence of the epistemic justification of individual beliefs on the justification of the beliefs of larger social entities in which they participate. This is precisely why I will assume a classification that differentiates between the phenomenon of cognition on the individual and the social level: while individual epistemology primarily deals with the epistemic properties of individual beliefs, social epistemology is concerned with the epistemic properties of social entities and practices. Collective epistemology is important, but it is only part of an increasingly developed social epistemology that experiences rapid and exciting development in the new millennium. Collective epistemology is undeniably important, but it is only a part of the larger domain of social epistemology which is witnessing an exciting surge of development.[37]

***

This book aims solely to discuss the epistemic properties of democracy as a social system. It is not concerned with the epistemic properties of groups, institutions or similar social entities often explored within social epistemology. However, before addressing the principal topic of my book, I will attempt to explain and clarify the nature of collective epistemology, as well as its relation to social epistemology, by analysing the epistemic properties of institutions as collective entities. My current and main goal is to demonstrate that, regardless of the highly specific interests of this inquiry, central epistemological properties remain equally applicable to individual, social and collective epistemology. Although institutions are, as a phenomenon, different from individuals and generally irreducible to individual agents, the normative character of individual epistemology translates to both collective and social epistemology. It is equally valid to assess the epistemic success of individuals, groups, institutions and the social system at large – we can explore how they form their beliefs, judgments and decisions and evaluate their epistemic quality. I will attempt to show that it is sensible to discuss the epistemic virtues of institutions in the same terms as the epistemic virtues of individuals

37 This account of collective epistemology as a constitutive element of social epistemology is supported by Goldman and Blanchard, 2015.

and, as will be seen later on, the epistemic virtues of entire social systems. Keeping in mind the recent readiness to augment discussions in social epistemology with direct practical applications, these and similar research topics may further justify their status of something akin to a real-world epistemology.

1.5.1. *Epistemic status of institutions as collective entities*

In everyday speech, we don't only attribute virtues and vices to individuals, but also to various kinds of groups. We habitually say that the jury is 'fair-minded', the police is 'racist', the government is 'corrupted', the university is 'snobbish', or that the committee is 'tolerant'. It is just as common to hear that an institution 'made a good decision' or that it didn't 'recognize' its advantages, that it is 'considerate' of its employees by 'perceiving' their talents or that it wisely invests in science and culture. Even more precisely, we are accustomed to saying that universities are 'intellectually responsible' for the competences of young generations, that the government 'expresses a unjustified attitude' toward gender issues, that the jury made a 'rational choice based on the given evidence', that the committee 'irrationally privileges the free rider strategy' or that the media did not 'investigate the case in an intellectually conscious manner'. In doing so, we implicitly assume that these collective entities or institutions are certain kinds of agents, the bearers of epistemic features – states, attitudes, beliefs, actions or like – for which they can be blamed or applauded. A common objection is that such utterances are purely metaphorical and that they truly refer to individual members of the institutions or to the executive members ultimately responsible for institutional decision-making processes. I will tackle the questions of responsibly ascribing epistemic features to institutions and the meaning of ascribing virtues and vices to institutions. These questions require more comprehensive investigation of the nature of those collective entities, as collective agents, to whom we can ascribe virtues and vices.

Such a project of real-word or applied (collective/social) epistemology needs to begin by answering the following questions: What makes an institution a collective agent, or what makes an institution an epistemic collective agent? Does an institution display epistemic virtues as an epistemically autonomous collective or as a cluster of virtuous individuals? What, precisely, makes an institution an epistemically virtuous collective agent? I would like to argue here in favour of the following claims: (i) as a social entity, an institution is an autonomous epistemic collective agent; (ii) being an epistemic agent, the intellectual virtues (vices) displayed by institutions are identical to those displayed by an individual agent; (iii) the virtues (vices) displayed by an institution as a whole should not be reduced to the virtues (vices) of its virtuous (vicious) individuals, that is, a virtuous institution is not (necessarily) an institution of virtuous individuals (and vice versa). Finally, I would like to offer a preliminary general proposal of what should be taken into account when defining an epistemically virtuous institution.

***

Although various kinds of institutions can exhibit different degrees of structure and formality, they can all be identified as social or collective entities. The nature and ontological status of institutions or institutional facts has been meticulously elaborated by John Searle.[38] According to him, institutions differ from other collective entities, such as a group of people on board of the same bus, the owners of Swedish cars, participants of a cocktail party, or gay communities, in sharing a clearly outlined approach to constructing and defining their aims and social function, as well as to specifying their constitutive rules.

An institution is a social construct generated by *collective recognition* and *collective acceptance* of its specific *status function*. For example, a government is formed when individuals within a single society collectively recognize the need for a certain organizational body, and when they collectively accept to ascribe this organizational entity the goal, or the status function of managing the state. Similarly, the institution of a jury rests upon collective acceptance of its status function of making unbiased decisions on the basis of evidential proof. In order for these or other status functions or goals to construct an institution, they need to be collectively recognized, ascribed to a relevant collective entity and collectively accepted. An institution cannot exist unless its surrounding community collectively accepts its existence and the justification of its existence through its main purpose. This makes it essential for the community to collectively recognize the function, goal and purpose of the institution, as well as the

38 John R. Searle. 1995. *The Construction of Social Reality* (New York: Free Press); John R. Searle. 2010. *Making the Social World* (Oxford: Oxford University Press).

accompanying *constitutive rules* for attaining those aims. Only then can an institution attain its 'deontic powers', or its rights and obligations. The very act of recognizing and ascribing goals and purposes, such as accrediting universities with the purpose of providing higher education or assigning juries the goal of making unbiased decisions in court, enables institutions to fulfil their societal aims and functions.

An important aspect of Searle's theory of institutional facts is the stance that, in order for an institution to attain its goals and fulfil its status function, the existence of a collective goal or function ought to be founded on *collective intentionality*. In other words, status functions are intentionality-relative. For example, if a group of scientists wished to solve a certain theoretical or practical problem, they will divide their responsibilities on the basis of the collective intention to solve the problem, and appropriately coordinate their actions. By cooperating with each other, they will participate in the common aim through immediate individual intentions and actions. Likewise, members of a wider community share the intention of ascribing scientific-research institutions the status of problem-solving agents. However, it is important to accentuate that Searle contends that, although each individual has their own intentions and all intentionality takes place in individual minds, collective intentionality is nevertheless not reducible to individual intentions.

Full understanding of institutions requires the additional concept of constitutive rules. It could also be said that an institution is a system of (linguistically expressible) constitutive rules that we collectively agree to adhere to.[39] Collective acceptance of constitutive rules grants institutions social affirmation of its defined status function or goal. In his later book, Searle particularly stresses the importance of speech acts in accepting constitutive rules, creating status functions and, finally, constructing institutions. Namely, Searle asserts that speech acts, as declarations, "change the world by declaring that a state of affairs exists and thus bring that state of affairs into existence".[40] This renders the social obligation of citizens towards institutions inseparable from speech acts (both oral and written); an utterance, or the performance of speech or a linguistic act, makes the speaker obliged to adhere to their promise.

We can briefly summarize this discussion about the prerequisites of constructing an institution. Collective recognition or collective

---

39 Searle, 1995.
40 Searle, 2010., p.12.

acceptance within a community is necessary because an institution cannot exist unless a community collectively recognizes and accepts it by assigning the institution a 'status function'. Collective acceptance through declarative speech acts confirms that entities have come to possess certain status functions (by being represented as having those functions). Linguistically expressible constitutive rules establish institutions by specifying the target of our collective intentionality. So, the whole of institutional/social/collective reality is derived from the collective acceptance of declarative speech acts related to the ascription of status functions to entities.

This leaves us with the following question: are such constructed institutions the type of collective agent that can be ascribed epistemic states and be evaluated as virtuous, or not?

1.5.2. *Institution: from a collective entity to collective agents*

As I have previously emphasized, there are many types of collective entities or many kinds of groups: from merely statistical (a group of people who drive Swedish cars) and explicitly self-identified groups (gays) to more structured, procedurally organized groups (teams, committees, juries, governments, states, etc.).[41] However, not every collective entity as such is a candidate for being a collective agent. The fact that groups or collective entities can be radically different raises the question of defining those entities that can be ascribed the status of a collective agent. The status of a collective agent and collective agency is important for appraising collective (epistemic) conduct in terms of virtue and vice. In that sense, this question can be articulated as an inquiry about the necessary requirements for considering an institution, as a collective entity, an agent capable of exhibiting virtues and vices.

Let us consider three reasonable proposals of the preconditions for attaining the status of an agent: (i) structured constitution and conduct, which means that the entity needs to be at least loosely governed by a set of norms or procedure;[42] (ii) joint commitment to some future goal or the existence of volatilely accepted common goal of the entity;[43] (iii) the capacity of rational and reflective control of its goals,

---

41 Fricker, 2010.
42 Fricker, 2010.
43 Gilbert, 1989.

which presupposes the general account of agency as essentially tied to rationality.[44] Each of these proposals, as well as their combination, suggests potentially relevant conditions for attaining agency.

Given the aforementioned definition of the nature of institutions, it would seem that, among other collective entities, they are particularly capable of satisfying these conditions. An institution is a collective entity with a stable internal structure whose conduct is defined through a set of constitutive rules and corresponding procedures, recognized and accepted by the surrounding community. As we have had an opportunity to see, an institution necessarily practices joint commitment to its goals. An institution is actually constructed by collective acceptance of a status function and constitutive rules by its members as well as by the wider community. Finally, it would seem that the purpose of an institution (to serve a certain status function or goal) makes it obliged to exercise rational and reflective control of these goals through procedures which insure that the goals are successfully realized. Since an institution has to attain its goal, it needs to be constantly aware of the institutional *modus operandi*. So, if any collective entity can be a proper candidate for a status of an agent, institutions seem to be particularly plausible.

This also implies that, being an agent, institutions can be considered virtuous or vicious. But, what is actually meant when calling an institution virtuous? Sometimes collective epistemic features (virtues) may be a matter of a sufficient percentage or the number of members who display this trait as individuals. Intellectually virtuous members, as individuals, can make a collective agent intellectually virtuous (e.g. some research teams). However, is it realistic to expect that all, or the majority of members of an institution, will display comparable intellectual virtue? What majority would be necessary and/or sufficient for attaining the status of a virtuous institution? Or, does it mean that, apart from some misleading discourse about institutions as collective agents, there is no such thing as a virtuous institution, but only virtuous members of an institution? This leads to the question of whether an institution can display virtue even if its members, as individuals, are not virtuous. Or, can an institutional decision be irrational (or epistemically unjustified, of sub-optimal epistemic quality), despite

44 Philip Pettit. 2014. 'How to Tell if a Group Is an Agent', in Lackey Jennifer (ed.), *Essays in Collective Epistemology* (Oxford University Press), pp. 97–121.

extremely rational members who permanently generate rational individual beliefs and decisions?

The debate between *summativists* and *non-summativists*, a relevant topic of collective epistemology, may prove to be helpful. Summativists hold that collective epistemic phenomena – collective belief, collective epistemic justification, collective knowledge, collective epistemic virtue or like – can be understood entirely in terms of individual phenomena. On the other side, non-summativists differ by arguing that collective epistemic phenomena cannot be understood in terms of individual phenomena.[45] Some authors favour the clearest formulation of summativism, precisely articulated by Gilbert: a group G believes that p if, and only if, all or most members of G believe that p.[46] Namely, if we generally defined summativism as a stance that collective phenomena can be understood entirely in terms of individual phenomena, many non-summativists (such as John Searle and Raimo Tuomela) would probably fit the description of summativists, as at the beginning or the end we always return to individuals.[47] Similarly, Lahroodi defined summativism by writing that "a group G has the trait T if, and only if, all or most members of G have T".[48] The account may refer to as 'summative' because the group's belief, according to this interpretation, is a function of the sum of individual beliefs with the same content as that ascribed to the group. We ought to differentiate summativists and non-summativists within the debate about forming collective beliefs, from those who take a stance only regarding the issue of justifying collective beliefs. For example, Goldman defends a very specific summativist approach which considers justified collective belief the result or aggregate of the justifications of individual beliefs. Goldman calls the function which takes individual attitudes as inputs and yields collective beliefs as the output a belief aggregation function, and then proposes a way of aggregating the justification of group belief – a justification aggregation function.[49]

45 Jennifer Lackey. (ed.), 2014. *Essays in Collective Epistemology* (Oxford University Press)

46 Gilbert, 1989.

47 Deborah P. Tollefsen. 2015. 'Rewiew: Essays in Collective Epistemology by Jennifer Lackey (ed.)', <http://ndpr.nd.edu/news/essays-in-collective-epistemology/> [accesed 19 June 2017]

48 Reza Lahroodi. 2007. 'Collective epistemic virtues', *Social Epistemology*, 21: 281–297, p. 288.

49 Alvin I. Goldman. 2014. 'Social Process Reliabilism: Solving Justification Problems in Collective Epistemology', in Lackey Jennifer (ed.), *Essays in Collective Epistemology* (Oxford University Press), pp. 11–41.

On the other side, non-summativists' argumentation is grounded on the *divergence argument*: there can be divergence between phenomena at the collective level and the corresponding phenomena at the individual level. A collective entity can justifiably believe p despite the fact that not a single member justifiably believes that p. For instance, a jury as a group can justifiably believe that the defendant is innocent (on the basis of judge's rejection of some evidence), even though not a single juror justifiably believes this proposition because it is defeated for each of them as individuals by the actually reliable hearsay evidence.[50] A collective can possess a feature (virtue or vice) present in few or even none of its individual components. The group can also lack a feature, even though many or even all individuals possess it. For instance, a football team can be competitive even though none of its members are competitive individuals; the government can display nationalism, even though the majority of ministers are not nationalists; an institution can make an irrational decision even though its members as such are not making an irrational decision. Worries about collective judgmental rationality were first identified by Kornhauser and Sager, in the context of courts of law, resulting in what is known as 'the doctrinal paradox'.[51] They explicate an instance in which the final judgment of a group can be irrational despite the fact that the individual judgments of all the members of the body are rational: through a natural mode of aggregation, the majority vote, the collective agent exhibited inconsistence in affirming that the defendant acted despite being obliged not to act, while going on to deny that the defendant is guilty. However, each individual judge had a perfectly consistent set of judgments.[52]

---

50 Lackey (eds.), 2014.

51 Lewis A. Kornhauser and Lawrence G. Sager. 1986. "Unpacking the Court", *Yale Law Journal*, 96: 82–117.

52 This illustrative example conveys a trial in which three members of a jury decide on whether the defendant breached a specific contract by considering (i) whether he was obliged not to act and (ii) whether he had acted despite these restrictions. The first judge held that the defendant was obliged not to act and still acted, thus breaching the contract. The second concluded that, since he was obliged not to act and satisfied the obligation by not acting, he didn't breach the contract. The third judge didn't think that the defendant was obliged not to act, so the fact that he acted couldn't be considered a violation of the contract. To sum up – two judges rationally concluded that the defendant wasn't guilty, while only one thought that he was. Thus, the defendant was proclaimed innocent by majority vote. However, if we were to subject the decision making process to scrutiny, we would find that two judges held that the defendant was obliged not to act and another two held that he acted. In this sense, it would

Since it seems that there can be systematically rational group agents whose judgments are not suitably tied to those of their members, we can wonder about its implications for the epistemic virtue of rationality at the collective level.[53] There seem to be concrete examples of group beliefs/attitudes that do not necessarily reflect the beliefs/attitudes of individuals. Also, some virtues or vices are intrinsically tied to institutions as there is no lower level of group or institution independent features to which higher-level features can be reduced. Instead of being the mere by-product of some invisible hand (misunderstanding or lucky accident), these group features are generated by a specific inner structure aimed at attaining the collectively accepted common goal (attaining better ranking, reaching a rational or impartial decision, attaining a decision of the best epistemic quality, or like).

As we have seen above, Searle rejected the summative account by arguing that collective intentionality cannot be reduced to individual intentionality. Rather, he purports that individuals have the capacity of 'we believe' and 'we intend'.[54] Raimo Tuomela offers another account of group belief that rejects summativism, as there is no requirement that all or most members believe that p.[55] Gilbert outlines a classic non-summativist view known as the *joint acceptance account;* according to her, joint commitments are not reducible to a sum of individual commitments, but they *are* formed by each individual expressing their willingness to be jointly committed with others as a body.[56] Gilbert is not a non-summativist because she thinks that the individual is irrelevant to understanding collective phenomena – they are crucial

seem that the defendant was obliged not to act and still acted, which clearly implies his guilt. This would mean that the verdict of his innocence, aggregated from the final conclusion of all three judges, is an irrational decision – the majority held that he was obliged not to act, but still acted.

	Obliged not to act	Acted	Breached the contract
Judge 1	True	True	True
Judge 2	True	False	False
Judge 3	False	True	False
Court	True	True	False

53 Goldman, 2010a.
54 Searle, 1995., 2010.
55 Raimo, Tuomela. 2004. 'Group knowledge analyzed', *Episteme,* 1(2): 109–127.
56 Gilbert, 1989., 2004.

for understanding collective phenomena, but because she thinks that group belief (and group knowledge, as well as other group attitudes). cannot be reduced to summing up individual beliefs *with the same content as that attributed to the group.* Moreover, Gilbert attempts to accentuate that each feature manifests the willingness of individuals to collectively constitute a *plural subject* of the goal in question.

It ought to be stressed that non-summativists are not generally unified and that they disagree regarding the questions of whether groups are legitimate bearers of cognitive states or not (*epistemic agent collectivists vs epistemic agent individualists)* and whether group properties and states can (i) be explained solely in terms of a collection of individual attitudes suitably interrelated, or (ii) there is something irreducible about group attitudes (*reductionist and anti-reductionist*). John Searle, for instance, is an *anti-reductionist:* group beliefs cannot be reduced to a collection of individual 'I-beliefs' suitably interrelated. Rather, they are constituted by 'we-beliefs'. These are *sui generis* states. However, they are the states of individuals rather than not groups, so he is an *epistemic agent individualist.* Gilbert, too, is an *anti-reductionist,* because at the heart of group belief and group knowledge is a joint commitment that is not reducible to the personal commitments of individuals. But unlike Searle, she thinks that joint commitments constitute plural subjects to which beliefs may be ascribed. So she is an *epistemic agent collectivist.*[57]

It is possible to participate in the summativism vs. non-summativism dilemma from a balanced perspective: *weak* non-summativism and *strong* summativism have emerged as options respectful of the complexity of the issue at hand. On one side, weak non-summativism can engage the reasoning behind considering group beliefs a certain function of individual ones, though not as a mere numerical sum or aggregated percentage. Meanwhile, strong summativism remains open to interpreting group beliefs as an aggregate or the sum of individual ones, but presupposes a more complex form of aggregation than trivial additions or accepting the stance of the majority.

Some kind of non-summativism is additionally supported by the fact that the practices undertaken by institutions with the goal of generating beliefs and decisions of the best epistemic quality, or the goal of being virtuous – can differ from the practices which generate the best individual beliefs. For example, in order to make

57 See more in Fricker, 2010.; Lackey (eds.), 2014.

the best possible decisions, epistemically virtuous institutions do not have to encourage and reward only the best individual beliefs and the best individuals, as practices of rewarding and favouring epistemic diversity have continuously proven to be more fruitful. Epistemic diversity efficiently generates beliefs of high epistemic quality because it involves a wider and more complex evidential base necessary for developing a critical attitude towards the currently leading stance, thus providing a better context for argumentation and refutation. All of these features guarantee a better final epistemic result. In other words, emphasising the epistemic virtue of institutions in the endeavour of producing high-quality beliefs and making good decisions clearly isn't reducible to merely encouraging the virtue of individual epistemic agents. Rather, it argues for developing an epistemically optimal institutional environment for generating such desirable epistemic outcomes. For example, while some authors have defined this epistemically optimal institutional environment for attaining high-quality beliefs as a system of rewarding the institution's individual members[58], others accentuate the importance of developing strategies of intellectual engagement – an approach that encourages dialogue between individuals coming from different cognitive and epistemic backgrounds.[59] Certain authors have opted for strategically planned avoidance of rushed or premature consensus.[60] None of these cases reduces the methods of managing epistemically virtuous institutions to methods of merely encouraging the epistemic virtue of individuals – instead, they focus on the individuals' personal relations and the interplay between their beliefs.

Anyway, all kinds of non-summativism offer a template for arguing in favour of collective virtues, i.e. the epistemic virtue of an institution. The non-summativist approach explains the situation in which a collective agent possesses a virtue or vice – on the basis of joint commitment or collective acceptance of a common goal – regardless of the fact that the majority of its members lack the same virtues (or vices) as individuals. It is entirely possible that an intellectual virtue

58 Philip Kitcher. 1990. 'The Division of Cognitive Labor', *Journal of Philosophy*, 87: 5–22; Michael Strevens. 2003. 'The Role of the Priority Rule in Science', *Journal of Philosophy*, 100(2): 55–79.

59 Michael Weisberg and Ryan Muldoon. 2009. 'Epistemic Landscapes and the Division of Cognitive Labor', *Philosophy of Science*, 76(2): 225–252.

60 Zollman, 2007. See also Kevin, Zollman. 2010. 'The Epistemic Benefit of Transient Diversity, *Erkenntnis*, 72(1): 17–35.

(or vice) displayed by an institution cannot be found in all or most of its members. We have made it equally evident that institutional acts, procedures or methods of attaining epistemically high-quality beliefs and decisions are neither identical with nor reducible to individual approaches to forming epistemically valuable beliefs.

***

To summarize, we began with the assumption that it is common and intuitive to ascribe actions, intentions, motivations, and doxastic states to institutions. We have then proceeded to show that there are adequate reasons for considering such ascription ontologically and epistemically legitimate, rather than just metaphorical. Furthermore, we have proven that an institution is a collective agent that can both be ascribed epistemic states and be evaluated as epistemically virtuous or vicious. In this sense, institutions can be considered the same kind of epistemic agent as individual epistemic agents. However, we have also shown that the virtue of an institution diverges from the sum of the virtues of its members, and that encouraging the development of epistemically virtuous institutions isn't reducible to making each individual agent epistemically virtuous.

Given the aforementioned divergence, we must tackle the question of whether the epistemic virtues and vices of institutions can be considered identical to those ascribed to individual agents. Can we assess institutional beliefs and decisions using the same criteria used for evaluating individual beliefs? Can we meaningfully claim that an institution is a rational agent, that it generates truth-conductive beliefs, that it exhibits epistemic responsible decision-making, and like?

1.5.3. *Epistemic virtue of institutions*

It is interesting to note that, unlike individual epistemology, collective epistemology is unable to avoid metaphysics. Individual epistemology certainly presupposes that individual subjects exist, but doesn't have to argue for or against their existence or the existence of beliefs. Any commitment to a plural subject or institutional beliefs contains an implicit debate about the possible existence of plural minds (faculties, intentionality, dispositions, brains or such) of a metaphysically spooky sort. Despite possible doubts, Fricker comments that there is no space for spooky ontological commitment as joint commitment is definitely the combination of individual commitments – it is the pooling of wills or other resources such as faculties.[61] The same is claimed by Gilbert, who said that the pooling of wills generates an *as-if* group will "this will will be directed at an end, as if the wills belonged to a single person".[62]

Sarah Wright suggests that the virtues ascribed to groups are identical to those ascribed to individuals. She introduces the distinction between two types of goals: *telos* and *skopos* show how a theory of epistemic virtue might be extended to groups. While attaining truth is the *skopos*, our epistemic *telos* may be – believing well. In other words, besides our final goal of reaching the truth (which might be obstructed due to different reasons), we can strive to exercise epistemic virtues (of responsibility, carefulness, conscientiousness or like). Both individual and institutional virtues primarily remain focused on predetermined goals. In addition, Wright points out that we could either think of a group's goals as the mere sum of the goals of its individual members or as goals inherent to the group as a specific entity. For instance, the epistemic *telos* of an institution can be a long-standing disposition to believe well, "to believe in accordance with epistemic virtues".[63] Here, Wright clearly implies the fruitfulness of transposing virtue epistemology – and the focus of its epistemic evaluations on an agent's virtue – into the field of collective epistemology. If an institution is an epistemic agent with an epistemic goal, there is no reason not to ascribe the same virtues to individual and collective epistemic agents – such as groups, communities, social systems, institutions and like.

Moreover, this would imply that epistemic evaluation ought to focus on the epistemic agency of an institution, rather than remain restricted to its products, such as true beliefs: for example, we can claim that an institution exhibits virtue because it forms beliefs in an epistemically responsible manner – it carefully conducts institutional research before making decisions, it engages all available evidence, it encourages epistemic diversity in order to attain a broader evidential base, it encourages critical interaction and intellectual curiosity between different individuals, and like. Epistemic virtues are institutional features that enable their epistemic fulfilment and development, understood as successful attainment of the common goal or purpose. This approach is particularly valuable because it doesn't flee from the practical utility of normative approaches, which generate a critical stance towards different epistemic processes and their

61 Fricker, 2010.
62 Gilbert, 1989., p. 211.
63 Wright, 2014., p.126.

outcomes by precisely differentiating epistemic virtues from epistemic vices. Thus, this approach makes it equally possible to characterize an institution as epistemically thorough, conscientious and innovative, and as superficial, biased, overly cautious and inconsistent.

While some proponents of virtue epistemology consider epistemic responsibility the fundamental virtue due to its intrinsic importance for securing autonomous epistemic development,[64] others perceive it as an important as a means for attaining the epistemic goals of truth or justification.[65] Regardless of whether we understand epistemic responsibility as the responsible disposition of an institution that leads towards the final epistemic goal of attaining correct or truth-conductive beliefs and decisions, or as a desirable virtue in itself– there is a certain consensus that it is a generic concept of virtue from which we can infer all other epistemic virtues. It primarily emphasises the active role of an epistemic agent and the element of choice (motivation) related to epistemic agency. In that sense, epistemic responsibility can be understood as intellectual conscientiousness – the commendable incentive to attain truth or another epistemic virtue such as intellectual impartiality and openness, willingness to exchange ideas, awareness

---

64 For instance, Linda Zagzebski. 1996. *Virtues of the Mind: An Inquiry into the Nature of Virtue and the Ethical Foundations of Knowledge* (Cambridge: Cambridge University Press); Linda Zagzebski. 2003. 'The Search for the Source of Epistemic Good', *Metaphilosophy*, 34: 12–28; Code, 1987.; Fricker, 2007.; James Montmarquet. 1992. 'Epistemic Virtue', in Dancy Jonathan and Ernest Sosa (eds.), *A Companion of Epistemology* (Oxford: Blackwell), pp. 158-177; James Montmarquet. 1993. *Epistemic Virtue and Doxastic Responsibility* (Savage, Maryland: Rowman and Littlefield); Robert Roberts and Jay Wood. 2007. *Intellectual Virtues: An Essay in Regulative Epistemology* (Oxford: Oxford University Press).

65 For instance, Ernest Sosa. 1980. 'The Raft and the Pyramid: Coherence versus Foundations in the Theory of Knowledge', *Midwest Studies in Philosophy*, 5: 3–25; Ernest Sosa. 1991. *Knowledge in Perspective: Selected Essays in Epistemology* (London: Cambridge University Press); Ernest Sosa. 2007. *A Virtue Epistemology* (Oxford: Oxford University Press); Alvin I. Goldman. 1992. *Liaisons: Philosophy Meets the Cognitive and Social Sciences*, Cambridge (MA: MIT Press); John Greco. 1999. 'Agent Reliabilism', in Tomberlin James (ed.), *Philosophical Perspectives* (Atascadero, Calif.: Ridgeview Publishing Co.), pp. 273–296; John Greco. 2000. 'Two Kinds of Intellectual Virtue', *Philosophy and Phenomenological Research,* 60: 179–184; John Greco. 2002. 'Virtues in Epistemology', in Moser Paul (ed.), *Oxford Handbook of Epistemology* (New York: Oxford University Press), pp. 287–315; John Greco, J. Turri and M. Alfano. 2017. 'Virtue Epistemology', <http://plato.stanford.edu/entries/epistemology-virtue/> [accesed 19 June 2017]

of one's own fallibility, control of excessive epistemic enthusiasm, necessary caution, intellectual curiosity and courage, intellectual humility and kindness, and like.

To conclude, an institution is a collective agent that can exhibit epistemic virtues even when its individual members lack this virtue as persons (and vice versa). So, in order for an institution – to be epistemically virtuous – it is not required that all or most of its individual members are epistemically virtuous. It is required that an institution displays the epistemic virtue necessary for behaving in a way that produces beliefs and decisions of the highest epistemic quality. Being an epistemic agent per se, the virtues of an institution are the same as the virtues of an individual agent – thus, the institution can be subjected to the same evaluation as the individual agent. If the epistemic virtue of an institution can be considered an epistemic virtue at all, it needs to at least somewhat resemble the concept we are familiar with in individual epistemology. Otherwise, why would we think that institutional virtue is virtue? The theories and concepts of virtue epistemology, although tailored specifically for individual epistemic agents, can be successfully extended to collective ones.

***

The epistemic virtue of an institution relates to fulfilling the purpose, goal or status function defined by joint commitment or collective intention. If the purpose of an institution was to make impartial judgements, as is the case with juries, or to provide just and efficient leadership, as is expected from governments, we must inquire how epistemic virtue contributes to attainting these specific goals and purposes. Is the epistemic virtue of an institution reducible to merely practicing the kind of epistemic agency that most efficiently leads towards the goal, reminiscent to the ancient virtue of *techne?* Or should institutional virtue be understood outside the narrow scope of attaining goals, but as continuous cultivation of the dispositions and capacities necessary for systematically virtuous performances.

I will attempt to explain my account of institutional virtue on the basis of the ancient distinction between theoretical and practical epistemic virtues.[66] Ancient philosophy emphasises the unity of

66 Richard Parry. 2014. 'Episteme and Techne', in *Stanford Encyclopedia of Philosophy* <https://plato.stanford.edu/entries/episteme-techne/> [accesed 19 June 2017]

three different aspects of theoretical and practical knowledge. Plato, Aristotle and the Stoics not only share a common distinction between the theoretical and the practical, but also perceive virtue as the unity of theory and practice. Virtue is a kind of 'the craft of life' that presupposes conscientious understanding of the universe, the Stoics claimed. Practice needs to be grounded on an account, something that involves theoretical understanding, according to Aristotle.

According to Plato, whereas *techne* is associated with knowing *how* to do certain activities, *episteme* sometimes indicates a theoretical component of *techne* associated with understanding. Plato goes on to claim that *techne* is informed by knowledge of forms.[67] *Episteme* can be understood as an analysis (abstract calculation which judges or distinguishes the things we already know) and as commanding knowledge[68]. Aristotle describes three approaches to knowledge or epistemic virtue: *episteme*, *techne* and *phronesis*[69]. Whereas *techne* denotes technical know-how, *episteme* relates to theoretical know–why, and *phronesis* emphasizes practical knowledge. Aristotle stresses the tension and unity between theoretical and practical knowledge. While *techne* deals with things that change, in the sphere of variable (production, action, experience, context-dependent, goal-oriented)[70], *episteme* refers to something far beyond everyday experience, universals and necessity (scientific, abstract, analytical and deductive knowledge, first principles, truth and certainty).[71] However, Aristotle introduces also the additional concept of *phronesis*:

"We may grasp the nature of prudence (*phronesis*) if we consider what sort of people we call prudent. Well, it is thought to be the mark of a prudent man to be able to deliberate rightly about what is good and advantageous (…). So (…) prudence cannot be science or art; not science (*episteme*) because what can be done is variable (it may be done in different ways, or not done at all), and not art (*techne*) because action and production are generically different. For production aims at an end other than itself; but this is impossible in the case of action,

---

67 Parry, 2014.

68 Plato. *Complete Works*, ed. by John M. Cooper (Indianapolis: Hackett Publishing Co., 1997), *Statesman,* 259e.

69 Aristotle. *Nicomachean Ethics*, 2nd edn, trans. by Terence Irwin (Indianapolis: Hackett Publishing Co., 1999), *Nicomachean Ethics,* 384/322.

70 Aristotle, *Nicomachean Ethics,* 1140a1–23

71 Aristotle, *Nicomachean Ethics,* 1139b18–36

because the end is merely doing well. What remains, then, is that it is a true state, reasoned, and capable of action with regard to things that are good or bad for man. We consider that this quality belongs to those who understand the management of households or states".[72]

The Stoics make a similar distinction between two virtues – *techne* and *episteme*, two notions of knowledge and craft that flow together in forming the *science and art of living*. While *techne* is a systematic collection of cognitions unified with practice for some advantageous goal in life, *episteme* is secure and cannot be shaken for any reason.[73] Zeno considers *phronesis* to be knowledge (*episteme*).[74] According to Sextus, the Stoics say that *phronesis*, being knowledge (*episteme*) of the good and the evil, enables *techne* concerning life.[75]

It seems that these lessons from ancient wisdom lead to the conclusion that the notion of epistemic virtue refers not only to *techne*, understood as epistemic behaviour best suited to attaining a specific goal, but to the unity of *episteme* – the knowledge about what is real, *techne* – the knowledge about how to act, and *phronesis* – the knowledge about what is good or bad for people. In order to be virtuous, an institution ought to exercise thus understood epistemic virtues. A virtuous institution is not only virtuous on the sense of *techne* – knowing how to attain a desirable goal (efficiently), but also in the sense of *episteme* and *phronesis*. More precisely, an epistemically virtuous agent is an individual who is epistemically responsible in searching for what is real and its proper application to various situations in life, all while aiming for the good and avoiding the bad for people. Similarly, an epistemically virtuous institution is an institution in which scientific knowledge (knowledge about what is real) is applied in everyday life (knowledge about how to act) with the aim of improving the quality of overall life for all (knowledge about what is good or bad for citizens). A virtuous institution cannot be only technocratically virtuous, but needs to be much more.

---

72 Aristotle, *Nicomachean Ethics.* 1140a24–1140b12.

73 Hans F. A. von Arnim, (ed.). *Stoicorum Veterum Fragmenta,* 4 vols (Leipzig: Teubner, 1903-1924), Zeno, *Stoicorum Veterum Fragmenta,* I 73.

74 Plutarch. *Moralia,* trans. by W.C. Helmbold, Loeb Classical Library, vol. 6 and vol. 8, part 2 (Cambridge: Harvard University Press, 1993), *On moral virtue,* 441A.

75 Hans F. A. von Arnim, (ed.). 1903-1924., Sextus, *Stoicorum Veterum Fragmenta,* III 598.

Finally, let us return to the concrete issue of offering institutions plausible advice on being epistemically virtuous with regard to their foundational goals. We have seen that the shortcomings of the distinction between theoretical and practical epistemic virtues have been problematized since ancient times. Although it may be successful, an institution that merely develops know-how tactics for efficiently attaining goals in particular situations does not seem to display sufficient epistemic virtue. In order for an institution to be able to adjust to different circumstances and continuously attain its goals, it needs to ensure that its epistemic environment and conditions (procedures and practices) are based on theoretical epistemic know-why. Another crucial aspect of epistemic virtue is the development of practices that encourage epistemically just and morally appropriate beliefs. For example, institutions characterized by a strict social hierarchy tend to impose such moral prejudices that may endanger members of particular groups.[76] It is equally common to witness situations of testimonial injustice – unjustifiably reduced trust towards members of certain groups vulnerable to social prejudice.[77] Additional problems arise due to the fact that moral or cognitive prejudice are so deeply rooted and unconscious that they become difficult to neutralize or eliminate.[78] This is precisely why it should be explicitly emphasized that the task of attaining epistemically just beliefs must equally concern epistemically virtuous individuals and epistemically virtuous social institutions. For instance, educational systems that promote equality and make education more accessible to diverse social groups strive to protect the members of marginalized from experiencing testimonial injustice.[79] Thus understood, the unity of *techne*, *episteme* and *phronesis* constitutes the epistemic virtue of an institution.

---

76 Elizabeth Anderson. 2014. 'The Social Epistemology of Morality: Learning from the Forgotten History of the Abolition of Slavery', in Brady Michael and Miranda Fricker (eds.), *The Epistemic Life of Groups: Essays in the Epistemology of Collectives* (Oxford: Oxford University Press), pp. 75–94.

77 Fricker, 2007.

78 Linda M. Alcoff. 2010. 'Epistemic Identities', *Episteme*, 7(2): 128–137.

79 Elizabeth Anderson. 2012. 'Epistemic Justice as a Virtue of Social Institutions', *Social Epistemology*, 26(2): 163–173.

1.6. *Conclusion*

Social epistemology is a relatively new area of research that has witnessed a rapid surge of popularity in the last couple of decades. Although its legitimacy within the wider area of epistemology was initially questioned by certain epistemologists – and some doubts still remain – it has indubitably managed to become an important and exciting sphere of epistemological research. While some of its topics, such as the questions of testimony or conversational practices, have been the focus of numerous important philosophical debates prior to the advent of social epistemology, it can be considered a novelty within standard analytic philosophy inasmuch as it claims that the phenomenon of cognition is socially situated, making social entities a valid subject of epistemological evaluation. In this sense, it is sensible to consider social epistemology a new and interesting project of expanding traditional epistemological topics to new targets: groups, institutions, social practices and social systems.

Although social epistemology, including the sub-discipline of collective epistemology, extends epistemological research far beyond the limits of traditional epistemology, it is fully respectful of the essential features of traditional individual epistemology: the normative character of the discipline and the intrinsic and objective epistemic quality of doxastic states (regardless of whether it is defined as the feature of a propositions or as a virtue, whether it bears monist ties to truth or is understood as a broader plural value). Just like the epistemic value of beliefs, judgments and decisions is irreducible to political or social values, epistemic virtue can be related to ethical or political virtues, but cannot be reduced to them. This extension of traditional epistemology is congruent with the view that epistemology can and should be interdisciplinary and practically applicable; its role cannot be exhausted in providing explanations and theoretical evaluations of the beliefs of individuals, groups, institutions, social practices and systems, but in actively making recommendations for their improvement. In addition to standard theoretical values, social epistemology has the additional potential of being a real world epistemology. Thus, it could provide epistemology with the status currently ascribed to, for example, the philosophy of politics or ethics – the ability to, both individually and institutionally, affect the common good.

2.
EXTENDED EPISTEMOLOGY AND HYBRID VIRTUES

2.1. *Monism of truth and plurality of epistemic values*

'Truth' is traditionally considered the fundamental and primary epistemic aim and value in the same manner as, for example, 'good' is considered the fundamental ethical value. The same role is played by 'justice' in political philosophy or by 'beauty' in aesthetics. However, last two decades of research within standard analytic epistemology have witnessed increasingly intense debates about epistemic values and intellectual virtues – a trend that has led to the idea of plural epistemic aims and values as an alternative to the traditional value monism of truth.[1]

Discussions regarding epistemic values are partially dependent on different understandings of epistemology as a philosophical discipline or the appropriate scope of its topics. Should we accept the narrow definition of epistemology as a theory of knowledge, it would seem natural to set the truth of a belief as the primary epistemic aim. In this sense, an epistemologist should primarily strive to define the criteria of justification and analyse the concept of knowledge.[2] If, on the other hand, we opted for the wider account of epistemological research as an analysis of the very process of cognition – the different ways we form beliefs, produce various cognitive products other than beliefs (such as,

---

1 Jonathan L. Kvanvig. 1992. *The Intellectual Virtues and the Life of the Mind: On the Place of the Virtues in Contemporary Epistemology* (Savage, Maryland: Rowman and Littlefield); Jonathan L. Kvanvig. 2003. *The Value of Knowledge and the Pursuit of Understanding* (Cambridge: Cambridge University Press); Jonathan L. Kvanvig. 2005. 'Truth and the Epistemic Goal', in Steup Matthias and Ernest Sosa (eds.), *Contemporary Debates in Epistemology* (Malden, Mass.: Blackwell Publishing), pp. 285–295; Adrian Haddock, A. Millar and D. Pritchard (eds.). 2009. *Epistemic Value* (Oxford: Oxford University Press).

2 Marian David. 2001. 'Truth as the Epistemic Goal', in Steup Matthias (ed.), *Knowledge, Truth, and Duty* (New York: Oxford University Press), pp. 151–169.

for instance, assumptions and working hypotheses) and form doxastic states like being trustful or accepting the judgments of others, as well as other kinds of cognitive accomplishments such as finding meaning in the course of experiential information, solving problems, and like – then it would be possible to postulate different epistemic values such as genuine understanding, epistemic responsibility, adherence with evidence and like. A wider and more extensive account of epistemology consequently expands the scope of its topics, from defining and determining the conditions of knowledge to critically analysing various cognitive processes devoted to making decision, acquiring beliefs and knowledge, evaluating, retaining and revising beliefs and other doxastic states, assessing the influence of social circumstances on epistemic outcomes and like.[3] Cognitive accomplishments or successfully formed doxastic decisions don't necessarily need to be evaluated on the basis of their truthfulness – instead, cognitive efforts can rightfully be exerted with the goal of adjusting beliefs to experience, basing beliefs on evidential proof, seeking empirical adequacy, making rational assumptions, promising working hypotheses or justified guesses, attaining genuine understanding and theoretical knowledge, or conducting epistemically responsible research.[4]

It is possible to accept the list of epistemic values suggested by Jonathan Kvanvig and still maintain that truth is the only, ultimate or primary epistemic goal – in this sense, the mentioned values are instrumental inasmuch as they indicate that certain beliefs, hypotheses or assumptions are likely to be true, or that certain processes are reliable guides to truth[5]. This implies that, once we had finally attained a true

---

3 This account agrees with Locke's original definition of epistemology as a discipline that doesn't limit its research to assessing the possibility of attaining true beliefs, but which is also concerned with the processes of cognition and the scope of knowledge. (John Locke. *An Essay Concerning Human Understanding*, ed. by Nidditch, Peter H. (Oxford: Oxford University Press, 1690/1975). An extended definition of epistemology that includes the epistemic properties of social processes and institutions is also supported by Goldman, 2010.

4 Kvanvig, 2005. See also Jonathan Kvanvig. 2010. 'Virtue Epistemology', in Pritchard Duncan and Sven Bernecker (eds.), *Routledge Companion to Epistemology* (New York: Routledge), pp. 199–207.

5 This monist or reductionist account of truth as the only intrinsic epistemic value is defended by the likes of Laurence BonJour. 1985. *The Structure of Empirical Knowledge* (Cambridge, MA: Harvard University Press); William Alston. 1988. 'The Deontological conception of epistemic justification', *Philosophical Perspectives*, 2:257–299.

belief, all other epistemic values would lose their value. To illustrate this with an example, suppose that I had attempted to find out how to reach a certain cathedral. Once I had finally attained a true belief about the correct path, it would no longer be relevant what processes had led me to it, whether the outcome is congruent with my prior experience or whether I had consulted a sufficiently broad evidential basis.[6] Regarding this 'value problem', Kvanvig holds that epistemic value is not exhausted in external success – that is, the objective truth of a belief – but that important internal elements of autonomous value can be found within the very process of cognition. Knowledge (justified true belief) is, for example, superior to a mere true belief because it is attained by engaging in independently valuable intellectual activities (having sound reasons for believing and relying on convincing evidence makes a belief more coherent with its surrounding system of beliefs and allows for better understanding). Even though this attitude dates back to the beginnings of epistemological thought and the likes of Plato, its significance was recently reignited by virtue epistemology. Numerous proponents of this fruitful new approach argue that the value of true beliefs attained due to intellectual virtues – wisdom, understanding, epistemic responsibility and like – surpasses that of differently formed true beliefs, and particularly of those attained through lucky incidents. It should be emphasized that, in contemporary discussions, virtue epistemologists have played an essential role in promoting this pluralism of intellectual virtues, holding that they make one's intellectual life richer and more satisfying.[7]

It is important to note that Kvanvig doesn't only question the monism of truth or reductionism (the reduction of all values to the value of attaining truth or avoiding error), but also argues that every cognitive success is important in itself. Concepts such as knowledge, understanding, wisdom, rationality or empirical adequacy can thus be treated as separate epistemic values, rather than as mere instruments or supplements to the acquisition of truth. In this sense, cognitive accomplishments such as finding meaning in the course of experience or being epistemically responsible while making a decision can be explained without reference

6 This is known as the *swamping problem*: if properties such as evidence are merely the instruments of attaining a further good (truth), then the achievement of that further good renders the instrumentally valuable properties of a belief virtually worthless (for example, being based on sound evidence). For more, see Kvanvig, 2003.

7 For more, see Kvanvig, 2003., 2005., 2010. and Zagzebski, 1996., 1998., 2003.

to truth. To offer a simpler example, the empirical adequacy of a theory does not have to be understood as a property that supports the likelihood of its truthfulness. Instead, we can conclude that the theory is thus less likely to be (easily) refuted by experience[8]. In a similar manner, being epistemically responsible in forming a belief can be valuable in itself if it is understood as one's commitment to the epistemic duty to base beliefs on evidence, sound reasons and other epistemic standards of consistency and justification. Epistemic duty does not have to be a function of truth and can instead be understood as one's avoidance of being intellectually superficial, inconsistent, lazy, or like.

However, we are neither attempting to choose a side in the debate between monists (reductionists) and pluralists on the topic of epistemic values, nor do we aim to analyse the strengths of pluralist approaches – be it pluralism of additional values or pluralism of intrinsic epistemic values. We are primarily striving to point out the possibility, sensibility and, finally, the necessity of perceiving epistemology as a discipline that analyses and epistemically evaluates doxastic states, cognitive processes, epistemic acts and general events, instead of limiting the area of its concern to analysing the concepts of truth, justification or knowledge. Secondly, it is important to show that such an extensive account allows for more comprehensive definitions of cognitive achievements or successes and a greater understanding of the particular epistemic values inherent to different cognitive processes and activities.

In the light of our discussion on social epistemology, it is evident that this pluralistic approach to epistemic values is far better suited to the analysis and evaluation of the epistemic properties of social processes, practices and institutions. While explications of the concept of knowledge are abstract and unrelated to the real-life dimension of cognition, reflections upon the epistemic quality of institutional decision-making and the responsibility of institutions in defining procedures or solving problems, rather than upon their objective truth value, are a sensible and interesting cause for debate. The narrowness of the traditional account of epistemology is the precise reason why many refuse to accept the topics of social epistemology as real epistemological concerns. However, it ought to be noted that such criticism is becoming less frequent as numerous have welcomed the expansion of the area of epistemology and the prospect of making epistemic values less strictly tied to the truth value of propositions. Therefore, our final and repeatedly emphasized

8 Kvanvig, 2005., 2010.

goal is to demonstrate the validity and necessity of an extensive approach to epistemology in general, which then allows for better epistemic evaluations of those cognitive processes or intellectual activities (such as communicational acts, institutional decisions, decision-making processes in social systems and like) that were traditionally exempt from epistemic evaluations. In the end, it is particularly important to note that this extensive approach not only enables a more comprehensive understanding of cognition, but can positively influence the epistemic value of real cognitive acts in various social situations and thus produce more epistemically efficient solutions to problems.

2.2. *Social epistemology and virtue epistemology*

The value turn characteristic of the last two decades of epistemological research has given rise to a particularly influential position – virtue epistemology. It is a widespread and influential epistemological project whose aim is to expand the area of concern of epistemic evaluations and epistemic values. Evaluations are no longer focused on the truth-value of the proposition and instead emphasize the epistemic virtues of the epistemic agent. We need no further explications of this approach to see that virtue epistemology is a fruitful normative framework for the topics of social epistemology: for example, since epistemic evaluation is no longer limited to examining the truth of a belief, it is now also possible to evaluate the epistemic responsibility of individuals within the group, as well as the responsibility of groups as special entities and agents, in making decisions. It is possible, for example, to discuss whether political decisions are more epistemically justified if they are based on systematic analyses of available empirical material or on efforts to harmonize the existing attitudes of citizens with contrasting worldviews, even if they cannot be formally classified as true. Such considerations of the epistemic virtues of individual and collective agents are almost unimaginable within the traditionally narrow account of epistemological concerns.

***

Various epistemological positions developing under the aegis of virtue epistemology – despite offering different definitions of the nature of virtue or harboring different stances about epistemically relevant topics – all share two basic attitudes. The first is the foundational thesis of traditional epistemology (especially emphasized within standard analytical epistemology) that defines epistemology as a normative discipline. Virtue epistemology focuses on the normative aspect of epistemic evaluations, where normative standards and values are not considered conventional or relativistic, but are presumed to have some sort of objective validity[9]. The second attitude, however, substantially deviates from the traditional epistemological approach according to which an epistemologist ought to be primarily concerned with assessing whether a proposition, belief or doxastic state is true, justified, rational or like. Instead, virtue epistemologists center their evaluations on epistemic or intellectual agents – which can include collective entities such as groups, communities, social systems, institutions and like, as well as individual epistemic agents. The focus of epistemic research thus shifts to, for instance, the question of whether an epistemic agent genuinely understands what is happening (instead of whether they simply have a true belief) or whether they are epistemically responsible in forming beliefs in the sense that they make careful observations, infer valid conclusions, evaluate different hypotheses and analyze available evidence. An epistemic or intellectual virtue is the property of an epistemic agent that supports their intellectual growth and fulfillment, or that simply defines them as a virtuous epistemic agent.[10] That is why, although they emphasize the normative aspect of this approach, virtue epistemologists often readily engage with empirical data (psychological, social, political or historical) that may provide information necessary for conscientious epistemic evaluations. The key feature of this approach is its focus on assessing the epistemic agent and their cognitive and intellectual character in order to promote intellectual growth and well-being. In other words, virtue epistemology does not scorn the practical utility inherent to the critical attitude towards different cognitive processes and outcomes produced by its differentiation of intellectual virtues and vices.

---

9 As seen in the first chapter, Goldman holds that this stance separates real epistemological projects from the epistemological revisionism characteristic of various kinds of social constructivism, postmodernism and like. For more, see Goldman, 2010.

10 It is evident that virtue epistemology mirrors virtue ethics inasmuch as it focuses on agency and the agent (in this case, epistemic) and evaluates their achievements in the terms of growth and fulfillment (in this case, intellectual). Moreover, authors such as Zagzebski especially emphasize the importance of this analogy and their neo-Aristotelian approach to epistemology. For more, see Zagzebski, 1996., 1998., 2003. and Michael S. Brady and Duncan H. Pritchard (eds.). 2003. *Moral and Epistemic Virtues* (Oxford: Blackwell).

Advocates and sympathizers of virtue epistemology are roughly divisible into two large camps:[11] (i) epistemologists who purport that intellectual virtues refer to the cognitive abilities or disposition of the epistemic agent (perception, deliberation, memory, etc.) in the manner that, for example, an agent's keen perceptiveness is virtuous inasmuch as it leads to truth or knowledge[12] and (ii) epistemologists who believe that intellectual virtues are (character) traits that can be learned, so each intellectual agent is responsible for consciously developing virtues such as intellectual conscience or openness that will enrich their future intellectual accomplishments.[13] However, both camps postulate the promotion of intellectual or epistemic development as the final epistemic goal. It is possible to differentiate between conventional and alternative approaches to virtue epistemology in that conventionalists – even within an epistemological framework that evaluates the agent rather than the proposition or the mere outcome – still focus on the standard questions of contemporary Anglo–Saxon epistemology such as the definition of knowledge, scepticism or justification.[14] The alternative approach, on the other hand, is primarily concerned with the issues of deliberation or argumentation, communication, research, understanding and wisdom, as well as with the psychological, social, ethical and political dimensions of knowledge.[15] It is particularly important to emphasize that this is not a rigid division given that there are a number of topics on which virtue epistemologists agree and reach compromises. For instance, it is possible to define the epistemic responsibility of an agent as a reliable disposition that leads to truth[16] or to claim that justification or knowledge are states attainable by practicing intellectual virtues such as wisdom.[17]

---

11 For more, see Greco, Turri and Alfano, 2017.

12 Sosa, 1980., 1991., 2007.; Greco,1999., 2000., 2002.

13 Code, 1987.; Zagzebski, 1996, 1998., 2003.; Montmarqet, 1992., 1993.; Roberts and Wood, 2007.; Fricker, 2007.

14 Sosa, 1980., 2003., 2007.; Zagzebski, 1996., 2003.

15 Kvanvig, 2003., 2005., 2010.; Fricker, 2007. See also Wayne Riggs. 2002. 'Reliability and the Value of Knowledge', *Philosophy and Phenomenological Research*, 64: 79–96; Wayne Riggs. 2003. 'Understanding 'Virtue' and the Virtue of Understanding', in DePaul Michael and Linda Zagzebski (eds.), *Intellectual Virtue: Perspectives from Ethics and Epistemology* (Oxford: Oxford University Press), pp. 203–226; Wayne Riggs. 2006. 'The Value Turn in Epistemology', in Hendricks Vincent and Duncan Pritchard (eds.), *New Waves in Epistemology* (Aldershot: Ashgate), pp. 300–323.

16 Greco, 1999.

17 Zagzebski, 1996.

Virtue epistemology provides a normative framework and an open space for evaluating the epistemic properties of groups, communities, institutions or systems in a manner unimaginable during the primacy of narrowly understood traditional epistemology and its focus on the truth-value of propositions. For instance, the virtue of epistemic responsibility of an agent is often used as a generic virtue from which others such as cautiousness, curiosity, courage, etc. can be derived. Thus, it becomes possible to praise the epistemic attitude of the jury by applauding their epistemic caution and conscientiousness in considering the available evidence, even if it is not possible to assess their final judgment as either true or false. Similarly, we can commend a local government for developing a smart city by intelligently developing procedures capable of effectively addressing its citizens' problems, although we would be hard-pressed to evaluate their decisions as true or even as truth-conductive. This is applicable to a variety of cognitive processes inherent to social environments whose outcomes do not seem to correspond to an objective truth value. This concept of epistemic responsibility, which implies one's cautious or conscientious treatment of evidence in the decision-making process, is an indubitably useful normative concept for evaluating individuals and groups who make decisions within social systems. In that sense, it is fairly irrelevant whether this virtue is perceived as an instrument for attaining a truth as an epistemic outcome or whether it is inherently valuable in itself. By emphasizing the virtue of epistemic responsibility (instead of merely evaluating the justification or the truth value of the final proposition), we are shifting our focus to the active role of the epistemic agent and the element of choice (motivation) related to intellectual activity – an element important for researching the topics of social epistemology. Epistemic responsibility implies intellectual conscientiousness, the autonomous motivation to attain the best epistemic outcomes through intellectually unbiased acts – such as the readiness to exchange different ideas, to come to terms with one's own fallibility, to restrain excessive cognitive enthusiasm in favour of cautiousness and to nurture intellectual curiosity and courage, as well to cultivate intellectual humility, inclusiveness and kindness. The general concept of epistemic responsibility and the derived virtues support a novel approach to evaluating cognitive processes and achievements – such as scientific research, procedures of forming and analysing hypotheses and theories, decision-making processes in social collectives and ascriptions of trust in communicational acts – by evaluating the acts of epistemic agents. For instance, an innately curious scientist aware of his own fallibility and the possible influence of his preconceptions on future research seems to approach his epistemic task of research with responsibility, and thus has a greater chance of producing true outcomes. He is deserving of epistemic praise even if we cannot assess his ultimate epistemic outcome, his theory, as true. Likewise, a person who is epistemically just and who judges the credibility of another person with the awareness that she may be harbouring unjustified stereotypes and prejudices about the other's social group is more likely to successfully acquire and transfer knowledge. Virtue epistemology thus provides an optimal normative framework for discussing the topics of social epistemology inasmuch as it allows us to attribute cognitive successes or failures to individuals, groups or institutions – even when it would be dubious or downright impossible to assess their agency in terms of truth.

I will continue to show that virtue epistemology isn't just a fruitful framework for epistemic evaluations of acts performed within social environments, but that it has the additional value of being able to link itself with political, ethical and other evaluations – thus encouraging and legitimizing the epistemic assessment of social entities. Should we recall Foucault's 'knowledge of the oppressed or subjugated', his high regard for the moral superiority and different epistemic perspective of the disadvantaged explicitly assumes the stance that decisions, attitudes and beliefs have an additional ethical dimension. Foucault does, however, somehow infer epistemic value from moral status, which is an attitude that could, at best, be discussed. What I am actually trying to point out is that the focus of virtue epistemology on the agent, rather than on the proposition, makes it possible to complement common moral judgments about an individual's virtues and vices with an additional epistemic component, which has been inexcusably ignored – or reduced to mere ethical and political virtue.

2.3. *Hybrid virtues: the harmonization of epistemic, ethical and political virtues*

We have already stressed that social epistemology perceives cognition as a socially situated phenomenon. The aim of social epistemology, from its generally extended perspective, is to subject the beliefs, judgments, decisions, and doxastic states of epistemic agents, regardless of whether they are individual or collective agents, to epistemic analyses and assessments conscious of their origin, motivations and resulting consequences. In evaluating, for instance, the attitudes and epistemic behaviours of an individual, group or institution within a social environment, we realize that epistemic assessment is a single aspect of a much larger picture: every real-world attitude or decision of an individual, group or institution is difficult to separate from their ethical/political backgrounds and from the wider social context of cause and effect from which such a position/decision had stemmed. As an illustration, imagine a national security service institution that decides to subject Afro–American or Muslim passengers at airports to more thorough scrutiny. Even though their decision might be considered epistemically justified in that is was founded on statistical evidence which suggests that members of these groups are more likely to perpetrate criminal and terrorist acts, it is undeniably ethically and politically incorrect in discriminating the members of these groups. By their definition, epistemic assessments must be able to verify the reliability of used statistical data and evidence – however, they largely ignore the wider social and political context that caused such statistical data, nor do they take into account the economic and political consequences of putting such decisions into practice. The extent of such (possibly justified) epistemic assessments is clearly unable to encompass the wider legitimacy of a decision and, as such, is of questionable significance. In real circumstances, a thinking person would hardly ever accept the relevance of abstract epistemic assessments, let alone the idea that socially desirable decisions should be made on the basis of theory-laden epistemological evaluations. This withstanding, I do not think that such extreme examples should encourage us to dismiss epistemic assessments as socially irrelevant or inapplicable. Isolated ethical/political justifications of decisions and judgments cannot suffice because they lack the necessarily epistemic legitimacy, i.e. they are seldom decisions of the highest epistemic quality. We have already questioned Foucault's tendency to ascribe epistemic superiority to the attitudes of the subjugated on the sole basis of their oppression. Likewise, there are numerous empirical examples (more closely discussed in later chapters), which show that not even democratic decision-making – the gleaming ideal of ethically/politically desirable behaviour – will always produce epistemically valuable decisions. Just like abstract epistemic assessments cannot address all important aspects of social practices or decisions, isolated ethical and political evaluation are an equally inappropriate exclusive criterion for their acceptance or rejection.

Assessments of social practices and institutions require both an epistemic and an ethical/political perspective. A desirable framework for comprehensively evaluating beliefs, social institutions and practices in terms of intellectual, ethical and political values can be found in a new project called 'ethics of knowing'[18] – and especially in its promising concept of *hybrid virtues*. The project of developing a hybrid perspective promotes those epistemological assessments of social practices and institutions that have often been ignored or even intentionally isolated because ethical and political evaluations were thought of as exclusively appropriate for appraising social phenomena. The fact stands that assessing the epistemic properties of individual beliefs, social practices and institutions apart from their ethical and political aspects – its theoretical and methodological significance notwithstanding – is usually considered too abstract to relevantly evaluate the social desirability of institutions and practices. Furthermore, since standard analytic epistemology insisted on normative epistemic purism and focused on the individual epistemic agent without taking into account the social dimension of knowledge, it consciously limited the scope of epistemological research to abstract analyses of basic epistemological concepts such as knowledge, truth, justification or like. This tendency resulted in the widespread the marginalization of epistemological values in assessing the legitimacy of real-world social practices and institutions. Similarly, it gave rise to the unacceptable 'deconstruction' of epistemology as unnecessary and the consequent popularization of epistemic nihilism.[19] This absolute unwillingness to subject socially situated beliefs, decisions and procedures to epistemological assessment – inherent to traditional analytic epistemology – is the crucial reason behind the success of postmodern orthodoxy and general tendencies to renounce epistemology.

The new tendencies in social epistemology mentioned in the first chapter,[20] as well as the value turn which gave rise to virtue

---

18 Fricker, 2007.

19 See for instance in Rorty,1979.; Latour and Woolgar, 1986.; Barnes and Bloor, 1982. See also Michel Foucault. 1980. *Power/Knowlwdge: Selected Interviews and Other Writings 1972-1977*, ed. by Colin Gordon (New York: Pantheon); Michel Foucault. 1991. *Discourse and Truth: The Problematizations of Parrhesia*, ed. by Joseph Pearson (Evanston: Northwestern University Press).

20 Alvin I. Goldman. 1987. 'Foundations of Social Epistemics', *Synthese*, 73(1): 109–144. See also in Goldman, 1999., 2004., 2010.; Miranda Fricker. 2006. 'Powerlessness and Social Interpretation', *Episteme*, 3(1-2): 96-108. See also Fricker, 2007., Code, 2010.

epistemology, have provided a framework for comprehensive social assessments, which will no longer neglect epistemology. Fricker's promising concept of hybrid virtues – and corresponding *hybrid view* on virtues – provide concrete opportunities for assessing individual beliefs, social institutions and practices in a manner respectful to both epistemic and ethical/political values. For instance, her concept of *epistemic justice* is a paradigmatic hybrid virtue that unifies epistemic, ethical and political values. In this chapter devoted to hybrid virtues and hybrid thinking, I will briefly explain the complexity of epistemically assessing social phenomena – both in terms of relevance and (should we accept their relevance) applicability in real life.

A solution may be found in isolating epistemic assessments from all other values, thus opting for an attitude that disregards everything but the epistemological perspective. We could also claim that the task of harmonizing different virtues belongs to a discipline foreign to epistemology, or that they ought to be harmonized in the course of their practical implementation. I don't think that these choices seem wise. This dilemma is an integral element of the task at hand – an analysis of the epistemic features of democracy in the context of ethical/political assessments. Had I conducted an analysis just to conclude that a practice is desirable because it meets the epistemic criteria, regardless of the fact that it is undemocratic, my exploration of democracy would be reduced to mere theoretical speculation devoid of any applicable significance. Knowing that I aim to stress the necessity of including epistemological evaluations in comprehensive assessments of social practices and institutions, I will conclude this chapter by stating that an isolated, abstract and inapplicable epistemological assessment which is neglectful of other determinants of an institution's desirability can never lead to a meaningful outcome. The potential of epistemically assessing social entities and practices should be explored in the context of its harmonization with ethical and political evaluations – by creating a hybrid platform of values.

***

In the following section of this chapter, I will try to clarify the concept of hybrid virtues using the example of epistemic injustice, as articulated by Miranda Fricker. I will start by exploring her notion of testimonial injustice as a form of epistemic injustice or, more precisely, by questioning the epistemic and ethical justificatory status of credibility deficits. Fricker excellently pointed out the necessity and possibility of making hybrid assessments. On the other hand, I will also show that her account leaves the concrete application of hybrid assessments – the processes of harmonizing epistemic, ethical and political values – somewhat opaque.

It is crucial to note that the majority of real-world cases are difficult to assess because epistemic and ethical culpability don't necessarily overlap. For instance, Fricker's account of credibility deficits is a uniquely clear case in that it is both epistemically and ethically unjustified. However, her later example of credibility excesses is far more challenging to assess because it is not equally epistemically and ethically culpable. Even though further challenges arise in those hybrid assessments in which epistemic and ethical/political evaluation happen to be conflicted, I will show why the hybrid approach still remains more conscientious than any alternative method of conducting isolated evaluations. Particular emphasis will be put on social practices such as epistemic paternalism or epistocracy which clearly exemplify possible conflicts of epistemic and ethical/political values. In explaining the complexity of evaluating these two controversial social practices, I will attempt to propose a minimal condition for the justification of individual beliefs, social practices or institutions from the perspective of a hybrid view.[21]

2.3.1. *Testimony and trustworthiness: the case of epistemic injustice*

Testimonies of other people are a fundamental social source of knowledge. The statements and testimonies of others are the key source of information on the basis of which we form, retain, or revise our beliefs. A paradigmatic model of cognition in a social environment

---

21 It ought to be noted that the concepts of 'truth' or the value of 'truth' will prominently feature in this book as a generic assessment of epistemic value. As has been repeatedly emphasized, I accept a wider account of epistemic value that is broader and pluralistic. Although epistemic value is generally understood as epistemic success and expressed in terms of truth, it can also subsume the concepts of epistemic responsibility, conscientiousness, problem solving, empirical adequacy, understanding and like. More specifically, I derive my understanding of appropriate epistemic evaluations from recent achievements in virtue epistemology. My usage of the term 'truth' in this epistemically unconventional sense that equates it to general epistemic quality refers to the widespread equalization of epistemic value and the value of 'truth' in general discourses, much like the value of 'justice' in philosophy of politics can be equated with a range of values – such as inclusiveness, fairness or tolerance – that prominently feature in general discourses.

can be found in the process of assessing and ascribing the credibility of other people and the reliability of their words in order to accept, suspend or reject their testimonies. Accepted testimonies thus become appropriate foundations for forming our beliefs. Relying on Edward Craig, Fricker claims that the process of assessing another as a better or worse informant is a fundamentally epistemic practice that rests on our understanding of the concept of 'knowledge'.[22] Namely, the meaning of the concept of 'knowledge' cannot be grasped through abstractly analysing the verb 'to know'. Craig's professed *practical approach* to explaining the concept of 'knowledge' rests on the views (i) that we primarily need true beliefs in order to survive and that (ii) as an active agent, an epistemic subject can appropriately influence the world only if she can form true beliefs about the possible outcomes of her actions.[23] If we want to be able to attain true beliefs, we ought to develop collective or social strategies of gathering information. We form countless credibility judgments about the epistemic authority or the epistemic rationality of others on an everyday basis. However, Fricker brilliantly complements Craig by arguing that these strategies and credibility judgments are never socially neutral. Our estimates of the credibility or epistemic authority of the informant, as well as the reliability of their testimonies, often depend on the social identity of the informant – more precisely, on the stereotypes and prejudices associated with their social identity.[24] Such stereotypes and prejudices about social identity (contained in what is called the *collective social imagination*) often depend on social status, the position of power or powerlessness of the informant's social group. For instance, Shapin's famously outlined the influence of a scientist's social power and status on accepting scientific practices, methodologies and theories as true in 17th century England.[25] Having the status of a 17th century England aristocrat generally provided not only social privileges, but also the status of an epistemic and rational authority. English gentlemen

22 Fricker, 1998., 2011.

23 Edward Craig. 1990. *Knowledge and the State of Nature* (Oxford: Oxford University Press).

24 Fricker, 2007.

25 See more in Steven Shapin. 1975. 'Phrenological Knowledge and the Social Structure of Early Nineteenth-Century Edinburgh', *Annals of Science*, 32: 219–243; Steven Shapin. 1994. *A Social History of Truth* (Chicago: University of Chicago Press); Steven Shapin and Simon Schaffer. 1985. *Leviathan and the Air-Pump,* Princeton (New Jersey: Princeton Univrsity Press). See also Latour and Woolgar, 1986.

were held to be trustworthy with regard to almost all matters, while lower class men could be trusted with none. Even more unfortunate were women who were perceived as unreliable regardless of their ancestry. Gender and class identities correlated with social status in clearly determining who is deserving of trust, regardless of whether that person was really a 'good informant' who could contribute to the formation of true beliefs. Lorraine Code describes a contemporary example of unfounded police mistrust towards an African–American woman who wanted to file a racial incident.[26] Fricker tells a similar story of police officers who, while conducting a regular drivers check, exhibited an entirely ungrounded level of mistrust towards a young black driver who claimed to be the genuine owner of the car he was driving.[27] In addition, she illustrates gender-based denials of credibility with a fictional example of 'female irrationality' found in Patricia Highsmith's *Talented Mr Ripley*.[28] Independently of these examples, we witness countless situations in which some people are simply ascribed greater or lesser epistemic authority (and rationality) on the basis of their social status or their belonging to a particular social group – the uneducated as opposed to the educated, the unemployed as opposed to the employed, women as opposed to men, the poor as opposed to the rich, as well as various ethnical, racial, religious or ideological minorities or people affiliated with certain scientific fields – on an everyday basis.

It should be immediately pointed out that a mere affiliation with a particular social group and identity isn't always the irrelevant explanation of someone's increased epistemic authority about certain issues: a leftist may be a more reliable informant about unionism simply because they are more likely to be interested and informed about unions, just like a rich man is more likely to be knowledgeable about the life of the golden youth. Finally, it could even be assumed that English gentlemen were indeed more reliable informants because they had enough free time to seek information and because their social 'code of honour' would be seriously threatened had they been caught in a lie or a mistake. The epistemic discrimination shown here is not synonymous with the epistemic selection of good informants. Epistemic discrimination is a situation in which social and epistemic

---

26 Code, 1995.

27 Miranda Fricker. 2013. 'Epistemic justice as a condition of political freedom', *Synthese*, 190(7): 1317-1332.

28 Fricker, 2007.

injustice combine to attribute individuals with unjustified excesses or deficits of credibility in accordance with stereotypes about their social belonging and identity. More specifically, I am referring to situations in which a credibility judgment (or a judgment about the reliability of a testimony) is *epistemically* wrong because the attributed reliability and credibility do not correspond to the actual state of affairs for reasons unrelated to rational calculation, but instead caused by social injustice. Epistemic injustice is a situation in which social injustice, entrenched in the form of social prejudices, generates epistemic errors.

It is crucial to understand that such epistemic errors never remain at the level of a mistaken credibility judgment, but go on to produce additional bad epistemic consequences by excluding truly good informants and including those who are not, thus hampering the entire system of forming and disseminating true beliefs. Finally, this social and epistemic injustice instigates further social and ethical injustice towards those already subject to unjustified credibility deficits because they are prevented from participating in epistemic and social processes. Fricker perceives cases of *credibility deficits* (as opposed to excesses) as particularly malicious because they unable the subject to participate in conversations that hinge on trust: this exclusion does not only portray the cognitive abilities necessary for every individual's self-esteem as questionable, but discriminates against them as social beings. In this sense, Fricker considers epistemic injustice a *hybrid error* that is equally intellectually and ethically culpable. Epistemic justice, on the other hand, is a hybrid virtue that harmonizes epistemic and ethical values by neutralizing prejudices derived from social identities, thereby eliminating the systemic harm exercised upon vulnerable groups.

2.3.2 *Deficits and excesses of trust*

In order to fully understand the concept of epistemic injustice, we ought to delve a bit deeper into Fricker's account. Even though her elaboration distinguishes between testimonial injustice and hermeneutical injustice[29], I will remain focused on the aforementioned phenomenon of testimonial injustice in which the hearer does not accord the speaker the level of credibility that they are due, thus inflicting them with serious epistemic and ethical harm. Let me explain the problem in

29 Fricker, 2006., 2007., 2013.

a more detailed manner. A testimonial situation occurs when a speaker/informant conveys information to a hearer/audience. The hearer then makes a credibility judgment by ascribing a certain degree of reliability, credibility or trustworthiness to the speaker, finally making an epistemic decision of trusting, distrusting or suspending their trust. A testimonial situation can only lead to epistemic success if it fulfils two fundamental conditions: the speaker condition and the hearer condition.[30] A speaker fulfils their condition by the means of their reliability, that is, their epistemic and moral character – only a competent and sincere informant can be deemed epistemically responsible. Likewise, the hearer condition hinges on an epistemically responsible assessment of the speaker: the ascribed reliability needs to correspond to the real reliability of the speaker. It is important to note that in any testimonial situation, the hearer doesn't only assess (in accordance to their background evidence) the acceptability of the testified content, but also the speaker's general trustworthiness as an informant.

Fricker stresses that the hearer's assessment first undertakes the form of basic testimonial perception, later becoming a more sophisticated testimonial reflection about the speaker's trustworthiness. According to her account, even during the basic testimonial perception the hearer perceives the speaker as a member of a social group (defined by education, gender, age, class, regional background or like) and makes an accordant credibility judgment. What Fricker is trying to point out is that, consequently, all credibility judgements are inevitably infected by our stereotypes and prejudices. Stereotypes are social generalizations about the epistemic trustworthiness of informants (widely held associations between a given social group and one or more attributes) usually unrelated to the relevant criteria of reliability or accuracy. Moreover, there are prejudicial stereotypes which may affect the credibility that a hearer ascribes to the speaker inasmuch as they tend to inflate or deflate the credibility demonstrated by the speaker. Accordingly, Fricker mentions two types of prejudicial dysfunction in testimonial practice: (i) credibility excess or a situation in which the speaker receives more credibility than she deserves and (ii) credibility deficit or a situation in which the speaker receives less credibility than she deserves. For instance, cases of credibility excess can be found in situations in which a patient ascribes to her general physician, due

---

30 See more in Lackey and Sosa (eds.), 2006.; Jennifer Lackey, 2008. *Learning from Words: Testimony as a Source of Knowledge* (Oxford: Oxford University Press).

their professional identity, a specialized medical competence that they do not possess; or a testimonial situation in which a salesman ascribes more reliability to a member of privileged social group due to their class identity. Cases of a credibility deficit are, for example, a situation in which a man ascribes to his female colleague less reliability than she deserves due to her gender identity, or a situation in which a jury thinks that a black man doesn't deserve any credibility due to his racial identity.[31] In an aforementioned later article Fricker offers an example of a 'stop and search' case where racial prejudice incited the police officer to ascribe a young black male driver a deflated level of credibility when he stated that he was really the owner of his car.[32]

According to Fricker, while credibility deficits produce epistemic/testimonial injustice, cases of credibility excess do not. A case of credibility deficit results in the exclusion of the subject from a trustful conversation: not only it undermines his capacity for knowledge that is essential to his value as a human being, but by doing so it discriminates him as a social being. The hearer both deflates the speaker's credibility and commits an ethically/politically bad act by undermining the speaker's credibility as a person of knowledge. This renders the hearer's assessment culpable from both the epistemic and the ethical perspective: in addition to being epistemically irresponsible as a hearer, she is accountable for doing an ethically unacceptable act. Testimonial injustice, enacted in the case of a credibility deficit, is at the same time intellectually and ethically inappropriate. In such a case, the virtue of epistemic justice is genuinely hybrid in that it aims at both truth and justice. According to Fricker, epistemic/testimonial justice, considered either as an intellectual virtue or as an ethical virtue, stems from the same motivation of neutralize prejudice in one`s credibility judgment. While intellectual virtues generally postulate *truth* as their ultimate aim and moral virtues strive towards some form of *good*, hybrid virtues are oriented towards both truth and goodness. The hybridity of epistemic/testimonial justice depends only on the demonstrated "(...) *harmony of epistemic and ethical ends in the specific case of neutralizing prejudice*".[33]

As I have previously noted, Fricker chooses not to characterize credibility excesses as examples of epistemic/testimonial injustice

31 Fricker illustrates this at length using fictional examples such as Patricia Highsmith's *Talented Mr Ripley* by or Harper Lee's *To Kill a Mockingbird.* Fricker, 2007.

32 Fricker, 2013.

33 Fricker, 2007., p. 128.

since the consequences of such misjudgements aren't sufficiently severe. Even though some people in a consistently privileged position of social power might be subject to a variant strain of testimonial misjudgement, this in no way entails that any token cases of credibility excess constitutes an ethical wrongness.[34] A proper case of epistemic/testimonial injustice might be termed as a *systematic* testimonial injustice produced not by prejudice *simpliciter*, but by those particular prejudices that continuously follow the subject through different injustices (economic, educational, professional, sexual, legal, political or like). Epistemic/testimonial injustice appears in different degrees of severity: while sometimes a speaker's word is taken far less seriously than it would be had the prejudice been absent, but they are still believed, there are cases in which even a small credibility deflation is enough to entail that the speaker's word is rejected. Anyway, a case can only be considered epistemically unjust if epistemic culpability – based on wrongly ascribing reliability due to prejudice – results in serious ethical consequences. Fricker thus concludes that, even though cases of credibility excess imply epistemic culpability based on prejudice (of positive valence), they do not significantly ethically damage the speaker.

***

Keeping Fricker's stance in mind, we can wonder what a case of credibility excess can teach us about hybrid virtues. It is beyond doubt that cases of credibility excess cause epistemic wrongness on the side of the hearer who failed at their epistemic obligation to ascribe the speaker with a level of credibility akin to the actual state of affairs. Excesses, as well as deficits, violate the rules of a testimonial situation (the hearer condition), produce an epistemically unjustified belief and divulge the epistemic irresponsibility of the hearer. Fricker proceeds to recognize that the epistemic wrongness inherent to cases of credibility excess primarily pertain to the speaker: they can distort the speaker's epistemic character and thus be considered a wrong. While being ascribed excess credibility can be advantageous for a person of the ruling elite, of privileged education or of distinctive accent, its continuous and *systematic* exercise can imbue them with an epistemic arrogance that

34 Fricker also contends that not all sorts of credibility deficit are cases of epistemic/testimonial injustice: credibility deficits might simply stem from *epistemic error* (human judgment is fallible and unlucky epistemic mistakes are always possible) or may be produced by *incidental* cases of testimonial injustice.

puts a range of epistemic virtues out of their reach, rendering them closed-minded, dogmatic and blithely impervious to criticism.

We can begin by noticing that such systematic ascriptions of excess credibility also expose certain members of society to systematic *indirect* ethical wrongness. Privileging one group over another due to prejudicial stereotypes of positive valence automatically discriminates the 'opposite' groups by unfairly – yet implicitly – depriving them of the appropriate level of credibility. For instance, someone who readily ascribes excess credibility to male professors inevitably implies that the credibility of female professors is somewhat dubitable. Likewise, the fact that the socially privileged elite is attributed with excess credibility implicitly suggests that members of lower classes are perceived as agents deserving of less. The decision to ascribe a privileged social group with more credibility than they are due implies a certain sense of comparison, or the judgement that any other group can never produce as good an informant about the given topic. Prejudices of positive valence which underlie cases of credibility excess are a social flipside, a symptom of the negatively connotative prejudices that lead to credibility deficits. Therefore, entrusting privileged groups with excess credibility indirectly 'hits' the unprivileged subjects by exposing them to various systematic injustices (economic, educational, professional, sexual, legal, political or like). 'Positive' epistemic discriminations (based on prejudices of positive valence) remain discriminatory acts that unfairly target certain groups due to their group identity. At this point, it is important to emphasize that – even though Fricker correctly admits that credibility excesses are just as epistemically culpable as credibility deficits – she seems to have misjudged the gravity of their ethical culpability.

Secondly, it seems that we can summarize Fricker's conditions for epistemic/testimonial injustice in the following way: (i) the existence of prejudicial stereotypes about certain identities; (ii) a failed epistemic obligation on the side of the hearer, (iii) an epistemic wrong done to the speaker and (iv) direct and serious ethical harm for the speaker. As we have previously seen, even though cases of credibility excess can be deemed epistemically culpable, Fricker does not consider them *ethically* unjust because they do not inflict *direct* and serious harm upon the speaker. This gives rise to certain issues, as Fricker goes on to claim that credibility excess, although it does not strive towards truth, is still unproblematic from the hybrid perspective of harmonizing epistemic and ethical ends. While an ethical perspective may allow one to classify credibility excess as in-culpable behaviour, it would be extremely debatable not to classify it as culpable from the perspective of hybrid virtue. Fricker obviously privileges ethical values over epistemic and consequently fails to develop a genuine hybrid view on virtues that balances or appropriately harmonizes epistemic and ethical values.

Fricker must be applauded for recognizing and defining cases of credibility deficit as a clear example of epistemic injustice: both the value of truth and the value of good are jeopardized due to identity prejudices. However, cases of credibility deficit are so painless to assess from the perspective of the hybrid view is because both constituencies have the same negative valence: a victim is subject to both epistemic and ethical harm. The crucial question is how to evaluate, from the perspective of the hybrid view, cases whose difficulty surpasses that of credibility excess. We must find an appropriate approach for tackling cases in which epistemic and ethical constituencies do not have the same valence, such as in the example of credibility excess where an epistemic wrong is followed by (direct) ethical innocence. Moreover, there are interesting reverse cases in which ethical culpability inflicts no epistemic harm, such as the instances of epistemic paternalism and epistocracy. A hybrid view that aims to harmonize the assessment of epistemic and ethical values needs to define a proper framework for evaluating these attitudes, social practices and institutions. [35]

2.3.3. *Conflict between virtues: epistemic paternalism and epistocracy*

Cases of epistemic injustice are straightforward examples of coincident ethical/political and epistemic harm. They are straightforward inasmuch as they indubitably deserve condemnation and ought to be detected and removed by the means of effort. However, as we have seen, situations such as excessive ascriptions trust can be epistemologically unjustified without being seriously ethically and politically defective since they do not inflict direct and systematic injustice. It is also interesting to explore these more complex situations in which social injustice seems to produce epistemically good consequences and situations in which a socially correct act is accompanied or can lead to worse epistemic outcomes.

35 See more in Snježana Prijić–Samaržija. 2014b. "Hybrid Virtues". *Etica e Politica / Ethics and Politics*, 16/2: 1167–1180.

Let us start with a case of radical discrepancy between ethical/ political and epistemic virtues, a situation in which social discrimination is accompanied with epistemic non-culpability. Similar admittedly realistic situations are often defended in less balanced political discourses. It is claimed that methods of political correctness –introduced so as to foster multiculturalism and reduce discrimination – are either based or can lead to epistemically culpable behaviour. Should one rely on statistical proof that members of certain racial and ethnic groups more frequently perpetrate criminal and terrorist attacks, then a deficit of trust towards the members of these groups would seem epistemically justified. For instance, certain philosophers have have stated that the epistemic discrimination of and mistrust towards the members of particular racial groups – although it may seem socially incorrect – can not only be epistemically justified, but may serve as efficient means of preventing criminal acts or terrorist attacks.[36] They proceed by arguing that (certain) manifestations of socially unjust deprivations of trust cannot be held – on the basis of their ethical culpability – epistemically culpable. A credibility judgement of distrust based on someone's belonging to a particular social group can thus be epistemically justified. In a somewhat radical manner, the argument further contends that epistemically responsible behaviour may require and justify such manifestations of racial, ethnic or religious discrimination. It could be said that such views obviously consider epistemic discrimination (followed by ethical/political) on a racial basis a genuinely justified case of epistemic selection. While they may accept that it is indeed a case of social injustice (because the existing statistics imply a legacy of prior injustice that had urged members of certain races and ethnic groups to commit criminal and terrorist acts), it is maintained that epistemic responsibility may turn social injustice into an acceptable behaviour. Such a situation could be approached as a radical reversal of Fricker's credibility excess and numerous similar stories underlying Foucault's thesis about the 'knowledge of subjugated' – whilst they choose to tolerate epistemic culpability that facilitates ethical/political justification, this particular case doesn't only tolerate, but directly promotes ethical/political discrimination should it result in epistemic justification. Confronted with such radical tensions and the possible consequences of prioritizing

36 See, for instance, in Neven Sesardić. 2012. *Iz desne perspektive* (Zagreb: Večernji list).

epistemic values when assessing social desirability, many often resort – such as Fricker – to giving obvious primacy to ethical or political justifiedness. Such extreme disparities, however, are not the topic of our current discussion. Since no effort has been made to acknowledge both epistemic and ethical/political values nor to undertake a hybrid evaluation, such extremes can only serve as blatant examples of misusing allegedly epistemic ambitions to justify unacceptable ethical and political stances. It is also crucial to stress that such immoderate examples mustn't be misused to discredit all epistemic evaluations of social desirability, but ought to, reversely, be treated as an additional stimulus to our efforts to postulate a truly hybrid perspective capable of harmonizing epistemic and ethical/political virtues.

Let us proceed to other, more relevant examples of disparities between epistemic and ethical/political values. For instance, programs of affirmative action – which aimed to promote an ethically and politically correct balance of different social groups in institutions by the means of offering privileged treatment – are often condemned for worsening epistemic results. Examples of privileged treatment, such as increased university quotas for Afro–American students and a legally determined level of women in parliaments, have been dismissed as processes that deprive epistemically more deserving subjects. In that sense, these epistemically more desirable subjects are not only hindered from contributing to the system of disseminating knowledge, but undergo the systematic ethical harm of being prevented from participating in institutions. Advocates of affirmative action claim that the ethical/political welfare of these programs, measured in the terms of social justice, outweighs the consequent epistemic harm and injustice. Likewise, although democratic majority voting practices might be socially just and fair by including everyone in the decision-making process on equal terms, this kind of equity often proves inept at guaranteeing the epistemic quality of the resulting decisions. Should voters hold untrue beliefs or act in an epistemically irresponsible manner by focusing on their subjective interests, unqualified judgments and prejudices, the result of the majority vote (regardless of how equitable) will not generate the epistemic quality needed for efficiently resolving social problems and achieving longstanding common good. Many advocates of political and ethical virtues will be inclined to ignore these epistemic sub-optimalities so as to defend the advantages of democracy.

Furthermore, let us consider an example widely contested in discussions regarding the justification of expertism.[37] Experts in certain areas are the relevant epistemic authorities in that they are comparatively the best available guides to truth (or to the avoidance of epistemic errors). Judgments to trust experts most commonly lead to true beliefs. However, exclusively entrusting experts with key political decision-making roles is considered socially unjust, non-egalitarian, or non-democratic. Social justice demands for everyone to be treated as free and equal regardless of their expertise, thus allowing everyone to partake in making decisions. Instead of confiding in experts, social justice requires univocal consensus – which, as it happens, leads to epistemically sub-optimal beliefs/decisions. Even though expertism (which I will further discuss in the remainder of this book) can be considered socially unfair procedures or examples of elitist discrimination, they generally result in epistemically correct ascriptions of greater credibility to those more apt at making decisions. This case differs from the case of racial discrimination in that it is a far more scientifically justified example of epistemic selection than alleged statistical proof about the racial backgrounds of those who perpetrate criminal and terrorist attacks. In any case, the expertisms' kind of injustice is much less likely to produce epistemic errors. However, the epistemic judgments inherent to both cases imply certain social discrimination and injustice.

Although these particular cases are certainly illuminating, it might be wise to engage in a more comprehensive analysis of epistemic paternalism and epistocracy – examples that most explicitly demonstrate the conflict of epistemic and ethical/political virtues.

***

Epistemic paternalism is the ethically doubtful practice of communication control that can produce epistemically desirable consequence in terms of truth.[38]

---

37 See, for instance, in David Estulnd. 2003. 'Why Not Epistocracy?', in Reshotko Naomi (ed.), *Desire, Identity and Existence: Essays in honor of T. M. Penne* (Kelowna, BC: Academic. Printing and Publishing) pp. 53–69; David Estlund. 2008b. *Democratic Authority* (Princeton: Princeton Univeristy Press); Fabienne Peter. 2008. *Democratic Legitimacy* (New York: Routledge); Philip Kitcher, 2011a. *Science in a Democratic Society* (Amherst, New York: Prometheus Books).

38 The practice of epistemic paternalism is defended by Goldman. Alvin I. Goldman. 1991. 'Epistemic Paternalism: Communication Control in Law and Society', *Journal of Philosophy,* 88: 113–131.

Likewise, epistocracy is an ethically and politically dubious public decision making practice that privileges some people over others with the aim of generating outcomes of higher epistemic quality.[39] In spite of their epistemic merits, both practices are usually disapproved of due to ethical deficits – being acceptable from an epistemic perspective and unacceptable from an ethical one, their practical applications confront us with paralyzing conundrums.

Epistemic paternalism is a social practice of communication control or regulation of information that strives towards optimal truth-production. Goldman's defence of certain forms of regulation – as opposed to deregulation - of information imposes two general pre-conditions for the practice of epistemic paternalism: (i) epistemic paternalism may only be practised in sub-optimal epistemic circumstances and (ii) only (objective) experts can be the controllers of information.[40] Suboptimal epistemic circumstances are such in which a majority of people is inadequately informed, uninterested in numerous topics, insufficiently educated to absorb various topics, unmotivated to invest time and cognitive resources in seeking information, or simply devoid of the free time necessary for truth-searching. Goldman contends that in such suboptimal epistemic circumstances, controlling delivered information instead of facilitating the free circulation of ideas will produce more true beliefs. Besides the rather intuitive assumption that ordinary epistemic situations are sub-optimal in the mentioned sense, numerous scientific findings support the claim that the majority of people is, for various reasons, unable to make an epistemically reliable decision.[41]

---

39 The most notable proposals of various forms of epistocracy can be found in Plato's *kallipolis*, Mill's famous idea of plural voting and Schumpeter's elitist democracy. Plato. *The Republic* (Harmondsworth, UK: Penguin Books, 1974); John Stuart Mill. *On Liberty,* (New York: Oxford University Press, 1859/1960); John Stuart Mill. *Considerations on Representative Government* (Buffalo, NY: Prometheus Books, 1861/1991); Joseph A. Schumpeter. *Capitalism, Socialism and Democracy,* New York: Harper, 1942/1976).

40 Goldman, 1991., 1999.

41 Ahlstrom–Vij convincingly claims that widespread incompetence is well-documented fact. For instance, only 13% of the more than 2000 political questions examined could be answered correctly by 75% or more of those asked, and only 41% could be answered by more than half the public. Many of the facts known by relatively small percentage of the public seem critical to understanding the political world: fundamental rules of the game, classic civil liberties, key concepts of political economy, the names of key representatives, policy positions of presidential candidates or the political parties, basic social indicators and significant public policies. See

In addition to the fact that the majority does not have the capacity of making an epistemically good decision, these deregulated epistemic circumstances hinder the informed minority from properly influencing the opinions of the uninformed majority. Informed people are likely to refrain from disclosing what they (consider themselves to) know because of the informational pressure produced by the current majority position or the social pressure associated with the risk of being sanctioned as a dissenter.[42] Even if they had decided to disclose their information, the impact of that information on the deliberating group would be relatively negligible due to what is known as the *common knowledge/information effect:*

> "The influence of a particular item of information is directly and positively related to the number of group members who have knowledge of that item before the group discussion and judgment."[43]

Pressing further, recent psychological and neurological studies have shown that people in possession of knowledge tend to be highly skeptical towards their abilities, while underachievers readily overestimate their knowledge in comparison to the skills of others. In other words, since people who lack the knowledge or wisdom to perform well tend to be entirely unaware of this fact, their wrong choices are often supported by a strong sense of certainty.[44] We now may briefly conclude that Goldman's diagnosis of the epistemic features of ordinary situations has proven correct: only a minority of deliberators can be expected

---

in Kristoffer Ahlstrom–Vij. 2013b. 'Why We Cannot Rely on Ourselves for Epistemic Improvement', *Philosophical Issues* (a supplement to *Noûs*), 23: 276–296; Kristoffer Ahlstrom–Vij. 2013c. *Epistemic Paternalism: A Defence* (Basingstoke, UK: Palgrave Macmillan); Michael Carpini, X. Deli and S. Keeter, S. 1996. *What Americans Know about Politics and Why It Matters* (New Haven CT: Yale University Press).

42 See in Cass Sunstein. 2006. 'Two Conceptions of Procedural Fairness: Social Research', *An International Quarterly,* 73(2): 619–646.

43 See in Daniel Gigone and Reid Hastie. 1993. 'The common knowledge effect: Information sharing and group judgment', *Journal of Personality and Social Psychology,* 65: 959–974, p. 960.

44 Justin Kruger and David Dunning. 1999. 'Unskilled and Unaware of It: How Difficulties in Recognizing One's Own Incompetence Lead to Inflates Self-Assessments', *Journal of Personality and Social Psychology*, 77(6): 1121–1134; Robert A. Burton. 2013. *A Skeptic's Guide to the Mind: What Neuroscience Can and Cannot Tell Us About Ourselves* (New York: St. Martin's Press).

to be motivated and informed about the relevant matters and their influence on the less informed majority is negligible and not decisive.

Goldman stresses that epistemic censorship or regulation can be justified only if the distribution of information is controlled by experts. He obviously presumes that experts actually exist and differentiates between merely reputational experts and objective experts who are comparatively the best guides to truth (or at least to avoiding false beliefs). While reputational experts do not possess the knowledge and scientific responsibility necessary for justifying their status, objective experts conscientiously provide sound arguments and divulge solutions to problems. The latter are identified during what Goldman refers to as *truth-revealing situations*, instances in which someone's objective expertise becomes explicitly evident because they are seen successfully resolving a problem. Not only should such experts control the content of information that is conveyed to people (schools, commercials or like) with the aim of better truth-acquisition, but certain experts (for instance, judges) may withdraw true information from relevant people (jury) who are making a decision if they conclude that this very information may interfere with the formation of a true belief.

Knowing that it is grounded on empirically sound facts about human reasoning, epistemic paternalism genuinely seems like a superiorly reliable route to the acquisition of truth, correct answers or epistemically high-quality beliefs in society. On the other side, any practice of communicational control, even if we assume suboptimal epistemic circumstances and the existence of objective experts, implies a serious ethical problem of censorship that violates the value of autonomy and the rights of each person to freely access information. However, we are beyond the point of reaching the disappointing conclusion that epistemic paternalism is an epistemically desirable and ethically unacceptable epistemic practice. It would be just an unacceptable for epistemologists to accept a practice that is scorned by ethicists. The answer might lie in the perspective of the hybrid view, whose intention to harmonize ethical and epistemic goods provides us with a promising framework for evaluating epistemic paternalism as a virtuous and socially desirable, or an undesirable practice.

Similarly, any attempt to introduce the epistemic value of truth or correctness into a democratic decision-making process generates the serious problem of epistocracy, or the institutional practice which privileges the opinions of experts. If we are searching for truth, correctness, efficient solutions to problems or other outcomes of the highest epistemic value, there is no reason for us not to privilege the opinions of experts because they are trained to be more efficient in dealing with various problems. On the other side, it reminds us of Plato's *kalipolis,* a radical version of epistocracy, as wisdom-based political legitimacy, that is commonly regarded as democratically unacceptable.

In debates about the epistemic justification of democracy, numerous philosophers have postulated various arguments against epistocracy.[45] Some participants argue that the existence of experts in science does not imply that a similar status of expertise is appropriate for ethics or politics. The mere fact that someone may possess more knowledge is insufficient for justifying their coercion of others to obey their stance, partially because the other person might not agree that they are genuinely more knowledgeable about what should be done. Other authors add that, even if there *are* experts in ethics and politics, they should not be privileged because all citizens have equal rights to participate/vote. The idea of privileged experts, despite the attractive prospect of attaining decisions of high epistemic quality, distorts the ethical project of a democratic society. On the other hand, it seems valid to say that discussions in which all participants are treated as equals and which primarily strive to produce a universally satisfying judgment do not guarantee outcomes of high epistemic value. Viewpoints that postulate some sort of consensus as the aim of good deliberation would not be deserving of the label 'epistemic' because the attainment of consensus is not an epistemological contribution to democracy.[46]

Like in the case of epistemic paternalism, we cannot be satisfied with the repetitive conclusion that the desirability of epistocracy from the epistemological perspective does not rectify its ethical or political insufficiencies. There are several possible options available. Should we automatically conclude that they can never be justified regardless of their epistemic benefits because they are not ethically/politically acceptable? Should hybridity be perceived as a mere confirmation of the presence of both virtues? Or can we seek more sophisticated models of harmonizing epistemic and ethical/political values and outcomes? We are left with the task of determining the optimal hybrid model of harmonizing epistemic and ethical/political values.

45 See, for instance, Estlund 2003.; 2008., Peter 2008.; Kitcher 2011. See also Thomas Christiano. 2008. *The Constitution of Equality* (Oxford: Oxford University Press).

46 Goldman, 2010.

First of all, we must note that all of these cases indicate that epistemic virtue is not necessarily related to ethical/political or social desirability. Similarly, social injustice and epistemic errors aren't necessarily connected. There are situations in which social injustice does not lead to epistemic errors (expertism or epistocracy) and certain socially progressive practices can cause substandard epistemic outcomes (affirmative action). Numerous philosophers have attempted to resolve these conflicts or divergences of justice and epistemic success by exclusively opting for either epistemic or ethical/political values.

Since we are attempting to properly deliberate about more appropriate solutions to such conflicts, we need to realize that every occurrence of an epistemic deficit or surplus – regardless of whether they are caused by social injustice or by an attempt to generate social justice – remains an epistemic error. It is still the case of attributing someone more or less credibility than they are due. Every attempt to justify an epistemic deficit/excess is an attempt to justify an epistemic error, which is unacceptable. Regardless of whether it is the consequence of discriminatory or privileged treatment, not a single epistemically wrong credibility judgment can be justified from a strictly epistemic perspective. As Craig reminds us that an epistemic error implies the failure to detect a good informant, neither case can succeed at acquiring a true belief. We are thus confronted with the problem of conscientiously dealing with circumstances marked by epistemic error: should we justify them as long as they are combined with social justice or should we condemn them regardless of their ethical associations? In other words, although it was easy to agree that cases of epistemic injustice, situations of social injustice that produce epistemic errors, are unacceptable, we must decide how to evaluate concrete situations in which ethical/political virtues do not correlate with desirable epistemic outcomes.[47]

47 See also Snježana Prijić–Samaržija. 2007. 'Trust and Contextualism', *Acta Analytica*, 22(2): 125–38; Snježana Prijić–Samaržija. 2016b. 'Socijalna i epistemička (ne)pravda', in Prijić-Samaržija Snježana, L. Malatesti and E. Baccarini (eds.), *Moralni, politički i epistemološki odgovori na društvene devijacije* (Rijeka: Faculty of Humanities and Social Sciences, University of Rijeka), pp. 37–50.

2.4. *Three hybrid solutions: elitism, egalitarianism and situationsim*

There seem to be three hybrid positions at our disposal. Unlike approaches that opt for either the epistemic or the ethical/political values whilst entirely ignoring the other, hybrid positions acknowledge the necessity of harmonization. Authors who participate in this debate stress the importance of both elements of the evaluation.

While the first, *elististic* model, acknowledges the importance of assessing both ethical/political and epistemic virtues, it still emphasizes the primacy of epistemic outcomes. According to the elitistic model, which can be considered genuinely hybrid, a particular case amounts to epistemic justice only if it entails both epistemic and ethical benefits. Should it happen that epistemic error was caused by social injustice, we could speak of a case of full-fledged epistemic injustice. When confronted with conflicts between epistemic outcomes and social justice, however, we ought to give primacy to epistemic success. In other words, it is unacceptable to sacrifice epistemic success or overlook serious epistemic sub-optimality for the sake of achieving social justice. Similarly, certain instances of forfeiting social justice in favor of epistemic good could be justified – for example, expertism and epistemic paternalism are sufficiently epistemically benefital to deserve some kind of justification.[48] For the sake of clarity, it is important to acknowledge that the earlier example of a radical omission of social justice for the sake of allegedly epistemic criteria should never be confused with the elististic hybrid position – it entirely overlooks social injustice and doesn't consider it pertinent to assessments of social desirability.

	Social justice	Social injustice
Epistemic error	Unacceptable	Epistemic injustice
Epistemic success	Epistemic justice	Acceptable

Table 1. Elististic model

I have dubbed the second model *egalitarian* because it considers the protection of social justice a necessary prerequisite of epistemic

48 Plato, 1974.; Mill, 1859/1960., 1861/1991.; Schumpeter, 1942/1976. See also Max Weber. 1964. *The Theory of Social and Economic Organization* (Basingstoke: Macmillan).

justice. The epistemic condition is thus either of secondary importance or plainly derived from social justice. This model corresponds with the prior in considering cases in which social injustice causes an epistemic error – these are paradigmatic examples of epistemic injustice. Likewise, the paradigmatic case of epistemic justice is a situation in which social justice is accompanied by epistemic success. Both ethical/political and epistemological virtues are taken into account. However, this model deviates from the latter by accepting situations in which social justice produces worse epistemic outcomes, while rejecting those in which social injustice entails epistemic success. In other words, while programs of affirmative action would be acceptable, cases of privileging experts would not. Given her attitude towards cases of testimonial injustice – and particularly her readiness to overlook epistemic mistakes that do not jeopardize general social justice – Fricker's stance could be described as egalitarian, regardless of her declarative advocacy of the hybrid view.[49]

	Social justice	Social injustice
Epistemic error	Acceptable	Epistemic injustice
Epistemic success	Epistemic justice	Unacceptable

Table 2. Egalitarian model

While the third possible hybrid model can be understood as something akin to a compromise, it is conceived as a perspective sensitive to the multi-layered dynamics of the real social world. This *situationist* hybrid model concurs that the union of social justice and epistemic success represents the best possible circumstances. As in the previous models, a paradigmatic case of epistemic injustice is still found in those situations in which social injustice causes epistemic errors. However, this model is specific in fostering the idea that the acceptability of a particular state of affairs with conflicted ethical/political and epistemic values is determined by a highly situationist approach to harmonizing ethical and intellectual virtues. This means that misbalances between justice and truth shouldn't be resolved by automatically opting for either value with the aim of catering to an abstract theory. Both the elitist and the egalitarian model create explicit hierarchies of values in that

49 Also, see more in Estulnd, 1997., 2003.; Peter, 2008. Fabienne Peter. 2016. 'The Epistemic Circumstances of Democracy', in Fricker Miranda and Michael Brady (eds.), *The Epistemic Life of Groups* (Oxford: Oxford University Press), pp. 133–149.

elitists favour truth, while egalitarians give primacy to justice. What this ultimately amounts to is that elitists resolve conflicts by sacrificing justice, whereas egalitarians forfeit truth. The situationist model rests on the assumption that the equal importance of both values abolishes the prospect of setting unquestionable rules about resolving conflicts. Each particular situation requires highly individualized assessments of whether we can justify the 'sacrifice' of epistemic benefits for the sake of 'ensuring' social justice. It might be more appropriate to characterize the situationist model in terms of its efforts to optimally harmonize both virtues and preserve them to the highest possible extent, rather than in terms of sacrificing one virtue to the other. Using the specific example of affirmative action, we would have to estimate the produced epistemic damage and carefully consider whether the long-term epistemic benefits of, for example, including women in politics or science could ultimately contribute to truth. While the inclusion of plural perspectives and diverse backgrounds has obvious epistemic advantages, such policies may temporarily slow down research by producing new social dynamics and requiring the adjustment of different methodologies. We could similarly tackle the case of expertism by assessing whether we are facing a situation in which it would be more appropriate to allow everyone to participate (such as critical situations of defining social goals or resolving urgent issues) or whether decision-making should be left to experts (for instance, the cases that require sophisticated knowledge or controversial decisions about human rights marked by conflicting worldviews, in which the majority is likely to overcome the minority). Decisions to give precedence to a certain value should never seriously jeopardize the other. The very concept of 'localized' harmonization rejects the possibility of abolishing either value, instead opting for a 'calibration' that ensures better long-term epistemic outcomes while preserving social justice. In other words, this would render justification of racial discrimination as a necessary prerequisite of risk reduction – knowing that this would produce unfounded credibility deficits – entirely unacceptable. In the long run, such practice would only contribute to social injustice without guaranteeing the (already questionable) improvement of epistemic outcomes. It is generally difficult to conceive any feasible circumstances in which racial discrimination would improve longstanding epistemic outcomes. However, this also implies that it can be possible to justify in certain situation both epistemic paternalism and other forms of experts participation (as opposed to the egalitarian model) and social affirmative actions (which the elitist model would prohibit).

	Social justice	Social injustice
Epistemic error	Situational harmonization Acceptable/ Unacceptable	Epistemic injustice
Epistemic success	Epistemic justice	Situational harmonization Acceptable/ Unacceptable

Table 3. Situationist model

2.5. *Situational hybrid view in social epistemology*

My defence of the hybrid model as optimal in comparison with the traditional 'power' play between ethical/political and epistemic values, as well as of its situationist version as best suited to real social dynamics, still offers only a limited conclusion. Instead of trying to propose an elaborate version of the situationist hybrid model, I am merely arguing that it is comparatively more capable of resolving conflicts between epistemic and ethical/political virtues. It is specific in allowing for situational, contextual or local harmonization of virtues. This hybrid model provides the existing plurality of intuitive stances regarding the role of experts, epistemic paternalism or affirmative action with a framework for thoroughly appraising concrete epistemic and social relationships. The point is that, for instance, we can neither dismiss affirmative action and similar fairness-oriented social practices on the basis of their epistemic dubiousness, nor automatically reject epistemic paternalism and the role of experts because of their apparent ethical/political opacity.

In advocating the situationist hybrid model, I am in no way attempting to argue that pure epistemological analyses of certain phenomena, such as expertism or affirmative action, are unnecessary. Likewise, I am not calling for the rejection of purely ethical or philosophical-political assessments. On the contrary, they are both necessary predecessors of any more comprehensive evaluation of real social circumstances. However, these isolated debates, as well as the hybrid approaches that appeal to the priority of either the epistemic or the ethical/political in circumstances of value conflicts, can never fully encompass the complexity of real social situations.

Secondly, it is important to emphasize that the hybrid model doesn't only explicitly oppose traditionalism, but also distances itself from any form of reductionism or orthodox claims about the „end of epistemology'. The hybrid model separates normativity from the *socially* independent idea of truth and acknowledges the fact that processes of acquiring beliefs can be unethical and unjust. In other words, it is equally respectful of the social character of knowledge and the attitude that distinctly epistemic criteria of evaluation (rationality, justification, truth, and ability to resolve problems) ought to be applied to beliefs and judgments. This model acknowledges the plausible idea that certain people are more knowledgeable than others while preserving ethical/political ideals and principles of fairness, plurality, participation, etc.

Thirdly, it is seldom easy to resolve circumstances of conflicted values. Estimating the extent to which it is justified to sacrifice epistemic values for the sake of social justice without jeopardizing the long-term acquisition of truth is a daunting task. It is no easier to determine how much social justice can be forfeited in favour of a successful epistemic outcome which might later support justice. These judgments should, besides the criteria of accurately assessing concrete circumstances (number and profile of involved and interested people, temporal scope, price, efficiency, or like) appropriately estimate the likelihood that the sacrificed value will later be redeemed. For example, we would need to carefully consider whether practices that momentarily jeopardize epistemic values – such as, for instance, affirmative action – could actually promote truth from some wider perspective. Bearing in mind these difficulties that cannot be resolved using a generalized theory, I find that it is still possible to outline the *minimum* conditions for fulfilling epistemic and ethical/political virtues.

The minimum condition for ensuring epistemic virtue is that epistemic agents do not, for instance, base their credibility judgments on false beliefs or prejudice. They must instead be conscientious or motivated by the desire to attain truth (or some other epistemical virtue that has objective validity) and avoid mistakes. On the other hand, ethical/political virtues can only be realized if epistemic subjects recognize the importance of pluralism, diversity, critical interaction and inclusion instead of egoistically preferring their personal stances. A credibility judgment that adheres to both of these generally articulated minimum conditions would be acceptable and valuable within the hybrid model, thus avoiding ungrounded deficits or surpluses of trust. Returning to the example of epistemic paternalism, any practice that favours the paternalism of experts while entirely ignoring the benefits of pluralism would not be acceptable. Similarly, programs of affirmative action that would allow newly privileged groups to yield results despite being intellectually lenient would not be justified. However, situational applications of paternalism that remain sensitive to pluralism by the means of specific decision-making processes or affirmative action initiatives – without forsaking the importance of meritocracy – could be deemed more acceptable. Nevertheless, the situationist hybrid model is inevitably limited by its obvious inability to imagine all possible particular local situations. Supposing that we accept this account of the minimum criteria, we must remain aware of the plausible objection that specific conflicts of virtues in real social circumstance will often be difficult to resolve. The best available approach to such cases of 'negotiating' or 'trading' between values can be found in the Aristotelian epistemic virtue of *phronesis* or practical wisdom – a wise person is one who can conscientiously assess the gravity of each relevant virtue in a given situation. It is practical *knowledge* about what is good or bad for people.[50]

2.6. *Conclusion*

Throughout recent decades, epistemology has undergone several significant expansions of its interests and topics. The first expansion, both the oldest and the most seldom questioned, encompassed discussions about cognitive processes such as perception, reasoning, memory, and so on, thus moving away from the traditional epistemic preoccupation with defining knowledge and providing a normative framework for assessing the justifiedness of beliefs. The second was related to the value shift that substituted the rigid monism of truth as the only real epistemic value with a pluralist account of values that can be considered an epistemic success or a guarantee of high epistemic quality – values such as, among many others, understanding, empirical adequacy and the reliable usage of available evidence. This type of expansion was most directly articulated in virtue epistemology and its efforts to change the target epistemic evaluations. Instead of evaluating the truth or justifiedness of a particular proposition, virtue

50 Aristotle, *Nichomachean Ethics*, 1140a24–1140b12.

epistemologists shift their focus to assess the epistemic virtues, such as epistemic responsibility, courage, curiosity, impartiality, conscientiousness, and the like, exhibited by epistemic agents. The third expansion of epistemic topics pertained to the legitimization of social epistemology, thus introducing the general notion of the social situatedness of doxastic states and the substantial expansion of research onto social entities and practices. It is important to note that each above mentioned expansion of epistemology, despite of their substantial broadening of traditional research topics, has retained the traditional epistemological normative framework: the objective validity of epistemic values and virtues. This explicit credence in the objective validity of certain phenomena renders them significantly different from all orthodox postmodern approaches to epistemic topics, which are generally characterized by epistemic nihilism and the reduction of epistemology to descriptive social sciences.

The final extension of epistemology, pertaining to the epistemic evaluation of social processes, practices and institutions, necessarily brought attention to the relationship between epistemic and political/ ethical virtues. It soon became evident that social practices such as trusting others in conversational situations can not be evaluated in purely epistemic terms, given that the causes of epistemic mistakes can be socially motivated. Likewise, social injustice can be generated by epistemic wrongdoings – such occurrences make it possible to speak about epistemic injustice or fair epistemic errors. Consequently, it was revealed as necessary to introduce a hybrid perspective or an assessment platform that would ground evaluations on attempts to harmonize epistemic and ethical/political virtues: a social practice or entity can and should be justified only if it fulfils ethical/political requirements while respecting or generating the epistemic quality of beliefs/judgments/ decisions. The hybrid perspective is particularly essential to social epistemology and its attempts to make epistemic evaluations socially relevant, broadening the criteria of social desirability: the epistemic justifiedness of social practices and institutions must not be ignored in favor of the ethical or the political.

However, the introduction of the hybrid perspective raised the issue of harmonizing epistemic and ethical/political criteria and virtues in circumstances of their divergence. It often happens that a social practice or institution prides itself with good epistemic results, but cannot be held ethically politically acceptable (epistemic paternalism, epistocracy). Similar scenarios may also occur in reverse, with social entities that fulfil all ethical/political desiderata, but result in epistemically suboptimal outcomes (affirmative action programs, democratic majority voting). It has been shown that, despite the declarative hybridity of seemingly balanced approaches, attempts to resolve conflict tend to sacrifice one kind of value to the other. Moreover, it is becoming increasingly evident that epistemic virtues are more commonly reduced to the ethical/political. We have tried to show that the situational model within the hybrid position – which is sensitive to the local and highly contextual properties of each situation – seems like the most promising method of generating evaluations equally respectful of both values.

3.
EPISTEMIC JUSTIFICATION OF DEMOCRACY

3.1 *Social epistemology and the epistemic justification of democracy*

Recent discussions within social epistemology have commenced the practice of evaluating the epistemic justification of democracy. This topic, primarily discussed by philosophers of politics, was introduced as a necessary precondition of democratic legitimacy that ought to join the ranks of ethical and political justification. Philosophers of politics have long held that democracy, in addition to being justified as a politically and ethically just system, should also be an epistemically justified social system, that is, a system that produces decisions of the highest epistemic quality. Despite the fact that it is a distinctly epistemological topic, the question of the epistemic features of democracy has only recently gained momentum due to its reclamation as a legitimate interest of social epistemology. As I have emphasized in the first chapter, the expansionist approach to social epistemology is explicit about its interest and intention of assessing the epistemic features of democratic decision-making procedures and the influence of social systems on epistemic results.[1] Although it is unnecessary to debate the interdisciplinary nature of this subject – which includes epistemological, philosophical-political and ethical considerations – the initial motivation for introducing the topic of democracy to social epistemology is intrinsically epistemological. Social epistemology has the task of critically exploring the epistemological properties of social institutions and systems in order to evaluate and ultimately improve the systems of forming and revising beliefs, making judgments, decisions and policies. It thus encourages more epistemically responsible or rational, justified and true epistemic outcomes, or at the very least aims to hinder those that are irresponsible, irrational and unjustified.

---

1 Goldman, 2010.

However, as I have previously pointed out, the necessity of finally analysing democracy from an epistemic perspective makes it neither possible nor desirable to conduct isolated and abstract epistemic inquiries. I see far more potential in a debate that presumes a hybrid perspective and approaches the justification of democracy by assessing its harmony of ethical/political and epistemic values. In a similar vein, the recent trends in philosophy of politics and social epistemology that have advanced the practice of evaluating the epistemic effect of democracy perfectly correspond to the basic features of the hybrid perspective.[2] If democracy or models of democratic decision-making must be both ethically/politically and epistemically justified, then any justification that can be considered meaningful and effective requires the harmonization of epistemic and ethical/political desires and virtues.

***

I will start with two assumptions which currently don't require particularly detailed explanations, thought this in no way implies that they couldn't be fruitfully discussed in some other circumstances. The first concerns the necessity of the epistemic justification of democracy, or the stance that the legitimacy of all institutions and systems – and particularly democracy as a comprehensive social configuration – must be based on adequate evidence that they, as social structures, maximally cater to the formation of high quality epistemic beliefs or decisions. In other words, these beliefs or decisions must be true or truth-conductive, justified, efficient at solving problems, correct or derived from arguments/reasons, epistemically responsible or like.[3] The second

---

2 Estlund,1997., 2008b.; Code, 2006.; Fricker, 2007.; Peter, 2008.; Kitcher, 2011. See also Thomas Christiano. 2012. 'Rational Deliberation between Experts and Citizens', in Mansbridge Jane and John Parkinson (eds.), *The Deliberative System* (Cambridge: Cambridge University Press), pp- 27–51.

3 Determing which epistemic values ought to be given primacy when evaluating the epistemic quality of democratic decisions or epistemic justification of democracy surpasses the scope of our current interests. An epistemic perspective obviously requires different approaches to defending the thesis that a democratic system is legitimate as long as it efficiently resolves the problems of its citizens (this pragmatic thesis is supported by, for instance, Philip Kitcher), claiming that it can only be legitimate if it makes decisions on the basis of reliable and truth-sensitive mechanisms (as suggested by Goldman and Christiano) or proposing, as is my intention, that an appropriate normative framework for evaluating democracy has be at least somewhat related to virtue epistemology. However, this chapter rests on the stance that assessments of social institutions ought to involve epistemic values. We can

preliminary assumption is that deliberative democracy, in contrast to aggregating democracy, has in its foundations the additional benefits of encouraging public debate as an *ethically*, *politically* and *epistemically* optimum property of democracy.[4] This assumption entails the thesis that the emphasis on discussion inherent to deliberative democracies already contains an initial epistemic advantage that requires more careful scrutiny. Namely, deliberative democracy rests on the idea that the legitimacy of fundamental political stances must be based on public discussions between citizens as such practice could improve both political and epistemic decision-making, thus facilitating the achievement of ideals such as rational legislation, participatory policies, civic self-management and public autonomy derived from civic deliberation. In short, since my aim is neither to discuss the legitimacy of democracy as a political system nor to compare deliberative and aggregative democracies, I will presume that deliberative democracy is most likely – at least in comparison with other available systems – to produce decisions of high epistemic quality. My primary aim is to determine which forms of deliberative democracy and public debate optimally support the production of epistemically desirable decisions while being ethically/politically justified.

Presupposing, above all, the importance of the epistemic justification of deliberative democracy, it is important to note that many philosophers of politics ignore or even dispute the relevance of any epistemic justification in determining democratic legitimacy. This stance stems from the fact that they don't assess legitimacy in terms of decision-making processes, but instead focus on justifying democratic states

---

only proceed to further identify the relevant epistemic norms, values and duties after we have preliminarily agreed on the importance of assessing the epistemic justification of institutions, practices and systems. It is crucial to note that any aforementioned approach to epistemic values can only pertain to our discussion about the epistemic justification of democracy if it adheres to the fundamental claim that epistemic values possess a certain objective validity. For more, see Goldman, 2010.; Kitcher, 2011.; Christiano 2012.

4 While advocates of aggregative democracy portray voting as the only and most important feature of democratic decision making, arguing that the aggregation of individual preferences most accurately corresponds to a collective choice (for instance, Kenneth J. Arrow. 1963. *Social Choice and Individual Values*, sec. ed. (New York: Wiley)), proponents of deliberative democracy deem that decision making processes ought to be more complex. A responsible decision making process should ensure that voting is preceeded by public debates, thus encouraging equal and just civic participation in expressing their individual stances. For more, see Bernard Manin. 1987. 'On Legitimacy and Deliberation', *Political Theory,* 15: 338–368, and Peter, 2008.

and democratically elected governments[5], presupposing the political concept of justice as the justification of political, social and economic institutions in a pluralist democratic society.[6] On the other hand, some authors consider epistemic justification relevant, but remain focused on elaborating the epistemic features of aggregative democracy. This can be illustrated by broad discussions about the famous *Condorcet Jury theorem* or the view that correct decisions can be attained by democratically aggregating different stances.[7] I, in no way, consider these attitutes unfounded or easily refutable. However, although I will occasionally reflect on their arguments, my starting assumptions are that (i) the epistemic justification of democracy is necessary for ensuring its legitimacy and that (ii) deliberative democracy, owing to its respect for reasons and debate, is more likely to be epistemically justified.

In order to clarify these assumptions, I will begin this chapter by briefly outlining the basic historical tenets of deliberative democracy and its epistemic justification. I will, then, shortly delineate the possible tensions between epistemic and ethical/political justification as a key challenge for hybrid evaluations of delibarative democracy. I will conclude by identifying three possible approaches to the hybrid justification of deliberative democracy: proceduralism, consensualism and reliability democracy. Although all three approaches are very convincing in the light of their efforts to balance epistemic and ethical/political justifications, I will attempt to further explore which one should be given primacy.

3.2. *Epistemic justification of deliberative democracy*

The concept of deliberative democracy is a relatively new occurence in political philosophy and is almost inherently interconnected with the stance that, in order to be fully legitimate, democracy needs to be an epistemically justified system. Namely, the very notion of a deliberation or discussion-based democracy implies the attitude that legitimate legislative and other issues ought to be based on public civic

5 For example, Weber, 1964.

6 For example, John Rawls. 1993. *Political Liberalism* (New York: Columbia University Press).

7 For example, Christian List and Robert E. Goodin. 2001. 'Epistemc Democracy: Generalizing the Condorcet Jury Theorem', *The Journal of Political Philosohy*, 9(3): 277–306; Robert E. Goodin. 2003. *Reflective Democracy* (Oxford: Oxford University Press).

debate. The introduction of public debates implicitly respects both the epistemic ideal of rational legislation, the political ideal of participatory politics and ethical ideal of civic self-management. Such public debates between citizens are expected to produce rational solutions to political problems by the means of converging attitudes or reaching a rational and widely acceptable conclusion.

The idea of deliberative democracy originated in the modern liberal theories of Thomas Hobbes and John Locke who, while portaying the plurality of interests as a source of civil conflict, also emphasized the necessity of public reason.[8] Similarly, James Harinngton and Jean Jacques Rousseau emphasized the desirability of establishing civil harmony on common interests, values and traditions, presuming some kind of consensus and public reasoning (civic republicanism).[9] Theories that accentuated the importance of participatory democracy throughout the 20th century generally associated it with the introduction of public civic deliberation as a prerequisite for achieving high quality decisions. In the 1960s, authors such Hannah Arendt and John Dewey depicted public debate as an important element of participatory democracy that respects the independence and autonomy of citizens within the process of synchronising beliefs.[10] The idea of participatory democracy undertook its final form in the 1980s; Joseph Bessette clearly states that true democracy demands that its citizens accept their civic position and the idea of the common good, opting for deliberative democracy as the optimal framework for achieving the common good through discussion, public reason, rational argumentation and rational decision-making.[11] Jon Elster may have offered the most concise definition of deliberative democracy as a practice of rational agreement about the common good,

---

8 Thomas Hobbes. *Leviathan* (Harmondsworth, UK: Penguin Books, 1651/1968); John Locke. *Second Treatise on Civil Government* (Indianapolis, IN: Hackett, 1690/1980).

9 James Harrington. *The Commonwealth of Oceana and A System of Politics* (Cambridge: Cambridge University Press, 1656/1992); Jean-Jacques Rousseau. *The Social Contract* (New York: Pocket Books, 1762/1967).

10 Hannah Arendt. 1958. *The Human Condition* (Chicago: University of Chicago Press); John, Dewey John. 1976. 'Creative Democracy: The Task Before Us', in Boydston Jo A. (ed.), *John Dewey, The Later Works, 1925 – 1953.* (Carbondale and Edwardsville: Southern Illinois University Press), pp. 224–230.

11 Joseph M Bessette. 1980. 'Deliberative Democracy: The Majority Principle in Republican Government', in Goldwin, R. A., and W. A. Schambra (eds.), *How Democratic Is the Constitution?* (Washington: American Eterprise Institute), pp. 102–116.

and of public debate as an instrument for improving political decision-making. Moreover, he portrays the educational consequences of discussion as an additional epistemic value of this type of democracy.[12]

In contrast to these theories, the 1950s were marked by elitist approaches suspicious of the idea of public debate. For example, Joseph Schumpeter argued that the fact that citizens are politically uninformed, apathetic and easily manipulated makes any increase in their participation a threat to stability. Similarly, pessimistic realists such as Max Weber thought that there was no common good that everyone would agree upon by the means of discussion, proceeding to argue that optimal governance must include a governing elite – democracy should be reduced to negative controlling leaders by maintaing the propect of their failure to be reelected.[13] A different approach to criticising deliberative democracy didn't stem from elitist or pessimistic anti-populist theories, but from the economic theory of democracy, better known as the rational choice theory. Proponents such as Anthony Downs applied economic categories to politics and argued that parties function as entrepreneurs competing for political consumers. According to this theory, citizens are portrayed as passive consumers who primarily practice political democratic control through voting, while the political process is seen as a struggle for power between conflicting parties rather than as a search for the common good.[14] Since periodic voting in elections wasn't perceived as a mechanism for aggregating individual interests or preferences, any claims that it could be improved through discussion with the aim of achieving the common good were rendered irrelevant. Namely, given that there is no common good that would be acceptable to all citizens/consumers, encouraging discussions that could allegedly produce better rational decisions about this generaly acceptable outcome would actually make no sense.

These opposing arguments about the role of public debate in democratic processes have postulated one of the key epistemic dilemmas that will continue to emerge in discussions regarding deliberative democracy: does public debate ensure better decisions than those made by elected educated representatives? We could roughly formulate it as a clash

---

12 Jon Elster. 2002. 'The Market and the Forum: Three Varieties of Political Theory', in Christiano Thomas (ed.), *Philosophy and Democracy* (Oxford: Oxford University Press).

13 Weber, 1964.

14 Anthony Downs. 1957. *An Economic Theory of Democracy* (New York: Harper).

between consensualism and expertism.[15] Namely, while proponents of deliberative democracy have generally emphasized the importance of achieving a rational consensus (about the common good) by the means of civic participation and public debate, its critics have stressed that the effects of discussion (among uneducated, passive and easily manipulated citizens) are overemphasized and that rational decisions can only be attained by promoting the stances of the educated few.

I will not proceed to indulge in a discussion of whether we should opt for a participatory pluralistic (forum) model or a market economic model of rational choice, nor will I discuss whether introducing deliberative democracy, as a positive civic direction, is better than reducing democracy to negative civic control. Overwhelming emphasis will be put on the epistemic justification of deliberative democracy as a model of democracy based on public debate. This short historical view is useful in that it clearly conveys the continuous scepticism that has trailed the concept of deliberative democracy since its advent; can participation and public debate, as such, produce quality epistemic decisions, i.e. what are the conditions and goals that public discussion must satisfy itself to be a generator of rational use of common reasons and instrument of making epistemic optimal decisions. In short, presupposing that deliberative democracy is by definition an epistemically more promising decision-making system, and that rational and reason-based public debate is unquestionably epistemically valuable in comparison to making decisions with no prior discussion, we can ask the following question: can deliberative democracy be justified as a social system from a hybrid perspective that unites epistemic and ethical/political justification?

3.3. *Conflict between epistemic and political justifications of deliberative democracy: democracy and truth*

Before proceeding to discuss the epistemic justification of deliberative democracy, it is important to realize that most polemics will revolve around the tension between the epistemic and political justification of deliberative democracy. We have already seen that the conflict can be addressed as the task of harmonizing epistemic desiderata, producing decisions of high epistemic quality, with the

---

15 Goldman introduces this distinction in one of his first works on social epistemology. See Goldman, 1987.

political imperative to preserve the values of equality, freedom and comprehensive civic autonomy. Of course, this conflict can also be resolved by unilaterally favouring the importance of one set of values over the other. However, as we have repeatedly pointed out, harmonizing epistemological and ethical/political virtues within a united discussion is much more desirable than remaining entrenched in isolated camps of either epistemology or ethics and political philosophy. Moreover, when confronted with conflicts between epistemic and ethical/political values, hybrid evaluations of social systems such as deliberative democracy emerge as a natural and preferable analytic framework.

It is important to note that these tensions between epistemic and political goals in justifying deliberative democracy largely relate to the role of citizens and the role of experts in debates and decision-making. Due to their education and training, experts are better at making correct decisions, or decisions that more efficiently resolve problems, than other citizens (or are at least comparatively better at avoiding bad decisions). On the other side, the exclusion of citizens from the decision-making process is anti-democratic. The second chapter on the hybrid perspective has already presented several examples of conflict between political/ethical and epistemic values: epistemic paternalism is a politically and ethically dubious practice of communication control that can produce epistemically good consequence in terms of truth (epistemic quality) due to role of experts; epistocracy is a similarly politically and ethically dubious practice of privileging experts in public decision making due to their ability to generate outcomes of better epistemic quality. According to many advocates of deliberative democracy, the decision to assign experts a key role almost automatically generates a democratic deficit.[16]

Extensive arguments against the practice of privileging experts in debates and decision-making processes were offered by critics of epistocracy, a system in which – owing to their privileged role and heightened capacity to make decisions – experts would actually rule, thus excluding citizens from societal decision-making processes. Proposals to reconfigure the role of a experts in society are often associated with Plato's concept of philosopher kings, Mill's account of plural voting, or Schumpeter's and Weber's elitism.[17] Although markedly different,

16 For more, see Estlund, 2003.; Peter, 2008., 2016.

17 Plato, 1974.; Mill, 1859/1960., 1861/1991.; Schumpeter, 1942/1976.; Weber, 1964.

all of these systems stemmed from the same conviction that there are serious epistemic limitations to a democratic deliberation in which uninformed, variably educated, egoistically motivated and manipulable citizens make decisions that might be far from optimal – these decisions wouldn't only jeopardize the fundamental epistemic value of truth, but would likely prove entirely inept at solving problems. However, most participants in this debate, that had originally belonged to philosophy of politics, have offered diverse arguments against the privileged treatment of experts in debates and decision-making processes.

We can begin by mentioning several examples. From the perspective of striving to secure each individual's ethical and political autonomy, it seems unjustifiable and anti-democratic to delegate all public decisions and practices to a select few. Despite the fact that experts, due to their knowledge, information and professional training, are the best available guides to epistemically high-quality decisions, there are serious reasons not to favour their stances in making decisions. The mere fact that experts might be more knowledgeable about what to do cannot justify their coercion of others to obey, partially because they may not take into account the gravity of individual perspectives.[18] Experts should not be privileged because all citizens have equal rights to participate/vote. Apart from this ubiquitous objection with regard to the equality, freedom and autonomy of each individual, it is also possible to question the experts' expertise. Claims that experts are not really the best guides to epistemically high-quality refer to the fact that experts are equally susceptible to being affected by their personal values and interests. Instead of being independent of values and interests, expert stances are infected by their special interests, ideological presuppositions and inequalities of power – as such, they can not reflect common human ends and the interests of a vast number of people.[19] This inability to avoid bias is considered a substantial threat to the traditional understanding of expertise as necessarily interwoven with objectivity and neutrality. Furthermore, it is possible to deny the very existence of relevant expertise in the domain of political decision-making or to claim that there are no experts in politics and ethics analogous to those in science. It is also argued that – since we have no way of adequately assessing moral expertise – there is no sufficient criteria for determining moral experts. Even if

18 Rawls, 1971/1999.
19 Estlund, 1997., 2003.; Peter, 2008.

we presumed that relevant inequalities in moral competences actually exist, there could be no strict definition of moral expertise that would be generally acceptable.[20] Likewise, one could draw attention to the fact that many experts are not objectively credible, but rather maintain their unjust status on the basis of reputation. It is also argued that no aspect of expertise protects citizens from possibly corrupt systems and governmental disregard for the common good. Others have pointed out that laymen lack the necessary knowledge to determine the real abilities of an expert and thus may find it difficult to fully trust them.

Many of these objections, even when just superficially enumerated, seem quite persuasive – hence, each of them will be individually tackled in the remainder of this book. However, it is crucial to begin by distinguishing two major types of objections: while some criticisms are intrinsically linked to the democratic deficit generated by privileging experts, others refer to various system's imperfections or failures associated with the possible role of the expert. This distinction is important because the first group outlines the fundamental challenges of epistocracy as a political system, and the other warns about possible systemic epistemic deficiencies that ought to be amended with appropriate mechanisms of democratic control.

Nevertheless, this debate gave rise to an important dilemma – truth and/or democracy. While it may seem as if this was a choice between non-democracy and democracy, it is in fact a symbolic simplification of the conflict between epistemic and ethical/political values in justifying democracy. Namely, if our primary aims were truth, high quality decisions, efficient problem-solving, or epistemic virtues such as epistemic responsibility, conscientiousness, curiosity and courage, there would be no reason not to privilege the opinions of experts despite our deep democratic convictions about the equality of all citizens. Therefore, every democratic society needs to confront the crucial problem of adequately integrating truth and values of democracy. More precisely, we need to attune the plausible idea that some people know more than others (which is an epistemically important fact that must not be ignored) with our commitment to democratic ideals and the principles of freedom and equality.

Even in these early stages of merely outlining the problem we can determine the most promising direction. I will take the side of those authors who argue that experts and ordinary citizens ought to divide

20 Christiano, 2008.

labour in public discussions and decision-making processes. This stance clearly implies the assumption that there can be a fully functioning democratic division of labour.[21] Rejecting all expertise is just as non-democratic as annulling any division of epistemic labour by delegating all decision-making to a small number of authorities. However, we must begin by inquiring whether it is possible to responsibly divide epistemic labour:

> "(...) the process of deliberation requires a division of labour (...). But the division of labour has traditionally been a problem for democracy and a problem for an egalitarian society. (...) The question is how can we enjoy the advantages of the division of labour in politics while treating each other as equal?"[22]

3.4. *Hybrid view and deliberative democracy*

The most daunting task of any position striving to harmonize and simultaneously foster both epistemic and ethical/political values of democracy is, therefore, to resolve tensions generated by the role of the expert: can we consider a democratic division a realistic prospect? How can we harmonize epistemic desiderata with political/ethical imperatives, the inclusion of experts with egalitarianism, the priority of the decisions of high epistemic quality with autonomy of each citizen?

We can discern three broad answers to this challenge of value harmonization. The first is the argument that harmonization is unnecessary because the political aim ought to be given primacy, while epistemic justification is of secondary significance (if any at all).[23] While the prioritization of ethical/political values might stem from the lack of an obvious solution to these tensions, it is more often a mere dismissal of the importance of epistemic justification of democracy – a rejection of the view that epistemic justification should play a role in assessing the social desirability of a system. The second answer

---

21 Kitcher, 2011.; Christano, 2012.

22 Christiano, 2012., p. 28.

23 John Rawls. 1997. 'The Idea of Public Reason, Postscript', in Bohman James and William Rehg (eds.), *Deliberative Democracy: Essays on Reason and Politics*, (Cambridge. Mass: MIT Press), pp. 93–144; Gerald Gaus. 1997. 'The Idea of Public Reason, Postscript', in Bohman James and William Rehg (eds.), *Deliberative Democracy: Essays on Reason and Politics*, (Cambridge. Mass: MIT Press), pp. 93–144.

is somewhat milder in claiming that, although it is necessary, the harmonization of values requires no division of labour as democratic procedures entail inherent epistemic values. This stance is defended by epistemic proceduralists, theorists known for criticising epistocracy and general attempts to criticize the experts' substantive role in democratic decision-making processes.[24] The third stance acknowledges the need for harmonizing values and considers a democratic division of labour possible. We can distinguish two approaches encompassed by this answer: consensualism and reliability democracy. In the following chapters, I will subject these positions – proceduralism, consensualism and reliability democracy – to more detailed scrutiny. Before I begin, I will briefly explain the rationale underlying mentioned solutions to the tension between epistemic and ethical/political virtues.

Non-epistemic justification of deliberative democracy. Certain philosophers of politics who defend the non-epistemic version of deliberative democracy and reject the necessity of harmonizing values claim that the significance of deliberation is not in producing more informed decisions, but rather in approximating the intrinsic standard of political equality. Deliberation has the instrumental value of resolving disagreements as it is a mediating mechanism by which all parties seek public, rational and impartial adjudication of their differences – as in the example of Gaus' *adjudicative democracy.*[25] Others – although they, taken at face value, agree that deliberation generates an epistemic advantage – actually reduce all advantages of discussions to ethical/political benefits. They generally advocate some sort of proceduralist position: (i) fair deliberative proceduralists argue that epistemic justification demands that all citizens have an equal or at least a fair chance to reason in discussions prior to voting,[26] (ii)

---

24 Estlund, 1997., 2003., 2008b. and also David Estlund. 2008a. 'Epistemic Proceduralism and Democratic Authority', in Geenens Raf and Ronald Tinnevelt (eds.), *Does Truth Matter? Democracy and Public Space* (Springer: Dordrecht), pp. 15–27; Peter, 2008., 2016. and also Fabienne Peter. 2013a. 'The Procedural Epistemic Value of Deliberation', *Synthese*, 190(7): 1253–1266; Fabienne Peter. 2013b. 'Epistemic Foundations of Political Liberalism', *Journal of Moral Philosophy,* 10(5): 598–620.

25 Gerald Gaus. 1996. *Justificatory Liberalism: An Essay on Epistemology and Political Theory* (Oxford: Oxford Universty Press); Gaus, Gerald. 2012. *The Order of Public Reason: A Theory of Freedom and Morality in a Diverse and Bounded World* (Cambridge: Cambridge University Press).

26 Bernard Manin. 1987. 'On Legitimacy and Deliberation', *Political Theory,*

rational deliberative proceduralists claim that procedural epistemic value lies in identifying good reasons, rather than providing fair access to discussions about reasons.[27] Although it may seem as if they still take the epistemic goal into consideration, neither form of deliberative proceduralism is really an epistemic view because they primarily understand deliberation as a political process with a desirable *political outcome* (consensus, agreement through public reason), rather than as an epistemic process with a desirable *epistemic outcome*. Any outcome of rational and fair deliberation – characterized by public reason – is acceptable independently of its epistemic value.[28]

Epistemic proceduralism. However, there is another proceduralist standpoint that explicitly advocates the necessity of harmonizing genuinely epistemic and political desiderata – epistemic proceduralism. Epistemic claims, as they emphasize, need not appeal to a procedure-independent standard of correctness or truth. At the same time, epistemic value can neither be identified with mere deliberation as such nor with whatever citizens may agree upon. Democratic procedures, which appropriately satisfy the conditions of fair, inclusive and pluralistic deliberation, also possess the imperfect tendency to produce *epistemically* correct outcomes. For instance, a procedure such as majority rule is legitimate because it is both fair (democratic rationale) and epistemically superior to alternative procedures (epistemic rationale).[29] Even though they may not be equivocal in identifying the real epistemic rationale, representatives of epistemic proceduralism eliminate the role of experts (including any division of labour between citizens and experts) due to its allegedly non-democratic character and exclusively derive both epistemic and ethical/political values from fair democratic procedures.

15: 338–368; Cass Sunstein, 1993. *The Idea of Democracy* (Cambridge: Cambridge University Press); Cass Sunstain. 2006. 'Two Conceptions of Procedural Fairness: Social Research', *An International Quarterly,* 73(2): 619–646; Frank Michelman. 1989. 'Conceptions of Democracy in American Constitutional Argument: The Case of Pornography Regulation', *Tennessee Law Review,* 56(2): 291–319.

27 Seyla Benhabib. 1996. *Democracy and Difference* (Princeton: Princeton University Press); James Fishkin. 1992. *The Dialogue of Justice: Toward a Self-Reflective Society* (New Haven: Yale University Press).

28 For more, see Estlund's brilliant analysis in Estlund, 1997.

29 Estlund, 1997., 2008.

Democratic division of epistemic labor. The third approach argues that democratic division of labour is capable of embracing the role of experts without resorting to the undemocratic practice of epistocracy. In its contemporary form, *consensualism* sharply recognizes that actual deliberations between experts are often infected by their special interests, ideological presuppositions and inequalities of power, and that they – as such – cannot reflect human ends or the interests of a large number of people. Consequently, no epistemic and ethical/political values can be based on blind belief in the expertise of official experts (scientists) or the notion that their stances are untainted by their values (and therefore objective and superior to the value-judgments of other groups). However, it is argued that it is possible to reach a consensus between equal and free citizens while still delegating a special role to experts. In this sense, public discussion should produce a sort of rational or informed consensus based on a non-egoistic and disinterested adjustment of personal beliefs and preferences to the stances of experts. This adjustment ought to be achieved through the iterated processes of trusting experts, learning from experts, being tutored by experts or like. Such deference to experts is appropriate because experts may help citizens overcome the limitations of their knowledge – and thus more effectively formulate and pursue their autonomously chosen goals.[30]

Similarly, advocates of *reliability democracy* claim that the rejection of epistocracy does not entail the rejection of expert participation altogether, i.e. their inclusion in the division of epistemic labour. Since experts can improve the epistemic quality of decision-making, they need to be given a role in deliberative democracy; we can not take democratic deliberation seriously if ordinary citizens will generally ignore the relevant specialized scientific knowledge in deliberating on issues that require such knowledge.[31] While citizens essentially must be a driving element that decides on the goals of a society, experts should use their special expertise to determine how to implement those goals. The entire process must rest on reliable democratic mechanisms of a truth-sensitive deliberative process.

It could be objected that these proposed forms of division of labour do not harmonize the values: they should be dismissed as undemocratic because they treat intrinsic political values (fairness, plurality, etc.) as a mere instrument for attaining the only important goal –

30 Kitcher, 2011.
31 Christiano, 2012.

truth, correctness or like. Any such instrumentalisation of political values underestimates the significance of individual agency and the irreducible value of pluralism by assuming that the correct outcome can be reached without the participation of all relevant individuals.[32] In brief response to this complaint, it could be argued that citizens are obviously expected to manifest certain deference to the community of experts, but not the kind of deference/trust in experts that disconnects a citizen from the decision-making process and invokes an element of epistocracy. Approaches that defend the division of epistemic labour are, as it is suggested by the very term, motivated by the explicit intention to harmonize epistemic and ethical/political desiderata to the highest possible extent.

***

This short overview has already presented the potential of the hybrid approach's fresh perspective on justifying deliberative democracy: it is not possible to adequately analyze and evaluate the epistemic features of democracy without taking into consideration its ethical/political traits nor *vice versa*. As we have seen, the hybrid approach is faced with the challenging task of realistically harmonizing epistemic and ethical/political values without reducing the epistemic to the political or the political to the epistemic. We can conclude this chapter with the previously mentioned promising account of the minimum conditions that make deliberative democracy justified. Firstly, deliberative democracy will be epistemically justified if epistemic virtues can be attributed to epistemic agents (individuals, groups, institutions) participating in discussions. Epistemic agents must act in an epistemically responsible manner, be adequately informed and unwilling to rely on false beliefs or prejudicial stereotypes. They should be epistemically conscientious or eager to attain knowledge about what is generally good for people, which includes a justified trust in experts. Secondly, deliberative democracy will be ethically/politically justified if the epistemic agents who participate in public discussions (individual, groups, institutions) can be ascribed the ethical/political virtue of responsibility or conscientiousness. This would imply that they will not egoistically prefer their own stance over the stances of other epistemic agents – including experts – but would rather remain sensitive to irreducible values of pluralism, diversity, critical interaction and inclusiveness.

---

32 Peter, 2008.

The key question is how deliberative democracy can ensure the harmonization of these epistemic and the ethical/political virtues of responsibility and conscientiousness. In tackling this question we will analyze three hybrid approaches that seek to reconcile the epistemic and the ethical/political justification of deliberative democracy: (1) epistemic proceduralism; (2) consensualism and (3) reliability democracy.

3.5. *Conclusion*

I have started from the assumption that the epistemic justification of democracy is necessary for its final and comprehensive legitimacy. It is insufficient for a system to be merely ethically and politically justified, but it must also be recognized as capable of generating epistemically high quality decisions. Likewise, I have assumed that deliberative democracy – given that it exhibits, along other democratic features, a heightened awareness of the importance of public participation and civic debates – is the best form of a democratic system. It was immediately evident that insistence on the epistemic justification of democracy introduced certain tensions into debates about justifying democracy. While these tensions had stemmed from abstract principles they soon manifested in realistic circumstances of having to choose between epistemic and democratic values. This finally articulated the dilemma between democracy and truth.

This conflict inexorably requires a conclusive answer to the issue of harmonizing epistemic desiderata – the production of epistemically high quality decisions, with the political imperative of preserving the values of equality, freedom and individual civic autonomy. Tension between the epistemic and the political goal in justifying deliberative democracy largely stem from assessing the role of experts in discussions and decision-making processes. It is argued that – due to their education and specialized training – experts are better at making correct decisions and decisions apt at efficiently solving problems than the average citizen. However, the practice of unilaterally privileging experts seems inevitably anti-democratic.

Tensions derived from this conflict of values can, of course, be solved by arguing in favour of only one group of values and the dismissal of the other, as was often comfortably done by epistemologists and philosophers of politics. Instead of choosing to remain entrenched in either the epistemological or the ethical/political camp, I will opt for the hybrid perspective – a unified model that assess social systems by balancing both values. The extended domain of social epistemology provides us with conceptual tools and an excellent theoretical framework for giving a carefully deliberated answer to the dilemma between democracy and experts (truth).

4.
DEMOCRACY AND PROCEDURES: DO DEMOCRATIC PROCEDURES INSURE EPISTEMIC QUALITY?

4.1. *What is proceduralism?*

I will begin from the aforementioned stance that the proper justification of deliberative democracy ought to be hybrid. Instead of being limited to the ethical and political justifications of democratic legitimacy, it must also provide the epistemic justification. This chapter on proceduralism is the first in a series of analyses of different hybrid approaches to justifying deliberative democracy.

Proceduralism is based on the general thesis that the legitimacy of a decision depends on the internal qualities of the decision-making process. More precisely, legitimate democratic decisions are those that are made through procedures in which all voters are treated as free and equal. In this chapter I will attempt to show that the mere procedural correctness of a democratic debate, despite being ethically and politically justified and in contrast to the stances of its advocates, cannot sufficiently guarantee the epistemic quality of decisions. I hold that the standard criteria of epistemic justification, including process-independent epistemic values such as truth, truth-conductiveness, correctness, epistemic responsibility and problem-solving, ought to be somehow introduced into the position of epistemic proceduralism in order for it to be at all relevant to the epistemic justification of democracy or to genuinely include a hybrid perspective. We are otherwise simply dealing with yet another reduction of epistemic values to ethical/political desiderata.

In the first part of the chapter, I will briefly clarify proceduralist views in order to make sense of what we are talking about when discussing the epistemic approach to procedural justice. I will try to accentuate the importance of clearly distinguishing epistemic from non-epistemic approaches – such as political or ethical justifications of proceduralism – which have repeatedly exhibited their proclivity for essentially rejecting the hybrid approach to evaluating social practices, institutions and systems. In the second part I will briefly outline the main proceduralist critiques of rival epistemic approaches to justifying deliberative democracy – veritism and pragmatism – and which derive their motivation from presuming certain process-independent epistemic values. In the third part, I will attempt to delineate certain critical outlooks on epistemic proceduralism by distinguishing strong (pure) and moderate epistemic proceduralism. I will argue that, while the strong model cannot ensure the epistemic justification of deliberative democracy, the moderate one may only prove to be valuable if it approaches the qualities of veritism or pragmatism.

4.2. *Epistemic and non-epistemic proceduralism*

We can begin by recalling that there are several kinds of proceduralist approaches, some of which we have already encountered in the previous chapter about the prospects of harmonizing ethical/political and epistemic virtues: (i) fair proceduralism, (ii) fair deliberative proceduralism and (iii) rational deliberative proceduralism. While fair proceduralism claims that a fair procedure of majority voting is sufficient for making democratic decisions legitimate, fair deliberative proceduralism rests on the premise that the legitimacy of a decision requires that citizens have equal (or at least fair) chances of presenting their arguments in discussions prior to casting their votes. Rational deliberative proceduralism doesn't only derive the legitimacy of a decision from a fair voting procedure and a fair approach to pubic reason, but demands a procedure capable of recognizing good arguments.[1]

Critics of *fair proceduralism* often emphasize that a mere fair procedure in which everyone can vote and decisions are made by majority rule neither ensures the epistemic quality of decisions nor epistemic legitimacy. The fairness of such procedures completely overlooks the epistemic quality of reasons that underlie the voters' attitudes. A procedure of choosing one among several conflicting preferences articulated by different citizens by flipping a coin would be just as fair and just as indifferent towards any underlying rationale: given that all individuals are equally likely to get elected by flipping a coin, the procedure could obviously be considered fair

1 Estlund postulated this excellent analysis of different kinds of non-epistemic proceduralism. Estlund, 1997.

and, consequently, legitimate. In other words, fair proceduralism is insensitive to the underlying rationale. Seeing that it completely ignores the nature and quality of the citizens' reasons behind making certain decisions, this case reduces epistemic legitimacy and epistemic virtues to epistemically irresponsible and unconscientious decision-making.

According to *fair deliberative proceduralism*, epistemic legitimacy depends on impartiality to the beliefs and arguments of individuals, rather than – as in the case of fair proceduralism – on impartiality towards their preferences and interests.[2] Although this account of justification recognizes both the underlying rationale and the epistemic virtue of impartiality, fair deliberative proceduralism sets no particular independent standards for assessing the quality of these allegedly unbiased reasons. A discussion can be neither epistemically justified nor responsible if individuals and society are indifferent to the quality of the content of the discussed epistemic reasons. Likewise, a fair procedure of discussing reasons can only improve epistemic legitimacy and fairness if the presented views are epistemically founded and stable. Should we agree that our only goal is to ensure fair civic access to discussions and a space for voicing reasons (regardless of their quality), the procedure will not have epistemic quality as any reason will ultimately be the same as any other.

The third approach of *rational deliberative proceduralism* recognizes the particular value of good reasons in addition to the mere value of ensuring that those reasons are fairly discussed.[3] Nonetheless, real epistemic legitimacy remains doubtful as the methods of recognizing good reasons and assessing their influence on the ultimate epistemic value of a decision are left entirely unclear. The inclusion of discussions and awareness of the value of reasons are primarily understood as parts of a political process that produces a desirable political result (conciliation or consensus), rather than as an epistemic process that generates a desirable epistemic result. The mere fact of conciliation in no way guarantees epistemic quality. To elaborate, any decision produced in a rational and fair exchange of argument-based reasons is considered acceptable irrespective of the epistemic quality of those reasons or the validity of their underlying arguments. This still makes it possible for any argument-based standpoint to be considered just as

---

2 Manin, 1987.; Sustain, 1993., 2006.; Michelman, 1989.
3 Benhabib 1996.; Fishkin 1992.

valuable as any other attitude supported by any kind of arguments. Although this view recognizes the importance of the epistemic virtue of responsibility – exercised through responsible argumentation, public justification and discussions about public justification – nothing is said about the criteria of recognizing the best arguments or the necessity of subjecting arguments to such assessments. The mere act of articulating arguments, despite its possible epistemic significance, does not automatically render a position epistemically valuable.

Despite the differences between these three proceduralist stances, it is possible to conclude that they evidently share an intrinsically non-epistemic approach. Democratic procedures are considered justified because they ensure a fair (plural, inclusive, impartial) decision-making process, and because they provide citizens with equal access to expressing their political beliefs and participating in the voting process with the result of, in best possible circumstances, successful conciliation. While this can be considered somewhat valuable, it is clearly insufficient. The political fairness of a procedure and the mere achievement of a common stance fail to fully account for the epistemic importance of democracy.[4] The thesis that democratic legitimacy necessarily requires epistemic justification rests on the assumption that – apart from the fairness of democratic deliberation and the achievement of consensus – democratic processes are or should be additionally epistemically justified in order to justify political authorities, governments and their legal manifestations. In summary, these forms of proceduralism are unsuitable for developing a hybrid perspective.

---

4 Conciliation or consensus – as the goal of a political procedure – can choose to satisfy epistemic requirements of different magnitudes: while minimum requirements reduce conciliation to a mere *negotiation* about mutually acceptable reasons and preferences, and while rational consensus demands that the expressed reasons and preferences aren't egoistically tied to personal interests, a genuinely epistemically valuable form of consensus rests on mutual reasons which aren't a mere (negotiated) intersection of different preferences, but which possess independent epistemic quality. Such reasons might have been attained through reliable (truth-sensitive) processes or have the potential to produce decisions capable of efficiently resolving citizens' problems. While fair procedures of attaining consensus are obviously desirable, they ensure little else but the consensus itself – let alone its possible epistemic value. For a more detailed account of different types of consensus, see Prijić – Samaržija, 2005.

4.3. *Foundations of epistemic proceduralism*

Joshua Cohen is certainly the father of 'real' epistemic proceduralism. Cohen stresses the significance of discussions in improving the epistemic quality of decision-making processes and precisely defines the procedural standard for assessing the epistemic quality of a decision: his ideal is a decision made in a model democratic procedure.[5] Such a decision is then the referential standard for assessing the epistemic value of other democratic decisions made in a concrete, real-world processes. The result generated by an ideal procedure is treated as an independent standard of validity applicable to current decision-making processes – to clarify, an 'independent' standard is 'a-specific-procedure-independent' standard. Note that this independent standard of assessing the epistemic qualities of decisions is not synonymous with the truth of political decisions. Cohen's standard does not presuppose realism or any other metaphysical concept of political truth or truth about the common good: the standard of the ideal procedure simply specifies those counterfactual conditions which cater to the best, most founded and most responsible discussions about political matters. In other words, it caters to a procedure that exercises the desirable epistemic virtues. Conciliation or a democratic decision made in an ideal procedure – a procedure that bases discussions on available information, rational arguments and a sound awareness of the common good, all while respecting the participants' equality and freedom – is correct in comparison with the sub-ideal approximations characteristic of actual democratic decision-making. Real decision-making processes (even though they aren't ideal) can, according to Cohen, provide the evidential bases of good political judgements as long as their structure remains respectful of this ideal. Cohen's approach nicely illustrates the features of a real epistemic procedural approach to justifying deliberative democracy (as compared to, for example, the fact that rational deliberative proceduralism stops being convincing after closer scrutiny) because it suggests that discussions ought to improve the epistemic quality of final decisions, rather than merely ensure the exchange of argument-based reasons.

Ranks of contemporary advocates of a real epistemic proceduralist approach to justifying democracy include certain influential authors

---

5 Joshua Cohen. 1986. 'An Epistemic Conception of Democracy', *Ethics,* 97: 26–38.

who aren't only critical of rival approaches linking epistemic justification to truth and solving problems, but who also question non-epistemic proceduralism. They unambiguously argue that a procedure must have intrinsic epistemic value which, however, cannot be reduced to its capacity to produce a true or a correct decision (whatever that may be) or a decision that efficiently resolves problems. In this regard, epistemic proceduralism first ought to explain how the impartiality and fairness of a democratic procedure ensure the consequent intrinsic epistemic value of the decisions made by such a procedure. David Estlund and Fabienne Peter compellingly defend a notion of *epistemic* proceduralism different from the aforementioned non-epistemic proceduralist approaches inasmuch as they explicitly claim that democracy must be epistemically justified and democratic procedures must have clear epistemic values.[6] While Estlund defends a more moderate version of epistemic proceduralism, Peter advocates the rather strong approach or *pure* epistemic proceduralism. In order to elucidate their positions, it is useful to learn from their criticisms of other non-proceduralist approaches which actually emphasize the importance of epistemically justifying democratic decisions. They both believe that the standard non-proceduralist approach to the epistemic justification of democracy pays the price of sacrificing political democratic values. By contrast, they consider epistemic proceduralism an option more capable of successfully balancing epistemic and democratic values. Though it is never explicitly mentioned, it is clear that their enquiry stems from a distinctly hybrid perspective as they aim to harmonize ethical/political and epistemic justification.

4.3.1. *Criticism of the standard approach to epistemic justification of democracy*

The standard approach to the epistemic justification of democracy rests on the view that democratic processes need to generate decisions which are correct from the perspective of some independent standard of epistemic value. I consider this position veritist because the postulated independent standard for assessing democratic decisions is usually conceived in terms of 'truth', truth-sensitivity, reliability, correctness, *truth tracking*, truth conduciveness and like.[7]

---

6 Estlund, 1997., 2003., 2008a., 2008b.; Peter, 2008., 2013a., 2013b., 2016.
7 Some kind of veritist approach is defended by, for example, Rousseau,

For instance, J.J. Rousseau's *correctness theory* argues that political decisions are legitimate only if they are correct, and their correctness is assessed on the basis of standards *independent of the procedure* by which the decision was made. In other words, according to Rousseau, the correctness of political decision must be assessed in terms of criteria unrelated to the fact that it was made in a democratic process in which citizens discussed or expressed their reasons and arguments. However, Rousseau does add that real democratic processes are so inherently correct that they will – under the right conditions – generally lead to such laws and policies which will be correct from the perspective of independent assessment. Among the ranks of modern authors, Goldman is a vocal proponent of the the veritist approach: he defends the concept of *reliability democracy* as a democracy based on reliable processes and quite unambiguously states that the consensus reached by the fair democratic deliberative processes does not automatically earn the badge of being epistemically justified.[8] No aspect of a fair procedure ending with a consensus constitutes an epistemological contribution to justifying democracy despite its obvious political justification. Rational public debate will only be epistemically valuable if it satisfies the condition of reliability or if it reliably leads to true beliefs.

Although advocates of epistemic proceduralism have abundantly criticized such approaches to epistemically justifying democratic decisions, I will focus on four fundamental issues: (i) the problem of instability, (ii) the problem of reliance or the tendency to support allegedly correct/true decisions, (iii) the problem of epistocracy, (iv) the problem of instrumentalizing democratic procedures.

The objection that standard approaches to epistemic justification produce instability stems from the difficulty of offering a singular definition of truth/correctness and the particularly dubious issue of assessing the truth/correctness of political decisions. It is difficult to agree upon whether a decision is true/correct or upon the extent to which a decision satisfies an independent standard of (political) truth. Given the fact that we do not know what a true/correct decision is or how we ought to recognize it, everyone can question or reject the

---

1762/1967.; Jean Jacques Rousseau. *Emile,* trans. by Allan Bloom (New York: Basic Books, 1763/1979).
1763/1979.; Goldman 1987., 1991., 1999., 2010.; List and Goodin, 2001.; Christiano, 2012.

8 Goldman, 2010.

legitimacy of a decision by refuting its truth or correctness (regardless of whether it was reached by majority vote or discussing good reasons and irrespective of whether it represents Rousseau's 'general will'). This notion of (political) truth is the precise cause of the instability which proceduralism successfully avoids, at least according to its proponents: while the majority will not accept that a decision is merely correct, most will accept the results of a democratic procedure or public debate even if they do not consider it correct or true.[9]

Standard approaches often commit the additional mistake of expecting that citizens will somehow spontaneously accept true/correct decisions on the sole basis of their correctness – which gives rise to the problem of deference. Epistemic proceduralists point out that this expectation is non-democratic because it is expected that, for example, a voter who defends the minority position suddenly concludes that he is wrong because the majority stance or the general will must be the true/correct attitude. Rousseau's account of the general will – understood as the most popular opinion – as the right stance is unacceptable inasmuch as it automatically dismisses the less popular attitudes as incorrect, thus urging citizens to accept as correct what they initially considered to be wrong. Should we assume that general will is definitely the correct attitude, then everyone who disagrees is condemned to an unacceptable situation in which their attitudes are not just in the minority, but inevitably incorrect. Knowing that democracy rests on the idea of unimpeachable pluralism, a standpoint which automatically disregards some citizens' opinions as wrong and incorrect and those of others correct (regardless of whether they are majority or minority views) cannot be considered democratic. Although democratic processes end up producing a final decision, it is not right to automatically and uncritically accept them as true/correct. Epistemic proceduralists emphasize that assessing the truthfulness/correctness of final decisions inevitably entails anti-democratic implications that hinder the pluralism of values and the legitimacy of diverse epistemic perspectives.[10]

The problem of epistocracy is commonly discussed in debates about veritism and more general polemics about the importance of epistemic justification in legitimizing democratic systems. I have already briefly mentioned the challenge of epistocracy when illustrating possible

9 Estlund, 1997., 2003., 2008a., 2008b.
10 Estlund, 1997, 2008a., 2008b.; Peter, 2008.

conflicts between epistemic and ethical/political virtues. Recalling its basic features, the assumption that the truthfulness of a decision is important for legitimizing democracy seemingly favors the practices of privileging experts and expertise as the best 'guides' to truth/correctness and allowing them to single-handedly make decisions. The most famous example of epistocracy is probably Plato's *Republic*, a community in which the legitimacy of decisions stems from the (objective) wisdom of the ruler that guarantees the truthfulness and correctness of his decisions. It is perfectly obvious that Plato's decision-making processes are entirely incompatible with any democratic procedure. Proceduralists argue that a democratic deliberative process cannot privilege anyone – not even experts – because citizens cannot be expected to follow the elite, but should rather exercise their equal access to making decisions. Choosing to introduce an independent criterion for assessing the epistemic quality of democratic decisions – such as the criteria of correctness, truthfulness, sensitivity to truth and like – inevitably entails the democratically illegitimate practice of privileging experts. Epistocracy gives rise to a number of additional problems. For instance, issues such as peer disagreement between experts and the acceptable authority on opting for a single expert most deserving of trust have been hotly debated. These polemics have cast doubt on the possibility of reliably recognizing those experts capable of arbitrating in matters of correctness/truth. Furthermore, some authors argue that there are no experts in political and moral matters, no objective and generally acceptable expertise, and, consequently, no foundations from which we can infer a political/moral authority.[11] It is claimed that there is no such conceptual connection between truth and democracy like the one linking truth and science. While democratic processes are obviously entirely unlike the structured methods of discovering truth in physics and medicine, those sciences still depend on the attitudes and research of relevant experts. From this perspective, accepting the views of experts seems reasonable. Nonetheless, political decisions aren't made in accordance to the rules of scientific seminars. This preliminary stance about the unfeasibility of appointing experts in political affairs can be alleviated by accepting the existence of experts and the superiority of their guidance to correct political decisions, and perhaps even by acknowledging the sheer possibility of settling on the best one among conflicted experts. Even if it were

---

11 Rawls, 1993.

so, expert stances cannot be imposed upon those of opposite opinions – particularly knowing that experts are not value neutral and that their personal interests and preferences still affect their views.[12] Epistemic proceduralists have concluded this discussion of epistocracy with a standpoint crucial for their position and for assessing the significance of epistemic justification: in politics, an attitude may be epistemically acceptable even if it is not true/correct.

Finally, Peter points out that veritist approaches instrumentalize the value of the democratic process and thus automatically undermine it by reducing the fairness of a democratic procedures to a means of achieving another goal – production and dissemination of knowledge or true/correct beliefs.[13] Veritism thus declares itself as an approach in which political and ethical legitimacy is merely the instrument of achieving an intrinsically valuable epistemic goal. It ignores the political value of democratic fairness. The instrumentalistic nature of this standard approach to epistemic democracy fails to acknowledge the irreducible value pluralism of individual action and the procedural epistemic value of collective discussions. An approach that focuses solely on the truthfulness/correctness of the final decision separates the value of the democratic process from the value of learning, thus overlooking that fact that procedural values are intrinsically epistemically valuable, according to Peter.

4.3.2. *Criticism of the pragmatist approach to epistemic justification of democracy*

The pragmatist approach to the epistemic justification of democracy differs from the veritist one in that it doesn't reduce the epistemic justification of democracy to the truthfulness/correctness of decisions produced in the democratic process. Pragmatism is an attitude that derives the epistemic legitimacy of democratic decision-making processes from the practical efficiency of the final decisions – more precisely, from whether the decisions can efficiently resolve the citizens' urgent and publicly recognized problems. Deliberative

---

12 Estlund, 2003.; Peter, 2008., 2016. It is important to note that critics of epistocracy aren't just epistemic proceduralists or those who deny the significance of epistemic justification. Christiano is, for instance, both an advocate of the standard approach to epistemic justification and a vocal opponent of epistocracy. Christiano, 2008.

13 Peter, 2008., 2016.

democracy is a form of decision-making that supports a collective approach to describing problems to the greatest possible extent, thus facilitating its effective resolution. In order to be at all successful, such collective inquiries require the democratic inclusion of all interested participants and directly oppose the exclusive epistocratic decisions inherent to veritism. Collective participation of all is a certain collective experiment about the optimal method of solving problems. Continuing Dewey's line of thought, Philip Kitcher develops the idea of an organized democratic science which optimally addresses current problems by relying on democratic procedures of public debate and participation. Progress, according to Kitcher, cannot be measured in terms of approaching truth because it is not progress *towards* truth; instead, it is measured in terms of moving *from* – solving a *significant* problem. However, it is important that Kitcher clearly emphasizes the role of experts in achieving the relevant epistemic goal of optimally solving the problem.[14]

Peter, however, holds that pragmatism is equally culpable of instrumentalizing democratic procedures and pure fairness. Although pragmatism significantly departs from the standard approach to epistemic democracy (which is why it is not vulnerable to the problems of instability, uncritically accepting allegedly true stances and epistocracy), it still reduces the value of fair processes of participation and discussion to their epistemic purpose of solving social problems. The pragmatist approach still fails to acknowledge the significance of value pluralism and individual action. Assuming a unanimous or consensual selection of a problem as more significant than any other – as well as the presumed consensus about the necessity of resolving the problem – contrast the irreducible pluralism of values that does not have to provide unilateral perceptions of problems or strive for the same goals when resolving them.[15]

This criticism of veritism and pragmatism, approaches that presuppose truth or some procedure-independent epistemic value, already makes it evident that the hybrid perspective will attempt to define the particular scope of including experts or the division of labour that produces the best possible decisions – understood as true/correct decisions or decisions that optimally resolve problems. Therefore, as we have repeatedly mentioned, any attempt to defend

14 Dewey, 1976.; Kitcher, 2011.
15 Peter, 2008.

epistemic justification from the hybrid perspective will depend on its ability to offer a solution that reconciles epistemic authorities with the democratic principles of freedom and equality.

***

I will continue by focusing on a more radical or 'pure' version of epistemic proceduralism in order to closely explore the theoretical scope of such an approach to epistemic justification. My aim is to show that this approach, despite its important inputs, can neither be an appropriate solution for epistemically justifying democracy by itself nor within the hybrid perspective. I will then consider a more moderate version of epistemic proceduralism that incorporates certain elements of veritism and pragmatism in order to conclude that they offer better frameworks for resolving the problem of the epistemic justification of democracy. However, I will finally conclude that proceduralism upholds an unsurmountable tension between epistemic and ethical political justification, which is particularly evident in its unilateral rejection of the role of experts and epistemic authorities in decision-making which, although it may seem attractive from the political perspective, can never be epistemically acceptable.

4.4. *Pure epistemic proceduralism*

Pure epistemic proceduralism rests on the assumption that the full epistemic value of a democratic decision-making process in the fair process itself, or, more precisely, in its procedural potential, rather than in the procedure-independent value of the achieved results. Epistemic value of democracy is unrelated to the truthfulness/correctness of the final decision or to resolving problems, which equalizes procedure-independent standards with the standards inherent to the fair procedure.[16]

As I have already mentioned, allegedly instrumentalist approaches that reduce fair democratic processes to the means of achieving another goal are, according to Peter, not only anti-democratic, but epistemically problematic as they neglect the epistemic potential of inclusiveness, diversity, individual action and value pluralism in making epistemically valuable decisions. Those civic interests, value systems and worldviews voiced in discussions should not be treated as instruments of ultimately

16 Peter, 2008, 2013a., 2013b., 2016.

achieving supposedly more neutral, objective and true decisions. The value of discussions and challenging different worldviews is not in annulling differences or achieving a more objective general stance that will then somehow diminish prejudice, but rather lies in the intrinsic epistemic value of fair discussion or deliberation. In short, pure epistemic proceduralism does not deny the necessity of defining a normative criterion as the basis for assessing knowledge production practices (public debates), but it separates this normativity from the criteria of truth/correctness or other procedure-independent values.

This makes it crucial to determine what is intrinsically epistemically valuable in a fair procedure. Peter opts for the intrinsic values of collective discussion or deliberation, the constructive function of deliberation, individual action and irreducible value pluralism, epistemic diversity, sustainable and durable critical interaction and a notion of epistemic inclusiveness unwilling to neutralize different interests and assumptions, but which rather accepts them as important epistemic resources. Collective action based on disagreement can be the motivational engine of evaluating and transforming injustice through democratic procedure. Interests, value systems and prejudice are epistemic resources that should not be avoided or neutralized; such behaviour would imply that they are treated instrumentally and negatively as constraints, rather than as valuable sources of the diversity needed for knowledge production. Criteria of correctness/truth and resolving problems are completely unnecessary because we can be sure that a fair procedure will, as such, necessarily produce an epistemically valuable result.

Looking at this brief summary of pure epistemic proceduralism, it is crucial to understand that it doesn't perceive the epistemic and non-epistemic rationales behind appraising the value of deliberative democracy as conceptually different. From her position – given that we are not dealing with any conflict between prioritizing a procedure's fairness or its epistemic value – there is no need to attempt to harmonize these values. On the contrary, the key thesis of pure epistemic proceduralism is that procedural fairness is simultaneously an ideal of political equality and epistemic value. Thus, every decision made in a fair, democratic and critical debate between representatives of different worldviews and values that is conducted in a transparent and non-authoritarian way is necessarily epistemically valuable.

Here we can distinguish between pure and moderate epistemic proceduralism on the basis of their attitudes towards the importance of truth/correctness and problem solving. Pure epistemic proceduralism is a strong version of proceduralism because it completely dismisses the standard of truth and all other procedure-independent criteria. The normativity of pure epistemic proceduralism forsakes the values of objective validity, neutralizing prejudicial constraints and other 'truth-sensitive' values that in any way presuppose the sheer existence of truth/correctness. Unlike its strong counterpart, moderate epistemic proceduralism still relates the epistemic value of public debates and democratic deliberation to truth/correctness or efficient solutions to problems, but it claims that the epistemic value of discussions cannot be reduced to the mere goal of producing correct or true beliefs. Attaining truth or making correct decisions cannot fully amount for the epistemic value of deliberation because discussions aren't reducible to their epistemic outcomes: while results are obviously important, the epistemic value of deliberation is not in the result, but in the procedure.[17] Whereas moderate epistemic proceduralism remains

17 Although Peter defends strict epistemic proceduralism in her book *Democratic Legitimacy* (Peter, 2008), she later embraced a more moderate stance, while maintaining that epistemic value can not be reduced to the truth/correctness of the result (Peter, 2013a, 2013b). Peter creatively grounds her tempered attitude on the recent surge of discussions regarding the possibility of reasonable disagreement. Epistemological debates about disagreement primarily explore whether participants in a discussion can form different attitudes if they have had access to the same evidence (presuming that they are of equal expertise). On the one hand, some philosophers argue that two peers who have access to shared evidential grounds cannot possibly reach a state of rational disagreement – they should either divulge which expert is correct or both suspend their opinions (David Christensen. 2007. 'Epistemology of Disagreement: The Good News', *Philosophical Review,* 116:187–217; David Christensen. 2012. 'Epistemic Modesty Defended', in Christensen David and Jeniffer Lackey (eds.), *The Epistemology of Disagreement* (Oxford: Oxford University Press), pp. 1–23; Adam Elga. 2007. 'Reflection and Disagreement', *Noûs,* 41: 478–502: Adam Elga. 2010. 'How to Disagree about how to Disagree' in Feldman Richard and Ted A. Warfield (eds.), *Disagreement* (Oxford: Oxford University Press), pp. 175–186: Richard Feldman. 2006. 'Epistemological puzzles about disagreement', in Hetherington Stephen (ed.), *Epistemology Futures* (Oxford: Oxford University Press), pp. 216–236; Richard Feldman 2007. 'Reasonable Religious Disagreements', in Antony Louise (ed.), *Philosophers Without Gods: Meditations on Atheism and the Secular* (Oxford: Oxford University Press), pp. 194–214. On the other hand, some philosophers hold that there are numerous scenarios that make reasonable disagreement possible. The most common rationale is that participants in a discussion can never possess entirely identical evidence – moreover, not even the experts who have scrutinized all available evidence

within the margins of the standard approach in that it acknowledges that decisions must in some way be related to the epistemic value of truth, pure epistemic proceduralism is a radical revision of the standard approach. I will attempt to show that the revisionist project of strong or pure epistemic proceduralism is not sustainable because it leaves the realm of epistemic assessments and reduces the epistemic justification of democracy to the political.

4.4.1. *Critical remarks on pure epistemic proceduralism: epistemic revisionism*

Before proceeding, it should be noted that strict or pure epistemic proceduralism suffers from excessive optimism regarding the epistemic value of deliberation: it argues that a fair procedure, by the virtue of its fairness, necessarily generates epistemically valuable decisions. For example, Peter writes, "If the procedure was genuinely fair, sexist proposals couldn't possibly be accepted".[18] While it is currently unnecessary to ponder upon the conceptual link between fairness and epistemically valuable decisions, we can ask a simpler question: aren't epistemically sub-optimal circumstances, such as deliberation between citizens, just as likely to produce epistemically sub-optimal

---

will entirely overlap. Certain evidence may be temporarily unavailable, the same evidence might be attributed different scientific weight and relevance in different scientific contexts, same data may lead to different conclusions in different clusters of knowledge and experts might justify the same evidence within different systems of epistemic norms (Sosa, 2010.; Alvin I. Goldman. 2010b. 'Epistemic Relativism and Reasonable Disagreement', in Feldman Richard and Ted A. Warfield (eds.), *Disagreement* (Oxford: Oxford University Press), pp. 187–215). Peter accepts Sosa and Goldman's stance regarding the possibility of reasonable disagreement (Opacity View). The mere possibility of reasonable disagreement, according to Peter, suggests that it is possible to have epistemically valuable attitudes that differ from each other – in other words, they are not both true/correct because two different positions can never be concurrently true/correct. She concludes that the truth of the outcome possesses distinct epistemic value, but keeps her distance by claiming that any attempt to assess the epistemic value of the decision must acknowledge the epistemic value of fair decision-making procedures (Peter 2013a.; 2013b.). However, her most recent article resorts to the old claim that emphasising the epistemic result instrumentalizes ethical/political justification, culminating with the view that truth does not live in politics. (Peter, 2016.).

18 Peter, 2008., p. 134.

decisions (even in the case of sexism). Should we push values and worldviews aside for the time being, the fact remains that participants in public discussions are insufficiently informed and mostly lack the necessary expertise for (directly or indirectly) making responsible decisions about numerous issues. We have already briefly mentioned empirical findings which have confirmed the view that most citizens are not only inadequately informed about the issues they are deciding upon (and are sometimes objectively hindered from becoming informed due to time-consuming everyday obligations and constraints on fully understanding the given area of expertise), but are also largely uninterested in investing their time and cognitive resources in learning about those issues or delving deeper into the problems. Many participants in decision-making procedures don't only lack the specific expertise and education necessary for understanding sophisticated topics or seeking additional training, but are also entirely unacquainted with the published programs of particular political parties, basic human rights and relevant constitutional directives.[19] Moreover, although deliberative groups often do include several professional and informed individuals, their influence on others is surprisingly weak. Empirical evidence suggests that the informed are reluctant to engage in debates with the less informed because they understand that the majority stance is too influential for them to somehow affect it. Similarly, they often succumb to the social imperative of agreeing with the standpoint of the majority, regardless of whether theirs might be different.[20] Even when the more informed actually articulate their views within a larger group, their stances fall victim to the influence of *shared knowledge* or shared information: "The influence of a particular fact was directly positively correlated with the number of members who had known that fact even before the group deliberated and made the final judgement."[21] In other words, the informed members of a deliberating group cannot disseminate knowledge to those who are not already at least somewhat

19 For example, American research has shown that 75% of examinants were able to correctly answer only 13% of the 2000 posed political questions, suggesting that a comparatively minor number of citizens understands and can critically assess the political concepts of civic freedoms and political economy, let alone recognize particular party members, the standpoints of presidential candidates, social programs or fundamental public policies (Carpini, Deli and Keeter, 1996., pp. 101–102).

20 Sunstein, 2006.

21 Gigone and Hastie, 1993., p. 960.

informed or at least somewhat professional. Consequently, the virtues of fairness, transparency and critical confrontation are insufficient for ensuring epistemically valuable opinions or decisions. The sub-ideal circumstances of everyday life undermine any notion of deliberative optimism because decisions will be affected by the inevitable deficit of information and expertise (time, education, etc.).[22]

It is possible that Peter challenges this argument for the simple reason that she doesn't perceive the fairness of a procedure as necessarily related to any level of information and expertise. In this vein, any fair discussion between participants can be deemed epistemically valuable regardless of their knowledge and expertise because its apparent drawbacks actually make it more inclusive and respectful of the irreducible plurality of social attitudes. It is true that critiques of deliberative optimism presuppose that an informed and expert citizen somehow ensures correct/true decisions. However, it is just as true that pure epistemic proceduralism ignores the epistemic significance of the way information and expertise influence the quality of decisions, instead entirely inferring epistemic quality from the sheer existence of participation and diversity.

In this vein, the second objection to strict or pure epistemic proceduralism points out that this approach significantly revises or even negates the fundamental epistemological understanding of epistemic values. If pure epistemic proceduralism's rejection of normative concepts of objective validity, correctness and truth may seem somewhat familiar, it is because epistemological literature commonly recognizes such attitudes as belonging to social *constructivism*. To exemplify, Peter states that:

> "(...) correctness is difficult, if not impossible, to determine. (...) Correctness alone, interpreted as a term that is independent from the procedure, is unattainable. However, if the procedure-independent standard is unattainable, it is difficult to imagine how democratic legitimacy may depend on the normative power of such a concept."[23]

Or:

22 For a 'pessimist' approach to deliberative democracy, see more in Kristoffer Ahlstrom-Vij. 2012. 'Why Deliberative Democracy is (Still) Untenable?', *Public Affairs Quarterly*, 26(3): 199–220.

23 Peter, 2008., p.133.

> "(...) The stance that prejudices can be treated as resources requires inclusive and public practices of knowledge production that facilitate interaction between different perspectives (...) political and epistemic justice are just two sides of the same coin."[24]

In contrast to the strong epistemic proceduralist assumption that any kind of truth or correctness is illusory, traditional epistemology and much of modern social epistemology are based on and largely determined by the view that normative standards of rationality and justification are neither conventional nor relativistic, but instead entail some kind of objective validity. Moreover, given that concepts such as knowledge and justification obviously presume the existence of truth or another normative notion similar to truth, they also presume that this truth is at least somewhat objective and non-constructed.[25] It is especially important to remember that our earlier review of virtue epistemology and epistemic justice has shown that – in real life – prejudices and stereotypes threaten the (traditionally understood) epistemic virtues of responsibility and conscientiousness.[26] Pure epistemic proceduralism thus veers dangerously close to Foucault's 'new' knowledge or one of the many forms of social constructivism – be it postmodernism, deconstruction or the 'strict program' – that explicitly reject traditional epistemological settings. These views explicitly are, and pure epistemic proceduralism seems to be, revisionist in relation to traditional epistemological conditions: unable to opt for epistemic relativism because of its compatibility with traditional epistemology (such as different forms of contextualism), they instead embrace a certain epistemic nihilism by claiming that truthfulness/correctness can not be determined at all because there are no foundations on the basis of which a decision would be true or more correct than another. This approach results in a negation of intrinsic epistemic values and a reduction of epistemic values to social facts (social practices and procedures, power relations, etc.). In other words, pure epistemic proceduralism is revealed to be an epistemically nihilistic and essentially non-epistemic project that calls for a radical revision of the traditional epistemological understanding of epistemic values.

Finally, and as a result, the epistemic status of strong or pure epistemic proceduralism is just as questionable as the statuses of the

---

24 Peter, 2008., p.133.
25 For objections to social constructivism, see Goldman 1999., 2010a.
26 Fricker, 2007.

aforementioned non-epistemic proceduralist approaches inasmuch as it replaces traditional normative epistemological concepts with the normative concepts of politics. Any attempt to regard the epistemic justification of deliberative democracy as worthwhile is thus entirely derived from the fact that it differs from customary political justification by presupposing that democratic legitimacy cannot be limited to political justification because it also depends on the epistemic quality of the decisions made in democratic decision-making processes. This is precisely why we cannot accept an approach that seemingly advocates the epistemic justification of democracy only to finally argue that epistemic value is entirely synonymous with the political value of a fair discussion. Such an approach negates the specific benefits of epistemically evaluating discussions because it reduces their epistemic value to the non-epistemic value of the fairness of the procedure.

An appropriately guided process of collective deliberation that respects the rules of reciprocity and mutual respect does not automatically generate – only in the virtue of its fairness – an epistemically valuable result. It is similarly unclear how political fairness can be conceptually synonymous with epistemic quality. I am in no way trying to claim that the virtues of reciprocity, equal treatment, mutual respect and irreducible pluralism aren't politically and ethically valuable – what remains unclear is the *exact* intrinsic epistemic value of inclusiveness, plurality, mutual respect, or critical confrontation, unless we choose to settle on their (evidential, perspectivistic) potential to lead to correct solutions, solutions capable of solving problems or truth-sensitive decisions. Moreover, I see nothing epistemically wrong in the much-criticized practice of instrumentalism and don't even consider it a threat to political values. From a strictly epistemic perspective, public debates and fair procedures are simply means of generating the best possible decisions in the presence of different systems of values. While such procedures are intrinsically ethically and politically valuable, they can have additional epistemic value. The possible epistemic value of, for example, ensuring that discussions are public and sensitive to diversity, neither distorts nor jeopardizes the ethical and political values of the procedure. Epistemic instrumentalization of fair public discussions does not entail their simultaneous political instrumentalization: a democratic deliberation or another fair procedure completely retains their intrinsic political and ethical value.[27] However, any inclusive and

---

27 Accepting epistemic instrumentalism isn't necessarily synonymous with

critical inquiry or discussion will obviously strive to adopt, retain and revise beliefs with the aim of settling on as many justified and rational beliefs as possible. It would seem downright questionable to accept critical discussions that encourage everyone to stick to their initial positions (whatever they might be) in order to preserve individual autonomies and the irreducible pluralism of civic attitudes.

Nevertheless, should a pure proceduralistic approach that rejects values such as truth and correctness still desire to keep the status of an epistemic approach, it would need to demonstrate what is specifically *epistemically* valuable in a fair procedure without resorting to the mere political value of fairness. At this point, I think that there are no good reasons for accepting strict or pure epistemic proceduralism as a persuasive epistemic justification of democracy.

***

This line of thinking seems to imply that far more potential could be found in a more moderate variant of epistemic proceduralism. I think that such moderate approaches are currently given two available options. On the one hand, it is possible to accept that there is one key epistemic value (truth/correctness, problem solving, etc.) and that fair procedures – transparent, inclusive, critical discussions with undeniable political and ethical values – are epistemically optimum means to reaching that aim. Such a moderate epistemic proceduralism would somewhat resemble the so-called standard epistemic justification of democracy, but would put a special emphasis on elaborating the epistemic quality of a fair procedure, understood as its capacity to generate true/correct outcomes or indirectly solve problems. On the other hand, it is also possible to defend a certain *dualism* of epistemic values: intrinsic epistemic value would be attributed both to the final outcome (a decision or a judgment) and the fair procedure. In this case, a valid decision would have to satisfy two conditions: (i) the condition of a *fair* procedure, which obviously demands for decisions to be made in a fair manner and (ii) the condition of truthfulness/corectness or problem

---

accepting the view that the political value of a democratic procedure boils down to its role in achieving the epistemic value of truth. Instrumentalists such as Goldman, Dewey or Kitcher definitely aren't trying to challenge the political and ethical values of a public debate. On the contrary, it is simply pointed out that, in addition to political values, public debates have the epistemic value of generating true/correct decisions or decisions capable of resolving problems.

soloving capacity. This dualistic position makes it possible to claim that an incorrect[28] decision may be *somewhat* epistemically valuable if it is made in a fair procedure and that we can speak of several epistemically valuable decisions that can not simultaneously be true – such as as in the case of rational disagreement.[29] Of course, this dualistic variant of epistemic proceduralism still faces the – though somewhat less urgent – task of explaining the conceptual link between fair procedures and epistemic values. It has to singularize the epistemically valuable aspects of a fair procedure without relating them to the possibility of correct outcome or their problem-solving capacities.[30]

4.5. *Moderate epistemic proceduralism*

As one of the most prominent advocates of epistemic proceduralism, David Estlund also supports the constitutive contribution of procedures to the epistemic justification of deliberative democracy. However, he maintains a clear distance from all non-epistemic forms of proceduralism, as well as from strict or pure proceduralism.[31]

Estlund argues that legitimacy – both ethical/political and epistemic – lies primarily within the procedure itself, rather than in the quality of the achieved results. While the standard approach to epistemic justification emphasizes that it is solely derived from the epistemic quality of the results of a democratic debate – decisions, judgments, etc. – which are assessed in accordance to the independent criteria of truthfulness/correctness or their problem solving capacity. Estlund emphasizes that the epistemic legitimacy of democracy rests within the procedure itself. This proceduralist epistemic justification is a crucial alternative to veritism because it puts emphasis on epistemic justification without referring to (metaphysical) truths or to the expertise of some individuals in comparison to others. According to Eslund, the veritist imperative of achieving the correct/true decision

---

28 Estlund, 1997., 2008.

29 Peter, 2013a., 2013b.

30 My research related to the basic postulates and subsequent criticism of pure proceduralism can be found in two articles: Snježana Prijić–Samaržija. 2014a. 'Epistemičko opravdanje demokracije: epistemička vrijednost proceduralne pravičnosti', *Prolegomena*, 13(2): 373-392; Snježana Prijić–Samaržija. 2017. 'The Role of Experts in a Democratic Decision-making Process', *Etica & Politica / Ethics & Politics,* 19/2: 229–246.

31 Estlund, 1997., 2003., 2008a., 2008b.

or judgement cannot convincingly persuade citizens to participate in public debates because there is no credible definition of a correct or true outcome that they could strive towards. Moreover, he particularly stresses that participants in public debates would be unlikely to uncritically accept truth and correctness as the goals of their discussion because such a choice implies that they would have to renounce their personal convictions if they differed from the outcome of the debate. While participants in democratic procedures will accept the legitimacy of a fairly made decision even if it differs from their position, this will never suffice to convince them that their personal stance is false or incorrect. Therefore, public debates don't have to produce a true/correct outcome, but rather aim to improve the quality of decisions by making them more rational, better grounded, and perhaps even more truthful and more just. It is crucial to notice that Estlund does not shy away from the concepts of truth or correctness. Also, unlike Peter, he isn't wary of relating deliberative procedures to truth/correctness, rationality or like – instead, he only refuses the veritist account of correct/true decisions as procedure-independent criteria for assessing whether a procedure is epistemically justified. The very concept of a deliberative procedure contains procedure-independent epistemic values which are neither truth nor correctness: democratic discussions have the intrinsic value of improving the rationality, evidential grounds and fairness of final decisions.

This marks the extent to which epistemic proceduralism diverges from, for example, fair proceduralism, whose advocates – much like Estlund – acknowledge the intrinsic value of procedures without immediately considering it a guarantee of epistemic justification. They only emphasize the importance of fair discussion and equality in voting. In contrast, Estlund argues that the democratic deliberative procedure possesses an *intrinsically epistemic objective property* of generating rationality, truth and justice – to a greater extent than any alternative procedure. This is the point when we have to explain why Estlund's epistemic proceduralism is described as 'moderate': when taking about decision-making procedures, he refers to their 'objective' epistemic property of improving rationality and truthfulness.

This is precisely what makes his version of proceduralism (unlike pure proceduralism, which, as we have shown, actually isn't an epistemic position) an inherently epistemic position congruent with «real» (social) epistemology. Unlike Peter, Estlund unambiguously argues that the fairness and democratic nature of a procedure do not automatically make it an inherently epistemically valuable deliberative procedure: ensuring that everyone fairly participatates by respecting values such as equality, freedom, irreducible pluralism and inclusiveness doesn't immediately ensure the equal epistemic influence of all participants or satisfy the condition of argument-based discourse in the relevant public arena. In other words, even if two equally fair procedures both satisfy the conditions of fair discussion, they can be epistemically unequal because one is epistemically superior. Estlund's epistemic proceduralism respects the epistemic criterion of correctness by accepting the existence of a certain connection between discussions and the goal of truth/correctness. However, according to Estlund, the purpose of a discussion should not be reduced to the truthfulness or correctness of its results (as was done by Plato, Rousseau, Condorcet, Goldman and even Cohen). Its purpose and epistemic virtue should instead be sought in the inherent epistemic properties of the debate itself.

Estlund claims that epistemic proceduralism evolved from the dialectical link between the fairness of deliberative procedures and the epistemic superiority derived from their imperfect tendency to produce epistemically correct decisions. Although epistemic value cannot be fully reduced to fairness, he argues for a profound connection between the political and the epistemic justification of deliberative democracy, the democratic political character of discussions and the epistemic quality of the final result.

The deliberative procedure, according to Estlund, is epistemically superior to the alternative procedure of privileging experts in making decisions. This suggests that he doesn't only criticize expertism, epistocracy and the practice of privileging expert views in terms of their previously mentioned non-democraticness, but also on the basis of their limited epistemic potential. The fact that all perspectives – including the perspectives of experts – are constrained by personal value preferences unite with the uncertain existence of expertise in the domain of morality and politics in order to render expertism epistemically less valuable than diversely argumentated public debates. Estlund argues that the epistemic value of a procedure does not principally depend on the participants' information and competences (their maturity, expertise, interest and sensitivity to rational argumentation), but on its structural and institutional features that generate desirable epistemic results. To sum up, decisions made in a deliberative democratic system are legitimate because deliberative democratic procedures – which rest on the equal participation of all and the privileging of none (due to their alleged expertise) – are epistemically optimal in comparison with any other ethically/politically acceptable decision-making process.

4.5.1. *Critical remarks on moderate epistemic proceduralism: between epistemic instrumentalism and value dualism*

Any critical review of Estlund's moderate epistemic proceduralism will struggle to detect whether it is closer to a mild instrumentalization of democratic procedures characteristic of the standard epistemic justification of democracy, or a certain dualism of epistemic values – the epistemic value of the procedure and the epistemic value of a correct/true outcome. Nonetheless, we will see that Estlund is satisfied with neither interpretation: while the first returns epistemic proceduralism to the petticoat of the standard approach which he wishes to shake, the second implies something quite similar to Leibnizian prestabilised occasional permanent connection of completely disparate values.

In order to fully grasp Estlund's proceduralism and his stance about the intrinsic value of the procedure, it's important to emphasize that he thinks that a procedure *can* be epistemically valuable regardless of its results. This is what Estlund is attempting to say when talking about its *imperfect* tendency to generate epistemically correct decisions. Although a procedure *tends* to produce epistemically correct/true decisions, it is not epistemically valuable because it increases the probability that the final decision will be true/correct or because it is an epistemically reliable process of achieving truth/correctness. A procedure is epistemically legitimate and valuable *irrespectively* of its particular final result even though it significantly contributes to it. In other words, the result of a good democratic procedure will be epistemically legitimate even if it is incorrect and a decision made in a democratic debate will have epistemic value even if it is untrue. Knowing that no advocate of the standard approach to epistemic justification would readily accept such a position, we could probably side with the interpretation that describes Estlund's approach as a certain dualism. Estlund thus enables a 'voter' who was left in the minority to claim that someone else's decision – even though he still perceives it as incorrect – morally and epistemically obliges him for strictly procedural reasons. The 'incorrect' decision retains both its moral and its epistemic value owing to the moral and the epistemic value of the procedure.

At this point, we must first inquire which specific procedure-related epistemic reason can epistemically justify the choice to accept an incorrect decision while knowing it is incorrect. While we could argue that an incorrect decision can be acceptable if we know that the procedure in which it was generated usually produces correct/true decisions, it would suggest that we are still seeking the value of the procedure in its fallible potential to generate truth/correctness. This is something that Estlund explicitly dismisses. Eslund clarifies the matter through the example of the Anglo–Saxon jury system. The procedure of determining guilt and passing the verdict includes complex features such as detailed scrutiny and disclosure of evidence, testimony, cross-examination and discussions between jurors. This procedure has an imperfect tendency to produce correct judgments: although the majority of decisions are indeed correct, mistakes occasionally sneak in. We can accept occasional mistakes as legally binding in the virtue of the fact that the procedure is generally epistemically valuable. The epistemic legitimacy of the decision therefore doesn't lie in its correctness (the judge can accept a wrong decision), but in the fact that it was generated by an epistemically valuable procedure. According to Estlund, the process of democratic deliberation does not have to be ideal to have epistemic virtue: ideal epistemic circumstances – in which everyone is informed about and interested in political issues, has enough time to seek evidence, favours the common good over their partial interests and appreciates good arguments, thus perfectly leading to correct decisions – are not *necessary* for epistemically justifying a discussion. It is sufficient to institutionally ensure a certain similarity between the ideal and the concrete epistemic circumstances: with time, mistakes and shortcomings will gradually wither away in the direction of more rational public deliberation that relies on increasingly dependable and generally acceptable decision-making processes.

Although his passionate personal conviction seems to evade the Scylla and the Charybdis of instrumentalism and pure epistemic proceduralism, Estlund still leaves us with a significant dilemma: what role does his theory actually give to the epistemic values of truth and correctness. On the one hand, Estlund is vocal in rejecting the veritist thesis that a procedure/discussion is epistemic only if it produces true or correct results/decisions. On the other hand, he claims that the epistemic value of the procedure is somehow indeed related to the truth/correctness of its outcomes (because it has an imperfect tendency to generate correct decisions). To make matters even more complicated, he rejects that the procedure has the *instrumental* role of increasing the likelihood of making correct/ correct decisions or being a reliable process of attaining true/correct decisions.

Eslund again seems to point towards two completely separate or intrinsic epistemic values, a standpoint which we have characterized as dualistic. There is no reason to dismiss any dualism of values as principally unacceptable. However, Estlund's dualism of epistemic and political values is problematic because he seems to claim that the epistemic value of a democratic procedure simultaneously is and isn't related to the truth. What could possibly explain the claim that the intrinsic value of a procedure (which is by definition incommensurable with the intrinsic value of truth) can still influence and even improve the truthfulness/correctness of decisions?

We have already discussed the value turn in epistemology and the subsequent advent of virtue epistemology. Instead of necessarily evaluating the cognitive successfulness of a doxastic decision-making process in terms of true beliefs, these approaches put emphasis on virtues such as epistemic responsibility, conscientiousness, curiosity and like. We can also recall certain views which have defended the pluralism of epistemic values. According to such approaches, cognitive efforts can be valuably directed towards, for example, adjusting beliefs to experience or supporting them with adequate empirical evidential bases. Other valuable achievements include genuine understanding, theoretical wisdom, rational assumptions, working hypotheses likely to be true and a commitment to epistemically responsible research.[32] Some authors who defend the pluralism of epistemic values or virtues still hold that truth is the only, the ultimate and the primary epistemic goal, while the mentioned values are simply instruments that indicate which doxastic states (decisions, beliefs, judgments) have the chance of being truthful and which processes are likely to reliably lead to truth.[33] Supporting this kind of pluralism can lead to the conclusion that, once we have achieved a true belief, all other epistemic values would be immediately rendered worthless. However, this interpretation obviously cannot be related to Estlun's standpoint as it clearly opposes certain fundamental proceduralist settings about the intrinsic value of the procedure.

---

32 Kvanvig, 2005., 2010.

33 This monist or reductionist view of truth as the only intristic epistemic value is defended by BonJour, 1985.; Alston, 1988.; Alvin I. Goldman. 1979. 'What Is Justified Belief?', in Pappas George (ed.), *Knowledge and Justification* (Dordrecht: Reidel), pp. 1–25; Alvin I. Goldman. 1986. *Epistemology and Cognition* (Cambridge, MA: Harvard University Press).

Other epistemologists claim that epistemic values aren't exhausted in external success (the truth of a belief) because cognitive processes include certain internal elements that entail independent value. This attitude is shared by many virtue epistemologists who claim that the intellectual success of achieving a true belief by exercising intellectual virtues is more valuable than the mere possession of a true belief.[34] In this sense, the epistemic value of the procedure and the true/correct decision trumps that of the true decision itself. Should we accept this interpretation of dualism, the procedure would have independent value in addition to that of true/correct decisions: we could thus ensure a wider evidential basis provided by all citizens, expand the domain of public reasoning and achieve decisions more congruent with the existing systems of beliefs, thus enabling citizens to immediately understand them. We still cannot be sure whether Estlund would accept this standpoint because the value of the procedure – although it's independent – is only auxiliary, while the value of truth/correctness is bestowed with central importance.

Estlund argues that a decision made in a good procedure has epistemic value although it is wrong: the procedure is not good because its resulting decision is likely to be true, but because it is simply valuable in itself. What is continually confusing in Estlund's dualistic stance is the downright bizarre thesis that the apparent value of a procedure is unrelated its potentially true/correct outcome, and yet – almost mysteriously – it somehow tends to result in true decisions. It becomes starkly obvious that procedures share a common feature with dependable processes of making right/true decision and that the properties of procedures at least somewhat resemble the properties of processes that lead to truth/correctness. These properties can encompass a wide array of possible features, ranging from a wide evidential basis and sensitivity to rational arguments, to the practice of neutralizing prejudice. It is apparent that every epistemically valuable aspect of a procedure seems to improve the final outcome of a discussion in terms of its truthfulness or corectness. However, Estlund does not want to confirm this.

We have repeatedly stressed Estlund's claim that a procedure is epistemically valuable even regardless of its untrue or incorrect outcome. I have also repeatedly written that a classical veritist/ instrumentalist would immediately reject the mere notion that a

34 Greco, 2000., 2011.; Sosa, 1980., 1991., 2007.; Riggs, 2002., 2003., 2006.

procedure (or truth seeking process) that doesn't lead to truth or correct decisions can have any kind of value. However, some (truth) monists agree with Estlund's stance by arguing that, in the case of attaining an untrue/incorrect belief, it's better to at least exercise epistemically responsible behavior (which usually results in truth) than to give up on both truth and a responsible procedure. Most virtue epistemologists (who are not dualists) would probably accept that mere external success or a true decision made without internal achievements – such as a good procedure or the practice of intellectual virtues – cannot be considered fully valuable. In short, it seems that Estlund's attitude is not so distant from the standard approach to epistemic justification as he sometimes lets it on. His ambiguity and inconsistency in clarifying what constitutes the epistemic value of a procedure and the somewhat mysterious nature of these values seem to be motivated by a desire not to question the ethical/political dimension of justification for purely epistemic reasons. In my opinion, Estlund doesn't disapprove of veritism because of its insistence on true/correct decisions, but because of the dangerous prospect of elitist and anti-democratic practices of favoring a privileged few. Let us recall his arguments that: (i) the truthfulness/correctness of the decision is an anti-democratic criterion for justifying a procedure because it entails the thesis that minority attitudes are wrong; (ii) the criterion of the truthfulness/correctness of the decision is inevitably connected to favoring experts, and any form of expertism or epistocracy implies the non-democratic practice of privileging a select few. In other words, Estund's primary motivation for rejecting the criteria of truth/correctness stems from the worry that emphasizing the epistemic value of procedures that produce true/correct decisions could become elitist and non-democratic, rather than from the epistemic reasons of refuting standard epistemic justification.

Although I argue that Eslund did not offer an acceptable alternative to the standard veritist approach to epistemic justification, the implications of his stance pose a realistic challenge for the hybrid position and the harmonization of epistemic and ethical/political values. Estund has profoundly detected the tension between ethical/political and epistemic justification, the tension between truth and democracy. His attempt to harmonize both types of justification forced him to sacrifice the normative criterion of true/correct decisions and settle on the imperfect tendency of procedures to generate true/correct decisions. Moreover, Estlund ought to be given credit for defending truth as much as he had deemed possible without jeopardizing democratic justification. This is more than what can be found in any other advocate of proceduralism.

We can conclude this chapter by noticing that Estlund couldn't offer a solution to the issue of privileging experts. He only leaves us with the strong impression that harmonizing truth and democracy won't be an easy task, and makes it evident that attempts of harmonization either resort to sacrificing epistemic virtues or make the mistake of misunderstanding their nature. This isn't entirely understandable because social desirability seems to be more dependent on ethical and political correctness than epistemic values. Should we recall Fricker's account on surpluses of trust, hybrid assessments of conflicted values seemed obliged to privilege the ethical and political consequences of different choices. However, since the aforementioned debates haven't exhausted every possible argument in favor of harmonization, it is unnecessary to give up and simply abandon the ideal of epistemic virtue by sacrificing it to the political. Nevertheless, neither pure nor moderate proceduralism succeded at offering an acceptable hybrid position. It could be said that they failed to offer a hybrid stance *at all* because epistemic justification was immediately either dismissed as secondary or downright sacrificed in favor of the political and ethical.

***

Since my primary motivation is to defend the possibility of harmonizing truth and democracy in a manner that doesn't immediately sacrifice epistemic quality in the slightest presence of tension, I will try to alleviate the proceduralist worry that truth and justice somehow inherently jeopardize democracy. To do this, I will have to demonstrate that it is possible to simultaneously preserve democratic values and provide experts – the best guides to true/correct – with a unique place in the decision-making process.

4.6. *Proceduralist critique of the role of experts in democratic decision-making processes*

We have repeatedly mentioned that the standpoint of epistemic proceduralism is among the more relevant and minutely elaborated positions in recent discussions about the epistemic justification of democracy. Proponents of epistemic proceduralism, including prominent supporters such as David Estlund and Fabienne Peter, claim that epistemically high-quality decisions can only stem from appropriate democratic procedures. It is crucial to note that both of them stress that no genuinely democratic procedure can cater to the privileged position of experts in decision-making processes. At first, many could probably agree with the proceduralist rejection of privilege as anti-democratic and inherently conflicted with the democratic notions of the freedom and equality of all citizens. Being a practice of favouring the elite, the privileged treatment of experts would thus seem particularly anti-democratic. While, for example, affirmative action and the general privileging of the marginalized or the underrepresented are not considered anti-democratic, the privileging of experts can hardly be justified in terms of democratic principles. However, a mere second glance shows that such an initial attitude introduces further dilemmas. The reasoning behind the exclusion of experts from decision-making processes reveals proceduralism to be a standpoint willing to sacrifice the epistemic quality of decisions and their truthfulness for the sake of maintaining fairness. Their justification of democracy is thus revealed to be almost exclusively ethical and political.

Epistemic proceduralists base their stance on a critique of the standard approach to the epistemic justification of democracy – the standpoint that democratic processes should generate decisions which can be considered correct from the perspective of some independent standard of epistemic value. This independent standard of assessing democratic decisions is usually defined in terms of 'truth' and 'truth-conduciveness' ('truth – sensitivity', 'problem solving', 'correctness', 'reliability' or like). Proponents of epistemic proceduralism have set forward various objections to such a justification of democratic decisions. An issue that has continuosly emerged as important is role of experts in decision-making processes, usually formulated as the problem of epistocracy. As the standard approach assumes that the truth/correctness of a decision constitutes democratic legitimacy, is highly unlikely not to privilege experts as the best 'guides' to truth/correctness who ought to be entrusted with making decisions. Proceduralists claim that, in a democratic debate, no one, including experts, should be in any way privileged – citizens cannot be expected to adhere to the stances of an expert elite instead of contributing as equals. Any attempt to introduce a 'standard' or independent criterion for assessing the epistemic quality of democratic decisions – be it the criterion of truth, correctness, truth-sensitivity, problem-solving or like – necessarily implies an anti-democratic tendency to favor experts as professional guides to truth/correctness. Epistocracy gives rise to numerous further issues such as the question of opting for the most credible expert within a dissonant group, or, differently stated, the problem of resolving disagreements between experts. Such cases raise the question of choosing experts who can act as arbitrators in matters of truth and correctness. As we have previously mentioned, certain authors claim that there are no genuine experts in political and moral matters because there is no objective and universally accepted expertise that could justify the ascription of such authority.

It is stated that there is no conceptual relationship between truth and democracy comparable to the one between, for example, truth and science. Democratic processes are certainly not comparable with the dependable methods of attaining truth in medicine or physics, scientific disciplines that rely on the stances and works of experts. While the conditions of science make the practice of privileging experts seem reasonable, political decisions are not made in a manner reminiscent of scientific seminars. One could possibly alleviate this initial rejection of the existence of experts by choosing to acknowledge their existence and consequent ability to act as guides to correct political decisions. We could even claim that it is possible to select the best among conflicted experts. However, even in such circumstances, the personal attitudes of experts cannot be imposed upon those who bear different opinions due to the fact that they can never be entirely neutral, being vulnerable to biased interests and preferences that may affect their stances. Epistemic proceduralists will conclude this discussion by making a statement essential to their position – in politics, a certain stance can be considered epistemically acceptable even if it is not true/correct. The epistemic acceptability of a decision is derived from the fairness of the democratic procedure – that is, epistemic value is mysteriously independent from truth and correctness. Particular credit ought to be given to Peter's lucid critique that the standard approach instrumentalizes the significance of the democratic procedure. Peter holds that its instrumentalization automatically devalues democracy, reducing it to mere means to attaining an alternate goal, such as the production and dissemination of knowledge or true/correct beliefs. According to Peter, the instrumentalizing nature of the standard approach to epistemically justifying democracy fails to acnowledge the irreducible pluralist value of individual agency and the procedural epistemic value of collective discussions. Furthermore, from Peter's standpoint, an approach which focuses solely on the truth/correctness of the final decision necessarily separates the significance of the democratic procedure from the merits of learning, thus failing to realize that procedural values contain intrinsic epistemic virtue.

In short, proceduralist critiques of the standard approach to epistemic justification have mostly, in a more or less explicit manner, rejected the privileged treatment of experts in democratic decision-making by maintaining that democracy can be epistemically justified without involving experts in decision-making processes. Fabienne Peter has undoubtedly offered an epistemically important articulation of the proceduralist objection to the privileged treatment of experts.[35]

4.6.1. *Epistemic instrumentalism and the authority dilemma*

Peter distinguishes between two kinds of decision making processes: (i) ones in which there are third-person authorities or experts and (ii) others in which there are no third-person authorities or experts. While the first decision-making process cannot be democratic, the second can. This seems to be entirely consistent with her earlier stances under the umbrella of pure proceduralism: a truly democratic decision making process excludes experts. The hidden premise here is again that politics is an area substantively different from science or other areas that involve experts. According to Peter, there is a certain intrinsic and insolvable tension between expert decisions-making processes and democratic decision-making processes.

The rationale behind the fact that democratic decision making processes exclude experts lies in the thesis that the epistemic value of a democratic decision-making process is not derived from its epistemic outcomes or, differently stated, the 'standard' of the correctness/truth of its resultant decisions. On the contrary, the epistemic value of a democratic decision making process lies in a fair and mutually accountable procedure of deliberation. She argues in favour of her thesis by recalling situations in which adjustments and reasonable disagreements are epistemically more valuable solutions than correct outcomes (decisions). According to Peter, the very existence of justified and reasonable disagreement between peers proves that (one) correct or true outcome is not necessarily an epistemically valuable requirement.

In contrast to Peter, I would like to argue that (i) even if we accept that the practice of privileging experts in decision making processes

35 Peter, 2016.

is not in itself democratic, there is a role for experts in a democratic decision-making process, (ii) the epistemic value of a democratic decision making process doesn't only lie in a fair deliberative procedure, but also the standard criterion of the correctness or truth of its outcome (rationality, justification, problem-solving capacity, truth-conductivness or like) and (iii) reasonable disagreement does not exclude the standard epistemic value of correct or true outcomes but, on the contrary, relies on it.

As a full-blooded proceduralist, Peter bases her stance on criticizing the fact that the standard approach presupposes the epistemic value of a true outcome. She ascribes to the standard approach the label of epistemic instrumentalism, that stance that it sacrifices democratic rationale to the epistemic one. More precisely, as we can have seen in the earlier account of epistemic instrumentalism, Peter is referring to the views that: (i) epistemic value is derived from epistemic outcomes, (ii) a correct decision is a desirable epistemic outcome, (iii) the epistemic justification of democracy depends on an epistemically correct outcome. Thus defined, epistemic instrumentalism seems to imply that democracy only has *instrumental value*. Peter claims that many epistemic democrats have, more or less explicitly, embraced the epistemic instrumentalist defence of democracy by arguing that democratic procedures are good means – or at least good enough means – for arriving at correct decisions (attaining the truth). They do this by claiming that the diversity of perspectives in democratic deliberation improves the correctness of the final decision, or that democratic deliberation insures a wider evidential pool for making the final decision, or even that the fairness and inclusiveness of democratic procedures generate the reliability necessary for attaining the truth. In one way or another, all of these approaches sacrifice the intrinsic value of the democratic procedure to the epistemic goal of attaining a correct or truth-conductive decision. In short, according to Peter, the main failure of epistemic instrumentalism lies within the assumption that the epistemic value of decisions is reducible to their correctness or truth-conduciveness.

Likewise, expertism is actually grounded on the same assumption that the epistemic value of democratic deliberation lies in a true/correct outcome (decision). Expertism, in contrast with the aforementioned positions, is really the stance that experts need to have a privileged role in the decision making process because they are, in comparison with other citizens, the most reliable guides to correct or true decisions.

If the legitimacy of a decision is in its correctness/truth, there is no reason not to additionally privilege the opinions of experts. For these very reasons, Peter believes that (despite the legitimacy of privileging expert opinions in different circumstances) experts and democratic decision-making cannot be harmonized.

However, if one wanted to reject expertism as non-democratic on the basis of such an argument, they would need to ascribe the same label to other non-expertistic stances that designate correct or true decisions as the goal of democratic deliberation. Peter is aware of the fact that the inclusion of epistemic outcomes or the criterion of correctness/truth into democratic decision-making processes generates the problem of specifying the participation of experts. However, she is also aware that she cannot reject expertism without simultaneously rejecting non-expertist attitudes that democratic fairness or inclusiveness improves the correctness of the final decision. Which is the exact reason behind her critique of epistemic instrumentalism. In short, Peter's reasoning commences with the premise that the practice of privileging expert opinions introduces illegitimacy into the democratic decision-making process (which needs to be based on freedom and equality) and closes with the conclusion that correctness and truth cannot constitute the epistemic value of democratic decision-making. Consequently, she not only qualifies expertism as a non-democratic or instrumentalist stance, but ascribes this label to an entire spectrum of viewpoints based on the assumption that only true decisions contain epistemic value.

In her most recent article, Peter articulated the problem of epistemic instrumentalism as *the authority dilemma*. If practical authority is justified on epistemic grounds, then legitimate practical authority is non-democratic. If, on the other hand, the practical authority of democracy wants to be legitimate, it must be justified on non-epistemic grounds. We can word this in an alternative manner: in those decision-making circumstances that involve a third-person epistemic authority, we can choose to adhere to those who know what the correct decision is and therefore accept a non-democratic decision-making process; if we insist on democratic decision-making then we can't defend the legitimacy of democracy on epistemic grounds, but must purely refer to practical rationale. The defence of democracy characteristic of epistemic instrumentalism thus undermines itself as the very epistemic circumstances it presupposes are incompatible with democracy.

This problem arises from a common epistemic instrumentalist presupposition about democratic legitimacy and epistemic authority, or the question of what constitutes the epistemic value of a decision-making process: if there is a correct decision to be made and if someone has legitimate epistemic authority to make claims about the nature of this correct decision, the epistemic case for democracy crumbles. The only way to sustain both the epistemic and the democratic justification of practical authority is to reject the assumption that the epistemic value of democracy lies in a correct or true outcome. Such a solution, consequently, points toward rejecting the role of experts in a democratic decision-making process.

Instead of epistemic instrumentalism, Peter proposes proceduralism and its procedural epistemic value as an alternative to the epistemic value of seeking correct or true outcomes. Her aim is to show that the deliberative democratic procedure itself, the process of exchanging reasons with others and of adjusting one's beliefs in response to their consequent arguments, may have epistemic value that transgress the value of making correct decisions. She perceives this procedural value of democracy as starkly contrasted to the previously criticized instrumental value of democracy.

4.6.2. *Epistemic instrumentalism vs political instrumentalism*

Firstly, I can agree with Peter that certain forms of the epistemic justification of democracy sacrifice democratic values to the epistemic value of correctness and truth. For instance, Plato's epistocracy, as the most radical form of instrumentalism, explicitly sacrifices democratic values to the epistemic value of truth. I also concur that such an epistocratic approach, which focuses only on the true outcome, cannot be justified because it ignores the values of the democratic procedure and of the learning process inherent to public deliberation and mutual accountability. However, it would be inappropriate to identify Plato's epistocracy with stances such as, for instance, Goodin's claim that democratic deliberation multiplies the perspectives or the diversity of evidence from which we aim to derive decisions of epistemically higher quality.[36] Goodin surely did not underestimate the epistemic value of collective deliberation, nor the value of mutual accountability.

Secondly, I agree with Peter's diagnosis of the problem as an authority dilemma: there is a clear and present conflict between the

36 Goodin, 2006.

epistemic and the democratic justification of political authority, or between political values and epistemic values in justifying democracy. In the justification of democracy, I concur with Peter's claim that the tension between the epistemic aim of truth and correctness on one side, and of democratic fairness on the other, cannot solved by epistemic instrumentalism because it either sacrifices or instrumentalizes democratic values to epistemic values. However, I disagree that any focus on standard epistemic outcomes such as correctness or truth *ought* to be eliminated from the epistemic justification of democracy.[37] I also disagree that the introduction of experts cannot, without exception, be considered democratic. Finally, I cannot agree that the epistemic justification of democracy should be reduced to democratic procedures (no matter how deliberative and fair they may be). Moreover, I would like to argue that Peter's proceduralist solution is a defence of political instrumentalism, which is just as incapable of solving the authority dilemma as epistemic instrumentalism. In providing arguments for this stance, I will rely on discussions about epistemic values in a social contex that were recently elaborated in social epistemology.

It is important to emphasize that traditional epistemology makes no reference to practical cognitive issues within the context of the real social world. Its focus was always on the acquisition of knowledge in idealized circumstances: individual epistemic agents are perceived as persons of unlimited logical competences and as asocial beings isolated from any socio-political context. Truth and rationality are detached from social power or any political dimension of belief formation. Instrumentalist approaches – which Peter continuously criticises – also assume this particular traditional approach to epistemic values. However, these traditional approaches are rivalled by an influential reductionist perspective promoted by contemporary movements such as postmodernism, social constructivism, sociology of knowledge and cultural studies that stresses the social aspect of knowing.[38] The reductionist approach proclaimed the death of epistemology, or, more precisely, the traditional epistemic concepts of truth, rationality, justification and so on. According to their claim that beliefs are mere social constructions of power, epistemic investigations would need to be reduced to deconstructions of beliefs to social power relations. Instead,

37 I have previously shown that it is mistaken to label any position that favours standard epistemic values over procedures as maliciously instrumentalist or likely to threaten ethical and political values.

38 Rorty, 1979.; Barnes and Bloor, 1982., Foucault, 1980., 1991.

I would like to advocate a third approach of 'truly' social epistemology, a stance positioned somewhere between traditionalist and reductionist extremes.[39] It assumes a social situatedness of knowledge (congruent with the reductionist approach) while maintaining the central classical epistemic values of truth, rationality, justification or problem solving (reminiscent of the traditionalists). Epistemic agents form, retain and revise beliefs/judgments/decisions under social influences, but they still need to be evaluated as more-or-less truth-conductive, rational, justified, epistemically successful in problem solving or like. While decisions are perceived as the product of a more-or-less fair decision making process, they nevertheless need to be evaluated as more-or-less justified, rational, correct or like.

This brief recollection of what social epistemology can teach us helps is to position Peter's proceduralist attitude towards the epistemic value of correctness or truth. It is obvious that proceduralism refers to the reductionist stance about truth or correctness. To clarify – in debates about democratic decision-making situations, Peter's proceduralism assumes a reductionist rejection of the stances that epistemic value lies in the epistemic outcome or that there are any valuable and objective epistemic standards (such as correctness or truth) independent of the procedure. Moreover, we can label her assumption that epistemic value cannot lie in a true outcome as a certain form of epistemic revisionism[40] due to the complete elimination of fundamental epistemic values (rather than a relativization or a certain sceptical scenario).

However, an attempt to position Peter's stance within the framework of social epistemology should not neglect her distinction between situations that involve and those that don't involve third-person authorities. While Peter does not fully deny the relevance of the epistemic value of truth in certain circumstances, she is suspicious of this value in the realm of politics – an area in which there is no objective experts. Keeping this mind, we can only articulate her

39 Fricker, 1998., 2007.

40 As we have seen in the first chapter, Goldman makes a distinction between three approaches to exploring the social dimension of acquiring knowledge: the first is limited to previously mentioned topics within (individual) epistemology that engage the social dimension in a more or less explicit way (*preservationism*), the second expands the realm of social epistemology to include new interdisciplinary areas (*expansionism*) and the third can hardly be considered a legitimate approach to social epistemology as it refutes the fundamental traditional epistemic values (*revisionism*), (Goldman, 2010a).

position as epistemic revisionism or reductionism within the domain of political decision-making processes. We thus need to restate our initial qualification: by claiming that the entire epistemic value of a democratic decision-making process is within a fair and mutually accountable procedure, Peter only accepts the reductionist approach to the *epistemic justification of democracy* and consequently rejects the core assumptions of (both traditional and truly social) epistemology. In her epistemic justification of democracy, traditional epistemic values are replaced with certain 'democratic procedural epistemic norms'. According to her opinion, an epistemically valuable decision is a social fabrication or the construction of a fair and mutually accountable deliberative process. As epistemic value lies entirely in the fairness of the procedure, there are no procedure-free norms of rationality, justification, validity or truth. In other words, the epistemic value of a decision is completely reducible to the political/democratic value of the procedure which generated that particular decision. It is worth mentioning that Peter does not reduce the general epistemic task to elaborating the social roots of a decision or to analysing the power relations inherent to the decision-making procedure. She preserves the normative component of epistemic evaluation that the reductionist approach habitually rejects. Socially unjust or politically unfair deliberations construct epistemically non-valuable beliefs. Instead of perceiving *every* construct (belief, decision) of deliberation as a significant epistemic outcome, we should only register the results of fair, inclusive and mutually accountable democratic deliberation as valuable.

Regardless of this important aspect of Peter's stance, she still utilizes the political instead of the epistemic evaluation of decisions in cases that don't involve any third person authorities. Consequently, such a position is nothing other than a form of political instrumentalism. Rather than a truly epistemic defence of democratic decision-making outcomes, Peter's epistemic justification of democracy is a defence of political constructivism based on a seriously revised version of epistemology, making her comparable to those who have declared the death of epistemology (in this domain of political decision-making processes). Peter claims that epistemic instrumentalism solves the authority dilemma by reducing democratic values to epistemic values and justifiably criticises such a stance. On the other hand, Peter's proceduralism solves the authority dilemma by reducing epistemic value to democratic/political value. Proceduralism sacrifices the epistemic value of decisions to their political value. Peter's alternative epistemic defence of democracy, which is affected by the authority dilemma, fails to solve this task in a manner reminiscent of the failure of epistemic instrumentalism.

Finally, the perspective of social epistemology helps us detect a possible inconsistency. Since such a reductivist epistemic approach is not assumed in situations that involve third-person authorities, we are left with two kinds of epistemological approaches: (i) traditional, for all situations involving third-person authorities, and (ii) reductionist, for situations in which there are no third-person authorities. In other words, while some decision-making situations still adhere to the epistemic value of truth and correctness, others don't. Even if we could accept her *political* explanation that the epistemic value of truth entails a democratically inappropriate role of experts, we would still need an *epistemic* explanation of what makes a democratic deliberation a particular kind of epistemic situation which renders a correct outcome dispensable. She claimed that democratic deliberation is exceptional because there are no third–person authorities and the epistemic value of truth/correctness is thus irrelevant. If truth/correctness is not problematic in some other discussions, what aspect of this particular kind of deliberation should make us epistemically doubtful about attaining truth? Aside from the politically doubtful role of experts, what is the *epistemic* reason behind excluding expertise from these deliberative processes? While reductionists are known to reject truth regardless of the situation, Peter develops a somewhat ambivalent position regarding the epistemic value of truth. Namely, her political instrumentalism does not offer an *epistemic* reason for rejecting the epistemic value of correctness or truth in political deliberations under the assumption that the political desiderata should be given priority.[41]

4.6.3. *Reasonable disagreement and proceduralism*

In an interesting development, Peter finds the foundation of her thesis that the correctness/truth of the final outcome shouldn' be the prioritized epistemic value in epistemology of disagreement, or, more precisely, in the 'opacity stance' presented by prominent advocates

41 My research related to the tension between epistemic and political instrumentalism has been published in the article: Prijić – Samaržija, 2017.

of reasonable disagreement.[42] Epistemology of disagreement argues that, in certain circumstances of persistent disagreement between two parties/peers (in which there is no third-person authority which can resolve the disagreement), epistemic agents have a reason to engage in deliberation with each other, accordingly adjust their beliefs and finally remain in reasonable disagreement. Peter holds that the existence of justified reasonable disagreement (in which both sides hold onto their conflicted beliefs) shows that the procedure of mutual accountability is an epistemically valuable procedure *per se* and that epistemic value thus does not lie in any procedure-independent correct outcome.

Firstly, it has to be emphasized that defences of reasonable disagreement within epistemology of disagreement come, without exception, from authors who (unlike Peter) prefer the traditional epistemological approach that unambigously portrays truth as the central and ultimate epistemic value. Debates within epistemology of disagreement focus on the particular problem of resolving situations in which the desired correct or true outcome is *impossible* to attain. Despite postulating reasonable disagreement as the only possible solution to such conflicts, not a single participant of these debates would desire to propose any substitution for truth. On the contrary, participants would unanimously try to divulge an appropriate solution or explanation only at the particular point of a discussion when it is not possible to attain a formally correct outcome.

Secondly, we need to register that situations of persistent disagreement are always perceived as clear cases of epistemic dissonance that ought to be resolved, rather than as a desirable epistemic solution.[43] Adjustments and reasonable disagreements, especially in concrete situations of decision-making, are sub-optimal epistemic solutions justified by the stance that correct beliefs are not possible to attain (yet). The mutual accountability inherent to adjustment practices or reasonable disagreement itself is not primarily a demonstration of the epistemic values of fairness independent from correct outcomes. This epistemic 'tolerance' and 'pluralism' doesn't arise from the fact that both parties accept that there is no correct epistemic outcome or that the shared evidence allows for different beliefs, but from the facts that *at this very moment* the shared evidence is insufficient for attaining a desirable

42 Sosa, 2010.; Goldman, 2010b.; Peter, 2013a., 2013b.

43 Linda Zagzebski, 2012. *Epistemic Authority: A Theory of Trust, Authority, and Autonomy of Belief* (Oxford: Oxford University Press).

common epistemic outcome (as exemplified by the Equal weight view or the Steadfast view) or that *principally* all relevant evidence cannot be fully accessed and shared by both parties (Opacity view).

The existence and justification of reasonable disagreement therefore neither prove nor illustrate the existence of situations in which the epistemic value of attaining correct or true outcomes can be rejected or replaced by the epistemic value of mutual accountability. On the contrary, it is based on the assumption that truth *is* the ultimate epistemic value – but that there are situations in which an agreement is (for different reasons) impossible to attain. It is fundamentally different from Peter's proceduralist claim that all situations which lack third-person authorities, who can solve the disagreement, warrant the rejection of the value of truth and its replacement with another epistemic value such as mutual accountability.

***

Peter is right to emphasise the fact that democratic and epistemic values can be conflicted: I have repeatedly stressed that political unfairness can generate epistemic success and that political fairness can generate epistemic culpability. Should we conclude that we ought to reject either one or the other as suggested by the authority dilemma, or assume either epistemic or political instrumentalism?

Most commonly discussed examples of epistemic culpability caused by political fairness are initiatives of affirmative action. As we have already seen, affirmative action programs that demand quotas for Afro–Americans at American universities or for women in parliaments are criticized as epistemically unjustified for potentially preventing epistemically more deserving people from attaining their earned positions and thus exposing them to epistemic and ethical/political (economic, educational) injustice. On the other side, there are situations in which epistemic benefits produce political unfairness, such as the examples of epistemic paternalism. Since experts are comparatively the best guides to truth (or at least to avoiding false beliefs), trusting experts usually results in justified beliefs. However, expertism, in addition to other kinds of epistemic paternalism, is usually seen as anti-democratic due to various reasons that we have previously discussed in detail.

In striving to equally appreciate democratic and epistemic values we should justify neither epistemic irresponsibility that leads to political fairness nor epistemic benefits that generate or assume political unfairness. As has already been mentioned above and throughout previous chapters, the veritist/elitist model responds to the standard approach to the epistemic justification of democracy by stressing the importance of epistemic outcomes. Given that this model identifies epistemic success as the necessary condition of legitimacy, decisions to sacrifice political fairness for the sake of epistemic goals become acceptable. While the veritist/elistist model could never accept a program of affirmative action, it could perceive some forms of expertism or epistemic paternalism as justified. As we have previously seen, this model bases its epistemic instrumentalism on the more or less traditional approach to epistemology. The second paradigm is the proceduralist/egalitarian model that puts emphasis on political fairness. Now an inverted scenario holds true – as political fairness is deemed indispensible for ensuring legitimacy, it becomes acceptable to sacrifice epistemic success for the sake of political fairness. Likewise, situations in which political unfairness results in epistemic success are completely unacceptable, while it is tolerable for political fairness to generate epistemic 'imperfections'. Whilst the proceduralist model readily justifes programs of affirmative action, it could never treat any form of expertism or epistemic paternalism as just. We have also seen that proceduralism/egalitarianism leads to political instrumentalism on the basis of its reductivist or revisionist approach to epistemic values.

It thus becomes necessary to propose a third approach – *situational hybrid model*. Even though they can be found under the umbrella of hybrid approaches, veritism/elitism and proceduralism/egalitarianism make clear and general value priorities regardless of the situation in question by deducing their assessment from their chosen resolution of the authority dilemma. Within the framework of the situational hybrid model, I insist on highly particular assessments of both political and epistemic outcomes in individual situations, and go as far as to plead for certain 'negotiation' or 'trade off' harmonizing procedures. It builds on the foundations of truly social epistemology by emphasizing the necessity of harmonizing epistemic and political values in a concrete real-world context. Instead of resolving cases of affirmative action by simply deducing our critique or apology from the principles of either veritism/elitism or proceduralism/egalitarianism, we need a more comprehensive analysis of their concrete and long-term epistemic and political outcomes. Actions that may immediately produce an epistemically sub-optimal outcome can be justified if there is reasonable likelihood that they will foster better epistemic results within a longer period. While programs of affirmative action may slow down or diminish the direct epistemic benefits of immediately employing the best possible candidates, they can prove to be epistemically far more valuable if they manage to improve the long-term epistemic capacities of producing correct outcomes by encouraging diverse evidential bases and plural perspectives. Moreover, the fact that these programs preserve and insure fairness creates a situation in which both values are properly harmonized.

Furthermore, the situational hybrid model enables us to assess the practice of epistemic paternalism as acceptable in some contexts, but unacceptable in others. It is unacceptable if it systematically violates the principles of epistemic and political autonomy despite its potentially good epistemic results. However, it can be acceptable if anyone who wants different information can easily access them by employing additional effort. For example, it is justified to only teach evolutionary theory in schools and exclude creationism if alternative information is still offered by churches or similar religious institutions. Jeopardizing the epistemic autonomy of children or the parents who want their children to be educated in accordance with religious doctrines is permissible for the sake of preserving the epistemic values of truth/correctness derived from a scientific or expert approach. In the same way and for the same reasons, it is justified to introduce sexual education in schools even if parents consider it a violation of their autonomy regarding the moral education of their children. On the other hand, media censorship that prevents the disclosure of truthful statistics about the perpetration of terrorist acts by minority groups can be justified if it seems likely that the public will, given its attitudes and prejudices, harbour uncritical resentment towards all members of minority groups.

We must notice that proceduralism/egalitarianism couldn't justify any of the aforementioned practices of epistemic paternalism and that veritism/elitism couldn't justify censoring true information for the sake of preserving stability. Moreover, Peter's account of situations that involve and those that don't involve third-person authorities appears far too vague to make a clear distinction between such situations and their allegedly substantial differences. It is highly unclear, for example, what criteria should be used for classifying school curricula – the content of school curricula is not exclusively the area of science, but a public space that must respect different doctrines, as well as foster inclusiveness and ethical/political autonomy. In addition to education, there are numerous similar social domains that interweave scientific and ideological/political content: public media, public healthcare, law and like. It seems safe to note that complex social situations appear to be far more numerous than those that are purely scientific or purely political.

While both proceduralism/egalitarianism and veritism/elitism derive their evaluations of real-word situations from ideal theoretical settings about the value of political fairness and truth, the situational hybrid model assumes that, despite their unquestionalble importance, neither value has a cross-situational robust character, but may instead be locally sacrificed in order to ensure the optimum balance of values in specific situations. In the example of school curricula, the autonomy of parents and their children should be sacrificed to preserve expertise and truth – for the sake of fostering a more just academic and social climate. Inversely, truth can be sacrificed to maintain social stability and equity – for the sake of ensuring a better context for future truth production. This doesn't mean that we have defined general rules – autonomy will not always be sacrificed to truth, nor will truth always be sacrificed to stability. Every occurence of conflicted values has a very specific context which urges us to estimate its particular costs and benefits with the aim of attaining the hybrid virtues of epistemic justice of fair truth. The epistemic instrumentalism of the veritist/elitist model and the political instrumentalism of proceduralism/egalitarianism are equally unacceptable positions.

The situational hybrid model similarly approaches the role of experts in democratic decision-making processes by seeking a specific harmonization of values. In the particular case of expertism, we could attempt to harmonize the epistemic and the political by introducing a division of epistemic labour. We could, for instance, leave decisions about social/political priorities to citizens while delegating dicussions about the methods of attaining these goals to experts.[44] In deliberative processes, decisions about the nature of the important issues can be tackled by citizens and experts can contribute through various forms of participation such as tutorials, supervision, education or appropriate representation of the marginalized or the absent.[45] Democratic desiderata can be preserved through *qualified* deference of citizens to experts. Any decision to trust an expert needs to be

44 Christiano, 2012.
45 Kitcher, 2011.

based on relevant evidence that confirms their trustworthiness and on democratic mechanisms of reaching consensus about the expert's trustworthiness.[46] Trusting epistemic authorities thus violates neiter the epistemic nor the political autonomy of each citizen (other than their epistemic and political egoism), but appears to be rational and grounded on democratic principles.[47] Each of these options will be further discussed in the remainder of the book.

Division of epistemic labour isn't a new principle unique to the situational hybrid model, but a precise framework for postulating different models of contextually harmonizing political and epistemic values. The harmonization of values inherent to the situational hybrid model tends to achieve the optimum balance of both epistemic and political values in each particular situation (not the abstract and absolute dynamics of political and epistemic values in all imaginable situations). 'Negotiation' or 'trade-off' scenarios in the division of epistemic labour sacrifice only the *absolute* values of either truth or fairness for the sake of hybrid values such as epistemic justice or fair truth, or, differently worded, for the sake of ensuring the best possible balance of epistemic and political values. Unqualified expertism of epistocracy cannot be justified in any 'trade-off' scenario: there is no epistemic benefit that can be justified by such a blatant example of a non-democratic procedure. At the same time, we can never justify an unqualified rejection of the role of experts: there is no real political benefit that inexorably *demands* the rejection of the epistemic values of correct/true outcomes or of the outcomes that resolve the problems of interested citizens.

The situational hybrid model disconnects normativity from both the concepts of the apolitical value of truth and the non-epistemic value of fairness, instead binding it to the idea that processes of forming true beliefs are socially situated.

---

46 Snježana Prijić–Samaržija. 2011. 'Trusting Experts: Trust, Testimony and Evidence', *Acta Histriae,* 19 (1–2): 249-262; Snježana Prijić–Samaržija. 2016a. 'The Division of Epistemic Labour in Democracy', *Anali Hrvatskog politološkog društva: Thomas Christiano's political theory: an exchange*, 12: 67–81.

47 Zagzebski, 2012.

4.7. *Conclusion*

We can conclude this chapter by stating that epistemic proceduralist have breathed new life into discussions about the epistemic justification of democracy.

The explicitly raised question of balancing between epistemic and political justification was often suppressed by privileging epistemic values or by, which was far more common, privileging political justification in discussions belonging to philosophy of politics. Since this debate was initiated in the domain of philosophy of politics, they valuably contributed by boldly pointing to the insufficiencies of the existing discussions. In short, proceduralists such as Peter and Estlund were the first to initate this debate and implicitly suggest a certain hybrid framework that transgresses the boundaries of philosophy of politics. Furthermore, epistemic proceduralists have presented convincing arguments against the prevailing standard approach to the epistemic justification of democracy. The particularity of epistemic proceduralism lies in their insistence that a democratic procedure must be epistemically justificatied, but that this epistemic justification cannot be reducible to truthfulness/correctness or any problem-solving capacity because it would jeopardize the independence of ethical/political justification. Epistemic proceduralists conclude that veritist and pragmatist approaches instrumentalize democratic procedures in favor of epistemic goals and generate a deficit of democratic fairness. In short, it was epistemic proceduralists who first questioned the relationship of democracy and truth and who must be commended for emphasizing the tension between democratic fairness and truth/problem-solving capacities.

However, I have tried to show that their criticism of epistemic instrumentalism actually strives to justify political instrumentalism. Both the strong and the moderate approach share the stance that standard epistemic values not only mustn't be given primacy when justifying democracy, but that they also can be legitimately sacrificed to democratical goals. In attempting to prove that a fair democratic procedure has an intrinsic epistemic value completely independent of the epistemic value of the final result – truthfulness/problem-solving capacity or like – they effectively reduced epistemic value to democratic fairness. The pure version of proceduralism was thus revealed as a reductionist and revisionist project that rejects standard or traditional epistemic values. Likewise, its moderate variety was shown to be a certain epistemic dualism that postulates two independent intrinsic epistemic values – the values of truth and epistemic value of democratic fairness. However, the exact intrinsic epistemic value of fair procedures, independent of the value of truth, was left highly ambiguous, as well as the relation between the epistemic and the political intrinsic values of democratic procedures.

The role of experts is a staple problem of epistemological proceduralism because it is closely bound to their rejection of the standard approach to epistemic justification and the significance of epistemic results. By denying truth as a criterion of epistemically justifying of democracy, they have also rejected every inclusion of experts in decision-making processes. It seems evident that their reasoning underwent an entirely opposite direction. Recalling their meticulously elaborated critical attitude towards any inclusion of experts in societal decision-making as an anti-democratic act of privileging the elite, their own theory seems to have them forced to exclude all notions of truth and problem-solving capacities. I have tried to argue – in contrast to the proceduralist standpoint and within the situational hybrid perspective – that any involvement of experts does not automatically have to be an apology of anti-democratic epistocracy and that it is possible to divide epistemic work in a manner that preserves both standard epistemic and ethical/political values.

In short, proceduralism resolves the dilemma between democracy and/or truth by opting to preserve democracy. Epistemic proceduralism was thus revealed as an attitude that, while seemingly emphasizing the importance of epistemically justifying democracy, failed to convincingly harmonize ethical/political and epistemic values.

p. 117 - 163

5.
DEMOCRACY AND THE EPISTEMIC VALUE OF CONSENSUS

5.1. *Ethical, political and epistemic value of consensus*

Unlike proceduralism, a stance whose vocal advocates and supporters seek to justify democracy in both political/ethical and epistemic terms, consensualism is not such a clearly conceptualized hybrid position. This position can be found in Goldman's discussions about social epistemology – he identifies the usage of consensus as the main criterion for distinguishing socially desirable practices as contrasted to veritism and expertism[1]. However, I think that this position can be found, although in varying degrees, in different perspectives that have been emerging throughout the history of epistemology and philosophy of politics. As a standpoint, consensualism reveals itself to be hybrid in its very definition – it portrays participation and conciliation as closely related to epistemic values. When speaking of consensualism, I am referring to the stance that decisions of highest epistemic quality are achieved by establishing agreement or consensus within a group, community or institution. While a successful consensus can be understood as the absolute conciliation of all participants, it can also be the agreement of an overall or even a relative majority. It can be more precisely defined as rational[2] or overlapping[3] (in an empirical or a normative sense[4]), as well as in other terms.[5] Regardless of the scope of consensus or the ways in which it can be attained or recognized, consensualism rests on the claim that any correct decision depends on

---

1 Goldman, 1987.

2 Lehrer and Wagner, 1981.

3 John Rawls. 1971, *Theory of Justice* (Cambridge, Mass: Harvard University Press).

4 Snježana Prijić–Samaržija and Nebojša Zelič. 2009. 'Overlapping consensus: normative understanding and doxastic voluntarism', *Croatian Journal of Philosophy*, 9(25): 101–115.

5 Snježana Prijić–Samaržija. 2005. *Društvo i spoznaja* (Zagreb: Kruzak).

the conciliation of all agents relevantly affected by that decision, and that epistemic and ethical/political values are best harmonized by the achievement of consensus. In order to fully understand this position, it is useful to briefly summarize the historical development of consensus as a simultaneously ethical/political and epistemic value.

Historically, consensualism is associated with Jurgen Habermas' stance that decisions of highest epistemic quality are achieved through rational consensus among equal citizens in ideal communicational circumstances. It is important to note that Habermas holds, in accordance with his consensualist theory of truth, that such a decision wouldn't only be politically and ethically optimal, but also *true*. To understand Habermas' view, it is important to realize that he perceives the consensual theory of truth as a model for elaborating the consensual theory of justice – which implies that truth cannot be separated from justice[6]. This renders Habermas' consensualism somewhat reminiscent of the hybrid view's harmonization of ethical/political and epistemic virtues.

To argue in favour of the consensualist theory of truth in epistemological discussions means to equate truth with idealized justification, a belief attained through a rational consensus in ideal communicational circumstances.[7] This approach is similar to the epistemic (or verificationist) theories of truth that equate truth with justified credibility (such as the stances of Hilary Putnam and Chrispin Wright). In his later works, Habermas advocates a 'pragmatic epistemological realism'[8] and speaks of truth as a successful representation of the objective world. However, when it comes to making decisions in a moral or a political context, Habermas puts aside metaphysical characterizations of truth or objective validity in favour of postulating consensus, intersubjective recognition, and justified claims as the best indicators of truth and epistemic correctness.[9] Various

6 Philip Pettit. 1982. 'Habermas on Truth and Justice', in Parkinson, G. H. R. (ed.), *Marx and Marxism,* Royal Institute of Philosophical Supplements (Cambridge: Cambridge University Press), pp. 207–228.

7 Jürgen Habermas. 1971/2001. *On the Pragmatics of Social Interaction*, trans. by Fultner, Barabara (trans.). Cambridge, MA: MIT Press; Jürgen Habermas. 1987. *Theory of Communicative Action* (Boston: Beacon); Jürgen Habermas. 2003. *Truth and Justification*, trans. by Barbara Fultner (Cambridge, MA: MIT Press).

8 Jürgen Habermas. 1998. *Inclusion of the Other: Studies in Political Theory*, ed. by Cronin, C., and P. De Greiff (Cambridge, MA: MIT Press); See also Habermas, 2003.

9 Habermas, 2003.

interpretations of whether this is a realist or an antirealist approach to truth, and whether inter-subjectively justified claims are an objective indicator of truth, can be delegated to a different discussion.

Habermas perceives deliberative democracy as an appropriate framework for managing discussions that can mimic the idealized concept of practical discourse or ideal communicational circumstances: a decision can be considered justified if everyone affected by that decision can accept it in a rational discussion.[10] He describes a rational discussion as an inclusive discussion between autonomous, responsible individuals who respect unbiased reasons and other agents participating in the debate. The legitimacy of any decision is thus dependent on a just and argument-based debate that concludes with a rational common acceptance of the decision by all interested citizens (who are affected by the decision) as free and equal agents.[11]

Knowing that his interest isn't limited to the principles of philosophy of politics, but that he addresses the epistemological issue of epistemically justifying deliberative democracy, it is not surprising that some authors consider Harbermas' account of deliberative democracy as an 'epistemic' theory. This is precisely why it seems justifiable to hope that Habermas' theory could resolve the tension between political and epistemological desiderata or articulate the hybrid attitude. Principles of deliberative democracy include important epistemic elements that guarantee epistemic quality: a rational discussion, exchanging and accepting epistemically valuable reasons and consensual decision-making as the ultimate signifier of right decisions. Habermas clearly advocates the attitude that rational discourse leads to a consensus that is both epistemically correct and politically acceptable for everyone.[12]

It's immediately evident that Habermas implicitly assumes the extremely optimistic stance that people will be prepared to put aside their moral beliefs, worldviews and interests regarding controversial political issues in order to achieve consensus through a rational and argument-based discussion.[13] It should be said, however, that Habermas is aware

10 Jürgen Habermas. 1990. *Moral Consciousness and Communicative Action*, trans. by C. Lenhardt, and S. W. Nicholson (Cambridge, MA: MIT Press); Jürgen Habermas. 1996. *Between Facts and Norms: Contributions to a Discourse Theory of Law and Democracy*, trans. by Rehg (William Cambridge, MA: MIT Press).

11 Habermas, 1998.

12 Habermas, 1996.

13 James Bohman. 1996. *Public Deliberation: Pluralism, Complexity, and*

of the sub-optimality of discussions in real social circumstances and acknowledges the role of institutions in conducting rational discussions and catering to a rational consensus: citizens should consider a law/decision legitimate if an, institutionally organized and managed, democratic process ensures that its final decisions are the fair products of a sufficiently inclusive deliberative process of forming beliefs.[14] Making prudent decisions is thus less dependent on the individual abilities of citizens who aren't ideal debaters (and which, as we have seen in the chapter on proceduralism, renders optimistic accounts of deliberation somewhat problematic), but rather on the aggregated prudence of de-subjectivised communication derived from the formal and informal methods of organizing discussions.[15] Habermas considers his position close to the stance of epistemic proceduralism because it derives collective reasoning from the application of democratic institutional procedures with the result of collective learning. However, Habermas strays from proceduralism by distinctly accepting the values of truth and correctness as the epistemic qualities of decisions. It should be noted that he is closer to Cohen than to Peter and Estlund because his criterion for evaluating epistemic quality is procedure-independent, but – unlike Cohen – his epistemic criterion of justification relies on the notion of truth rather than on an ideal procedure.

The fundamental problem of Habermas' consensualism, consensualist theory of making fair decisions, or his consensualist theory of justice[16], is its dubious application in conditions that are less than ideal. Achieving a rational consensus in idealized communicational circumstances – implying a sincere, tolerant, argument-based and informed, institutionally well organized and guided debate – is certainly an attractive and highly acceptable goal. However, any sub-ideal moral and epistemic circumstances render the concept of a 'rational' consensus entirely unclear. Methods of recognizing whether a concrete consensus can be considered rational or ideal become equally dubious.

Democracy (Cambridge, MA: MIT Press); Thomas McCarthy. 1998. 'Legitimacy and diversity: Dialectical reflections on analytical distinctions', in Rosenfeld Michael and Andrew Arato (eds.), *Habermas on Law and Democracy* (Berkeley: University of California Press), pp. 115–153; Georgia Warnke. 1999. '*Legitimate Differences*' (Berkeley: University of California Press).

14 Jürgen Habermas. 2008. *Between Naturalism and Religion*, trans. by Ciaran Cronin (Cambridge: Polity).

15 Habermas, 1996.

16 Pettit, 1982.

In simplified terms – since there is no standard referential value for assessing whether we have made a true decision, it is impossible to determine whether a particular decision is correct or whether it is close to being correct. The outcome of a rational consensus is almost always uncertain – a gamble or a matter of chance.[17] In that sense, we are perpetually suspended in an agnostic limbo where it is impossible to assess the correctness of a decision.

Habermas is aware that we can never be sure whether the attained consensus is truly rational, meaning that we can never be sure whether what was made is a correct (true) decision. It should be noted that this isn't just an example of typical consensualists' falibilism - the possibility that a decision is not correct even though it was thought to be or the attitude that any consensus is nothing but the best inter-subjectively verified decision. The sub-ideal circumstances in which real debates take place incite far weightier problems than those characteristic of pursuing a rational consensus: namely, it is possible to achieve a consensus on something that is evidently incorrect. No aspect of the discussion itself, the exchange of arguments and the act of consolidation eliminates the possibility that the decision is not only sub-optimal, but blatantly incorrect. For consensus to be rational, it is important for the debaters to be informed, sensitive to good arguments, eager to assess arguments without egoism, and like, which often doesn't occur in actual deliberations. On the contrary, we have witnessed terrible policies that had received consensual support. In short, although only a *rational* consensus is acceptable, actual consensuses rarely satisfy the conditions of rationality which imply an (almost) ideal conversational situation. Fallacies of collective reasoning inherent to everyday situations range from sub-optimally informed and insufficiently competent participants to the obscurity produced by group dynamics – from failures to resist the pressure of conformism and co-ordination (manipulation and like) to collective irrationality.

Either way, Habermas has excellently articulated the epistemic value of consensus: a fair, well-guided, informed and non-egoistic deliberation oriented towards consolidation generates choices of the best attainable epistemic quality. The ethical and political qualities of a discussion are necessary preconditions of an epistemically valuable decision, but cannot guarantee it on their own. Unlike prodecuralists,

17 Pettit, 1982., p. 209.

Habermas notes that, in addition to fairness, deliberation must satisfy the significant epistemic conditions of involving informed participants and being wisely guided by institutions.

Furthermore, we must not overlook the fact that consensualism is, as a position, inextricably linked to the work of John Rawls.[18] His consensus is different than that of Habermas: instead of defining consensus as the aim of a discussion, Rawls demands that the consensus be established at the beginning of the deliberation as a necessary precondition for the functioning of the public mind, which will then, naturally, generate another (rational) consensus at the end of the discussion. According to Rawls, the main shortfall of public debates is not in the private interests or potential epistemic incompetence of participants, but instead in the plurality of their comprehensive doctrines, worldviews or normative concepts of the (common) good. In order for a discussion to be at all *possible*, it is necessary to establish a consensus on the common values provided by public mind and reasonably acceptable by all involved parties. Rawls identifies this as an *overlapping consensus* on political values (which also comprise the basis of the Constitution). As long as we have reached this initial consensus, Rawls argues that any outcome of such a public debate should be considered legitimate – overlooking the correctness, epistemic quality and problem-solving capacity of the final decision, as well as its adherence to Habermas' account of ideal possible consensus (an approximation of a rational consensus in comparison with a consensus attained in ideal communicational circumstances[19]). The initial consensus guarantees the legitimacy of the resulting decision. In this regard, there are two reasons why Rawls is not a 'real' or epistemic consensualist such as Habermas. Firstly, it is evident that Rawls' defence of deliberate discussions or the usage of the public mind entirely lacks Habermas' epistemic motivation in which an attained consensus is also the epistemically best decision, but instead treats consensus as the functionally necessary foundation of a (reasonable) discussion. Secondly, for Rawls, the acts of engaging the public mind, postulating widely acceptable reasons and conducing rational debates in a plural society are primarily oriented towards political goals such as the formation and maintenance of a just society (all participants *functionally* partake in the debate as equals)

18 Rawls, 1971., 1993.
19 For a more detailed account of normative consensus as a starting point of discussions, see Prijic-Samarzija and Zelic, 2009.

irrespective of the epistemic goals of achieving true or high-quality decisions. It is therefore appropriate to speak of Rawls as an advocate of political consensualism, rather than hybrid.

5.2. *Consensualism vs expertism*

In contemporary debates about democratic practices, Philip Kitcher is certainly one of the best advocates of the position which we have been referring to as consensualism.[20] Given that Kitcher's stance belongs to an interdisciplinary area between social epistemology and philosophy of science, his perspective strays from political consensualists such as Rawls by its eager epistemic assessment of democratic decision-making. It must be noted that Kitcher does not evaluate the epistemic justification of democracy as a political system. Instead, he investigates the democratic functioning of scientific institutions which mainly have epistemic goals. Knowing that he discusses the optimal division of epistemic labour between experts/scientists and laymen best suited to achieving democratic goals, Kitcher is presented as an author aware of the necessity of harmonizing ethical/political and epistemic values.

Kitcher is deeply and permanently interested in possibility of simultaneously attaining democratic and epistemic goals. Namely, he wonders whether scientific institutions – as paradigmatically inspired by epistemic virtue – can simultaneously be politically justified. Philosophy of science, social epistemology, political philosophy and ethics have proven to be, in Kitcher's example, natural partners and allies in this applied project of democratically and epistemically advancing social institutions and practices.[21] In short, Kitcher is an indispensable reference in any discussion about consensus because he, instead of privileging scientists/experts, proposes a consensual approach to the

---

20 Kitcher, 1990., 2011a., 2011b. See also Philip Kitcher, 2001. *Science, truth, and democracy* (Oxford and New York: Oxford University Press).

21 E. Anderson named the branch of social epistemology interested in the particular epistemic strengths of institutions «institutional epistemology», and Goldman considers this a certain form of «applied epistemology», especially given his personal work on the epistemic potential of institutions and social practices such as law, the media and educational institutions. Either way, Kitcher and numerous other authors have provided research that illustrates the shift from the purely theoretical approach of traditional (individual) analytic epistemology in favour of applied research. For more, see Anderson, 2006.; Goldman, 1999., 2010a.; Goldman and Blancahrd, 2015.

functioning of scientific institutions. Despite never explicitly speaking of a hybrid perspective as such, he perfectly understands the necessity of this kind of assessment.

***

Kitcher's central question is whether a well-regulated scientific practice in a democratic society should be based on the consensus of all interested citizens affected by scientific research, or whether experts/scientists should enjoy a special status that would encourage all interested users/citizens to unanimously accept and promote their findings. This is the dilemma between consensualism and expertism: are the beliefs, judgments or decisions made by consensus epistemically and democratically more justified than those adopted in procedures that privilege experts?[22] Kitcher defends consensualism or the stance that social practices – in his case, science – produce epistemically best results when they are based on the consensus of everyone in a given society, rather than when they simply implement the decisions of scientists/experts.

Kitcher inquires what science should be like in a democratic society in order to be justified, given its inherent *raison d'etre.* Do science and scientists deserve the status of objective and neutral researchers whose superior positions allows them to demand that others believe their findings? Who should define the important issues that science ought to address? Should they be imposed upon society by scientists themselves or should citizens delegate them to scientists? Should a well-regulated scientific practice be based only on the research and attitudes of experts, or should non-experts participate in it?

Kitcher answers these questions in the manner of a true consensualist: the opinions of experts/scientists are not value neutral to the extent that would automatically guarantee their superior epistemic status, so a well-regulated scientific practice in a democratic society should be

22 In his very first works on social epistemology, Goldman distinguished three individual strategies regarding justification: consensualism, expertism and veritism (Goldman, 1987). His later works consistently defent veritism, the approach which primarily justifies those institutions and social practices that support the acquisition of true beliefs. Although it is currently currently unnecessary to embark on a more detailed analysis of Goldman's position, as it will prominently feature in the chapter on reliability democracy, I will use his classification of justificatory strategies and, for the time being, focus on confronting the criteria of consensus and expertise.

based on the consensus of all members of the community – regarding the issues that ought to be researched, as well as broader concerns. More specifically, Kitcher argues that public knowledge – which is essentially comprised of science – needs to be based on an ideal conversation that presupposes the mutual respect of all members of the community: "Science would be well-regulated if problems were specified in an ideal conversation, including all relevant views in conditions of mutual respect."[23] Such an ideal conversation aims to attain consensus: (1) the most desirable outcome of the conversation would be a complete consensus among everyone participating in the discussion, an unanimous acceptance of a certain option as best; (2) the next desirable outcome is the achievement of partial consensus, i.e., a significant overlap between different options; (3) the third desirable consensual outcome is achieved by majority vote; when participants in a debate fail to even partially agree, it is necessary to reach consensus through a voting procedure that considers the option supported by the majority a desirable consensus.[24]

Kitcher's model of addressing issues within a well-regulated scientific practice in a democratic society mirrors his restoration of the ethical project: he rejects any authoritarian conversation in favour of equitable participation of all interested parties. The only correct way of attaining a desirable attitude within such a project is through a public debate – one which participants enter as entirely equal, regardless of their expertise and social standing, and which aims to divulge a solution that will content everyone (or the majority). The privileged status of experts (of any kind, including scientists) contradicts the concept of such a project.

This consensual approach parallels Kitcher's account of the goal of a well-regulated science in a democratic society: the goal of science is not to uncover fundamental principles or to solve practical problems. It also shouldn't aim to solve practical problems through the study of fundamental principles. Well-regulated science seeks good for all people, which, according to Kitcher, doesn't only involve all and diverse communities, but extends to future generations. Science needs to attend to the needs and goals of all citizens, which actually means that it should appropriately address those issues that citizens perceive as problematic. Scientific progress is, consequently, not measured in

---

23 Kitcher, 2011a., p. 106.
24 Kitcher, 2011a., p. 115.

terms of its proximity to truth: there is no ideal scientific system that scientists need to create, form, discover, or attain. Scientific progress is not a dynamic act of progressing *towards*, but a progress *from* that is evaluated in terms of its problem-solving capacities. In the spirit of Kitcher's pragmatic naturalism, scientific truth is constituted as a tool for solving those significant problems that were defined in an ideal discussion. In short, scientific conclusions about major problems that ought to be addressed should stem from ideal conversations, discussions that satisfy the condition of mutual respect.

Although Kitcher never declaratively ranks himself among consensualists – and generally doesn't adhere to the terminology and classification of my books – it is quite evident that these attitudes make him a paradigmatic contemporary representative of this position. Unlike Habermas and his consensualist theory of truth, Kitcher argues for pragmatism: the aim of a public debate is to solve the problems of all interested parties by reaching a consensus. Unlike proceduralists, he defines the ultimate epistemic justification of deliberation in relation to the standard epistemic notion of the epistemic value of the final decision, rather than to the decision-making process itself. In other words, the resulting consensus of a public debate is not a goal in itself, but has to be evaluated in terms of its capacity to resolve problems. His direct and well-elaborated position encourages us to reflect upon the consensualist claim that epistemically justified/rational/desirable decisions in a democratic society, even in democratic science, need to be made by achieving consensus instead of by privileging experts.

***

We can distinguish two underlying rationales or two stages of argumentation that incited Kitcher's defence of consensualism: (1) consensus and conciliation most appropriately mirror democratic values, while the privileged treatment of any group, including experts/scientists, implies an evident democratic deficit; (2) the rival position that delegates a special role to experts in science stems from a wrong assumption, the myth of objective and value-neutral science (scientists). Kitcher also proves that democratic societies absorb the ideal of the common good from a primarily political perspective. This is why a scientific practice which strives towards that same goal should support democratic values and ideals.

Kitcher begins his argumentation by claiming that consensus is a genuine expression of collective will. Given that science endeavours to attain the common good, there is a natural and necessary link between democracy and science – democratic ideals and values should thus be appropriately applied to science. The role of science in a democratic society must not rival the principles promoted by democratic ideas and the values of public knowledge. The goal of an epistemic enterprise should coincide with the goal of democracy – the common good. In other words, democratic procedures and goals are necessarily connected to epistemic benefits. Expertism, as a position that delegates scientists a special role in forming and justifying beliefs, exhibits an evident democratic deficit by favouring an exclusive group of participants. Kitcher holds that democracy necessitates a clear commitment to equality, which includes epistemic equality: all citizens should take part in the debate and are, as equal participants, equally justified in expressing opinions that reflect their values. Recalling Plato's ideal state and its explicit articulation of privileging experts, Kitcher uses it to illustrate that expertism presupposes an authoritarian system and is, as such, deficient with regard to democratic values and ideals. According to Kitcher, existing scientific practices actually do favour experts and support a division of epistemic labour that delegates them a special, significant and fundamental role. And such an expertist practice is undemocratic.

In the second stage of his argument, Kitcher elaborates the thesis that experts/scientists have been wrongly ascribed a special epistemic status because their scientific approach was assumed to be objective and value neutral. This readiness to ascribe an objective value to expert positions stems from the myths of value neutral scientific research and the existence of objective standards uncorrupted by preconceptions, background theories, ideological presumptions, interests and unequal positions of power. Kitcher convincingly demonstrates that the attitudes of experts are necessarily just as value-laden as the attitudes of any other participant. History of science is a history of overconfidence and disappointment. As its legacy, the Enlightenment bequeathed the belief that the sciences (primarily natural sciences) are potentially capable of solving all imaginable human problems. Even governments were convinced of the prudence of investing in scientific research. However, recent debates have exhibited a certain scepticism, an ambivalent attitude, towards the unquestionable authority of natural sciences. The optimistic legacy of the Enlightenment is being increasingly called into question. Representatives of critical theory such Horkheimer and Adorno[25]

25 Horkheimer and Adorno, 1978.

introduced a radical criticism of scientism and postmodernism encouraged their refusal to attribute 'knowledge' and 'truth' to scientists.[26] Similarly, history and sociology of science revealed scientific inquiries to be an alternative manifestation of politics.[27] Kitcher claims that scepticism towards scientific authority wasn't produced by postmodernism or any other philosophical position. He instead offers an excellent analysis of the complex rationale that underlies scepticism: (1) particular areas of inquiry, such as evolutionary theory, molecular biology and many others, are suspect because of their perceived impact on popular forms of religious beliefs or their connected to dangerous and unsafe manipulation with human lives and the environment; (2) since enthusiastic scientists promised more than could be realistically expected from science, its actual results were perceived as scientific weakness and inefficacy; (3) comprehensive theories of *nature-in-general* (for example, the evolutionary theory or the mathematical tools of neoclassical economics) are perceived as disappointing due to their numerous unsuccessful concrete applications; (4) scientific institutions and scientists are perceived as separate from society and scientists are thought to be an overambitious and arrogant elite whose research generates serious risks and threatens the environment and human beings; (5) since scientists have failed to respect the value-neutral ideal of research untainted by judgements and preconceptions, the neutrality of science was disregarded as a myth. Kitcher concludes that the idealized image of scientists is a legacy of excessive optimism which ought to be rejected – scientists do not automatically deserve the privileged status of decision-making authorities.

Their existing scientific beliefs render them rather biased in picking out the scientific projects deserving of further research: some favour particular projects because they consider them better guides to the common good and others opt for approaches closer to their more specific scientific goals. Certain scientists orient scientific practices in a particular direction in order to increase the credibility of their own findings and others adjust scientific research to their own talents and abilities. Kitcher emphasizes that this bias isn't limited to the context of deciding upon what is important for science, but also extends to the context of justification. Objective evaluations of evidence and a

---

26 Derrida, 1976.; Lyotard, 1984.

27 Kuhn, 1962.; Foucault, 1980.; Shapin and Schaffer, 1985.; Latour, 1987.

normative criterion of sufficient evidential grounds are unattainable: procedures of verifying and proving findings are just as infected by personal values as the processes of scientific discovery and decision-making.

The authority of science – resting on the myth of unbiased and objective research – has granted scientists an unjustified and privileged position. Likewise, the existing expertistic division of epistemic labour caters to the subjective interests of scientists as a fixed social elite, while either rejecting or marginalizing alternative approaches. Since scientific research is generally not value-neutral, the only acceptable form of debate in a democratic society oriented towards the common good seems to lie in unrestricted distribution and competition of the ideas postulated by all participants. In spite of this conclusion, Kitcher diverges from social constructivists and postmodernists by refusing to perceive this analysis as an indicator that the authority of science should be generally abolished. He is equally unwilling to equalize science with other systems of beliefs or 'ways of life'. From Kitcher's perspective, the choice to articulate the contemporary ambient of disillusionment with science and recognize the value subjectivity of scientific research only aims to undermine official expertism and the tendency to infer scientific authority from the myth of value neutrality. The solution doesn't lie in delegitimizing science and the sheer existence of objectively valid beliefs/decisions, which is a notorious constructivist intention, but in introducing consensus as a remedy and as an expression of collective will.

Should we expand the topic and apply Kitcher's argument to the general epistemic justification of democracy, we would end up a full-fledged (pragmatist) consensualism founded on the following theses: (i) epistemic justification or epistemic quality of decisions cannot be reduced to truthfulness, but to their capacity to successfully resolve the problems of all interested parties (thus achieving the common good), (ii) epistemic and democratic justification of decisions/beliefs/judgments, but also of institutions and social practices, overlap in their aim of achieving the common good by solving the problems of all citizens; (iii) consensus of all interested parties is the optimum way of making decisions oriented towards this epistemic and democratic goal; (iv) privileging experts is contrasted to the consensual method and is a democratically and epistemically unacceptable way of making decisions.

***

I will proceed to show that consensualism in general, including Kitcher's meticulously elaborated stance, fails to respond to the challenge of harmonizing epistemic and ethical/political justifications of democracy because consensus is in itself an insufficient guarantee of epistemically valuable decisions. I will try to show that Kitcher's proposal of dividing epistemic labour between citizens and experts is far more acceptable than unqualified consensualism, but it remains unclear whether this improvement of consensualism can be considered a truly acceptable option.

5.3. *Enhanced consensualism and enhanced expertism*

It is beyond doubt that a consensus achieved during fair deliberation fulfils its ethical and political task. But does it satisfy the epistemic conditions? Every form of consensualism suffers from at least three obvious epistemic weaknesses: (1) delegation of decision-making to the (uninformed) majority; (2) the problem of conservatism; (3) the problem of isolation.

As previously stated in our discussion of Habermas' consensualism, any sensible contemporary defence of consensualism needs to acknowledge the sub-ideal epistemic circumstances of real social deliberations in which we attempt to reach consensus. Most potential participants are not just inadequately informed about the issue at hand, but are also predominantly uninterested, unmotivated to invest time and cognitive resources in learning about the topics that are deliberated upon, unwilling or unable to recognize their lack of knowledge and finally, too immature or poorly educated to grasp complex topics within a narrow timeframe. Such circumstances make epistemically valuable decisions seem rather unlikely. In other words, these sub-ideal epistemic circumstances (and the impossibility of ensuring an ideal conversation and a rational consensus) are precisely the reason why reliance on experts is treated as an epistemically desirable alternative. In *ideal* circumstances – where everyone is adequately informed and capable of making decisions, or at least capable of learning and retaining necessary information – consensus would have no relevant epistemic alternative. Every individual citizen would satisfy the conditions of being relevantly informed and un-egoistic. Since sub-ideal circumstances delegate the choice of scientific topics and research directions to an agreement between all participants, irrespective of their expertise and credibility, it is more than likely that the outcome will be unacceptable. It is obvious that interested debaters who lack information about the issue at hand or cannot adequately absorb it within a short time frame – regardless of whether they are deliberating about scientific research or other social practices and institutions – aren't equally equipped to make decisions as those who possess more information and who have been trained to deal with such topics. The faults of our epistemic reality, clearly illustrated by certain attitudes expressed during several elections and referendums, warn us that citizens seem more interested in ideology-laden issues such as the definition of marriage, religious clashes and polemics about immigration than in workers' rights, the quality of education or the importance of equality. Likewise, interests of the vast majority lie in topics such as football, celebrity culture and political gossip. Little respect is paid to the tedious issues of fiscal policies, social justice and human rights. In addition, it is highly unlikely that the uninformed and the unskilled (regardless of Kitcher's optimistic claims about their capacity for altruism) can assess the impact of their stances on the common good or the values underlying their subjective attitudes, rendering the problem-solving capacity of their opinions highly questionable. Keeping this in mind, it is evident that the consensus produced in such sub-optimal epistemic circumstances, which make it impossible to speak about an ideal public debate, probably won't be the best available solution. We have already pointed out that, as a result of the majority consensus, the uninformed attitude often prevails over the informed, thus producing a final decision wholly incapable of resolving the problem[28].

Secondly, a public debate that equally engages those who possess a certain degree of expertise and those who possess none at all can, at best, result in a consensual cross-section of their stances. Such a consensus will always be epistemically sub-optimal in comparison to solutions produced solely by experts, regardless of the subjective

---

28 We have already discussed this issue within the book. However, it must be added that even contemporary neuroscience has confirmed the perils of delegating decision-making to the uninformed. Recent studies have shown that being informed correlates with a skepticism towards the validity of one's own stances, while the less informed exhibit continuous overconfidence that they are right. All of this, of course, heavily influences their eagerness to agree with others in a discussion. For more, see Kruger and Dunning, 1999.; Burton, 2013.

values underlying their views. The choice to include a larger number of participants with different values and interests doesn't make the result epistemically more valuable purely because there are many of them. Numerous prejudices don't automatically neutralize prejudice due to their number. It is far more probable that the most popular prejudice will prevail. In other words, the resulting common good or the solution to the problem will be somewhat feeble because the final agreement will have to be acceptable to those who have hardly any knowledge about the problem. A layman simply cannot contribute to the solution in the same way an expert who possesses relevant knowledge. It should be emphasised that neither laymen nor experts are value-neutral. In that sense, even Kitcher's progress *from* will not be optimal, the epistemic goal of resolving the problem will not be optimally attained and any improvement will be slow(er) because participants will be more likely to agree on familiar options than to embrace controversial novelty. Consensus thus reveals itself to be an instrument of perpetuating the majority attitude and the existing social patterns, that can, at best, encourage policies of gradual progress. As such, it is *conservative* at its very core.[29]

In the end, it is possible to imagine consensual decisions that not only fail to resolve problems, but instead actually deepen them. No aspect of consensus guarantees that the conciliated attitude will adequately resolve the problem. Both history and contemporary society flood us with examples of consensual agreements starkly incongruent with the notion of the common good. We don't even have to reference the notoriously extreme example of Nazism as there have been numerous other consensual decisions that denied human rights and adopted racist, sexist and similarly oppressive laws. Just recall the currently widespread tendency of snubbing immigrants and refugees who are then, due to the pressure imposed by the frightened majority, treated in accordance to unpopular emergency measures. When there is no criterion of validity apart from internal agreement within a group, there is no factual evidence or epistemic virtue that can anchor their decisions in anything objectively valid. We have seen there is no moral value that couldn't be easily disproved because the majority can attain consensus about anything at all. This *isolation* of the value of the decision from any objective evaluative criteria renders consensus a potentially dangerous and perilous decision-making method.

---

29 Prijic-Samarzija, 2005.

Kitcher seems to be somewhat aware of these problems by rejecting 'vulgar' consensualism, the tyranny of ignorance potentially produced by some consensus. This is why he proposes a certain enhanced consensus, which acknowledges that (1) democratic division of labour implies a significant inclusion of experts, and (2) an ideal discussion presupposes conditions that favour knowledge and expertise.

Kitcher admits that consensus is a challenge for every democratic society given the fact that some people are more informed about certain issues than others. He contends that it is equally non-democratic to reject the obviously superior epistemic positions of some people as to uncritically delegate all epistemic labour to a small group of (alleged) authorities. Kitcher's account of an ideal discussion therefore requires that all participants are as informed as possible or at least adequately aware the importance of being informed (the *epistemic* condition of an ideal conversation), and that they non-egoistically respect the views of others in attempting to reach an agreement (the *affective* condition of an ideal conversion[30]). He argues that debaters should not rely on false beliefs about the world. They also have to be able to identify the desires of other participants and acknowledge the consequences of the institutional actions that are being deliberated upon. Furthermore, participants need to consider and compare different approaches in order to properly balance ethically permissible and factually grounded desires and demands.

Despite his initial insistence on the democratic values of consensus and the assertion that it produces the best decisions, Kitcher's optimum division of epistemic work still delegates a significant role to experts and their expertise: (1) he recognizes their existence and comparatively better capacity of resolving problems, and (2) postulates the ideal of expertise (as previously defined) as a fundamental precondition of an ideal discussion. Considering that sub-ideal circumstances make it desirable – due to various epistemic deficiencies – for all debaters to be in some way tutored by experts, Kitcher actually ascribes experts a special epistemic status implied by a certain social trust in the credibility of the expert community. This, however, also means that Kitcher's well-regulated science and decision-making process in democracy aren't actually based solely on mutually respectful conciliation between equals, but are largely informed by the legacy of expertism –

30 A similar approach to the method of rational consensus can be found in Lehrer and Wagner, 1981.

confident deference to experts. The role of experts is finally recognized and acknowledged to such an extent that the abundantly criticized practice of expertism was, for the sake of an argument, reduced to its most radical manifestation – Plato's authoritarian expertism. It is unconvincing to uncritically reject expertism because of the faults of its most radical version – Plato's concept of an expert group that decides on everything, while others cannot access the epistemic process.[31] Likewise, it seems unfounded to perceive the current state of disillusionment with science as a fact that attests to the inadmissibility of expertism. Despite all the challenges imposed upon scientific practice by contemporary democratic societies, and which Kitcher has brilliantly analysed, it is still the best methodological and procedural best framework for seeking truth – in comparison to alternative and marginal approaches or 'ways of life'.[32] There are, of course, numerous acceptable versions of scientific expertism – much milder than Plato's approach – that successfully avoid these challenges. The proposed enhanced consensus seems like a promising position capable of uniting the expertist and the consensualist rationale.[33]

Kitcher's final position, based on a non-egoistical and unbiased adjustment of one's own views to those of experts through the process of questioning one's own standpoint and learning from experts, could be characterized not only as enhanced consensualism but also as a 'limited' consensualism. It is a consensualism that recognizes the role of experts, but is primarily oriented towards the ideal of collective will and the democratic values of equal participation in the deliberative process.

However, if we accept the constraints imposed upon the initial version of consensualism, it is important to note that there is no significant obstacle to considering this position a certain 'limited' expertism. Apart from possible argumentative divergences, there seems to be no particular difference between 'limited' consensualism and a correspondingly 'limited' expertism that neutralizes potentially authoritarian expert elitism through democratic public debates between all interested parties. Accepting and

31 Even Plato proposed several control mechanisms aimed at neutralising the experts' subjective biases and attempts to misuse their privileged position, thus ensuring that they remain the objectively best guides to resolving problems.

32 Goldman, 1999.

33 Lehrer and Wagner's famous account of rational consensus can also be considered a good suggestion, although I must note that it is more reminiscent of enhanced expertism than true consensualism. Prijic–Samarzija, 2005.

recognizing the limitations – such as the fact that the attitudes of experts cannot be value neutral – 'limited' expertism has access to myriad available procedures that block the exclusivity (ideologies or biases) of expert attitudes, i.e., that prevent experts from imposing stances which cater to their personal interests and thus undermine the democratic desiderata of attaining the common good. For example, expertism can be restrained by the precondition of introducing and promoting epistemic diversity and inclusivity by making the political choice to reach numerous citizens with different epistemic backgrounds, thus ensuring a wider evidential basis for decision-making experts.[34] It could also necessitate the practice of 'advocating' non-experts; any scientific research or decision-making process should always consult, seek the opinions and acknowledge the attitudes of interested non-experts and alternative approaches.[35] Maybe it should be required for expert decision-making mechanisms in scientific research or political decision-making to undergo meticulous public scrutiny – they should transparently divulge the sources and intelligibility of their underlying rationale, goals, assumptions, results, finances and like.[36] This would neutralize the experts' subjective values and any possible 'politically-militaristic' practices of protecting their own elitist interests, simultaneously engaging diverse perspectives, plural opinions and broad evidential bases.

It is unnecessary to engage in a more comprehensive discussion about whether this is just a terminological discussion – which implies an absence of significant divergences between the positions of 'limited' consensualism and 'limited' expertism – or whether Kitcher could insist on actually substantial differences. It is important to note that Kitcher's position is undoubtedly characterized by the dual role of experts and consensus: Kitcher opts for consensual solutions when postulating highly generalized claims about about ideal conversational goals, but refers to experts in elaborating concrete problem-solving procedures. Knowing this, it seems important to summarize this discussion by concluding that both a well-regulated scientific practice and a desirable decision-making methodology in a democratic society require the fulfilment of two preconditions: (1) the condition of expertise or the epistemic condition; and (2) the condition of public debate or the democratic condition. We can repeat our claim that – regardless of how we may name and conceptualize

34 For example, see Miriam Solomon. 2006. 'Norms of epistemic diversity', *Episteme*, 3(1-2): 23–36.

35 Code, 2010.

36 Goldman, 1999.; Kitcher, 2011a.; Christiano, 2012.

the balanced standpoint between consensualism and expertism – both democratic scientific practice and democratic systems at large must optimally satisfy both preconditions, neither of which can be sacrificed for the other, identified with the other or reduced to the other.

***

We have seen that both proceduralist and consensual attempts to harmonize epistemic and ethical/political justification generally reveal themselves as inconsistent – primarily due to their continuous dread that introducing experts necessarily undermines the democratic goal. Both Habermas' and Kitcher's consensualism differ from proceduralism in appreciating the significance of the independent epistemic value of expertise and the corresponding independent value of the epistemic result (either as the epistemic value of truth/correctness or its problem-solving capacity). In this sense, consensualism is a genuine attempt to conceive a hybrid perspective that truly strives to harmonize epistemic and ethical/political values. While proceduralists reduce or sacrifice epistemic virtue to the ethical and political, refusing to acknowledge that decisions possess an epistemic value independent of the fair procedure, Habermas and Kitcher quite clearly postulate the importance of epistemic virtues (truth, correctness, problem solving) alongside the political and ethical.

However, the shortcomings of consensualism lie elsewhere: it has been shown that original consensualism (which opposes the inclusion of experts in the process of attaining consensus) doesn't suffice to guarantee the desired epistemic quality of decisions. A consensus attained as the result of decision-making processes in sub-ideal epistemic circumstances – often far-removed from Habermas' ideal of rational consensus in ideal conversational circumstances, or Kitcher's requirement of satisfying epistemic and affective conditions – simply cannot automatically produce epistemic quality. Even though deliberative democracy inherently includes the method of achieving consensus or conciliation in public discussions, it neither guarantees the epistemically most valuable solution nor does it even resemble a rational consensus in ideal conversational circumstances. Despite the efforts of the advocates of consensualism, it has again been shown that democratic justification simply does not automatically ensure epistemic justification unless it incorporates additional criteria of expertise. Consensual decision-making will, at best, ensure ethical/political justification, but not epistemic justification. Decisions made in such processes simply do not have the necessary epistemic value, so we can confidently speak about a certain indirect sacrifice of – potentially positive – epistemic values, in favour of the ethical and political.

The enhanced consensus finally offered by Kitcher delegates a special role to experts and is somewhat more convincing. However, it soon becomes evident that it is not just a request for consensus, but also an independent demand for expertise – which consensualists have often declaratively denounced as anti-democratic. This discussion about consensualism has reminded us about the challenges of harmonizing epistemic and democratic goals, and has emphasised the necessity of reconsidering and redefining the role of experts in democratic systems.

5.4. *Consensus and experts: consensus and dissagrements between experts*

I have repeatedly emphasized that relying on experts in decision-making processes entails certain epistemic and political challenges: (i) the epistemic consist of the fact that expert attitudes are not value-neutral, and even experts often disagree within their own ranks; (ii) the political challenge is principally reducible to the already elaborated thesis that relying on experts introduces the threat of epistocracy, which clearly opposes democratic values. Kitcher argues that both epistemic 'deficits' inherent to involving experts can be compensated a deliberative process oriented towards establishing a consensus: a public hearing in which everyone participates as an equal can neutralize the value-laden and subjective attitudes of experts, and the very act of consensus can neutralize the democratic 'deficit' generated by authoritarian expertism. However, as I have previously mentioned, there is a certain level of indeterminacy inherent to Kitcher's proposal, an ambiguous or even dual attitude towards experts: on the one hand, there is an evident reluctance to emphasize their importance, and on the other there is an equally clear awareness of the necessity of including experts and their expertise in discussions.

Aware of these circumstances, Kitcher finally postulates the redeeming idea of dividing epistemic labour: the aspects of epistemic labour most vulnerable to value biases should be left to conciliation, while those that require sophisticated knowledge should be delegated to experts. An idea that proposes a certain balance of consensual conciliation and expertise is a promising solution to harmonizing democratic and epistemic justification. What emerges as crucial is the issue of defining the appropriate degree of their participation in decision-making processes. I will proceed by scrutinizing and further elaborating Kitcher's proposal of an epistemic division of labour and the possibility to compensate for the democratic deficits of expertism by the means of consensus. This interesting proposition deserves more detailed elaboration in the context of harmonizing epistemic and democratic ideals.

***

Kitcher points out two problems characteristic of the epistemic status of experts: firstly, experts are neutral neither in their research nor in their attitudes, and there are disagreements between experts partially caused by their differing subjective values and interests. What happens if we delegate decision-making to experts – assuming that they will be able to resolve the differences between their values – and they continue to disagree? Whose decision should we accept? Wouldn't consensus genuinely be a better solution? Kitcher proposes the practice of resolving conflicts and disagreements between experts with a broad consensus between non-experts.[37] The democratic act of introducing non-experts in the role of unbiased citizens (within a wider public debate or civic jury) in order to resolve scientific problems that scientists themselves cannot unravel – despite its democratically desirable participatory element – has a rather questionable epistemic result: (1) it is rather unconvincing to entirely reduce disagreements between experts to differences in their background values, which is implied by Kitcher's solution; (2) it is particularly unlikely for non-experts to be sufficiently informed and professional to fully understand – and, finally, resolve – sophisticated disagreements among experts.

Even though disagreements between experts can sometimes stem from their background values, causes of particular disagreements are often far more complex: different available evidence and ways in which that evidence is incorporated into background knowledge (which is

37 Kitcher points out that disagreements between experts can slow down scientific progress and generally refers to disagreements caused by clashing background values. In this respect, he doesn't consider disagreements in science particularly unlike other instances of disagreement, such as those pertaining to politics and ethics. It is consequently suggested that disagreements ought to be resolved during public debates with non-experts, wherein the "conflicted" parties would explain their stances in a clear and comprehensible manner. Groups of previously tutored lay people with different background values could, in such a scenario, resolve the disagreement. Kitcher, 2011a., p. 220.

far more complex than matters of individual interests[38]), information processing standards and different evidential weighs that experts attribute to their evidence (and which do not necessarily have to be a consequence of value infection, or at least not only value infections). There are terminological disagreements among experts that are neither superficial nor value-laden, but that require sophisticated conceptual analysis. Furthermore, despite the respect that experts may exhibit towards each other, they often disagree with those who they do not consider their *epistemic peers*; they attribute them lower epistemic credibility or simply believe that they themselves possess better evidence and are more capable of learning from that evidence.[39] Disagreements are somewhat understandable because it is difficult to imagine a state of full evidential overlap, particularly in those complex systems of reasons that are not always available to conscious memory.[40] However, disagreements between experts definitely dot not exclusively stem from different value systems and can therefore be resolved by non-experts. Although discussions are commonly considered a fruitful remedy for disagreements, it is extremely unlikely for public discussions among non-experts to resolve disagreements between experts.

In spite of Kitcher's view, perhaps the curative and corrective potential of public debates and broad consensus should be sought outside their questionable ability to resolve disagreements between experts. In order to satisfy the epistemic goal, advocates of consensus should at the very least be able to prove that consensus is an epistemically effective method of resolving disagreements. They should show (1) that some aspects of public debates (among non-experts) contribute to optimally detecting and resolving significant problems and (2) why these particular features of consensus are a comparatively epistemically valuable method of resolving disagreements.

Not only has it been unproven that a broad public consensus could resolve disagreements among experts in an epistemically valuable manner, but it is equally dubious whether consensus among experts themselves could optimally settle their disagreement.[41] Extensive and interesting discussions within epistemology of disagreement

38 Sosa, 2010.

39 Goldman, 2010b.

40 Ralph Wedgwood. 2010. 'The Moral Evil Demons', in Feldman Richard and Ted A. Warfield (eds.), *Disagreement* (Oxford: Oxford University Press), pp. 216–246.

41 Lehrer and Wagner, 1981.

have revealed the unlikelihood that rivaling experts will be eager and able to reach a consensual solution. Even if evidential overlaps were attained, they would probably not suffice to automatically resolve the disagreement. Some philosophers within epistemology of disagreement argue that experts will be reluctant to revise their attitudes even if other experts, whom they consider competent and equally informed, think otherwise – simply because they think that they are right.[42] Others claim that such disagreements, if disagreeing parties are evidential and cognitive peers, should be resolved by both sides giving up or refraining from judgments until new circumstances arise.[43] We are given the third option of resolving disagreements by contenting that both rivaling attitudes are correct and allowing them to remain in a state of reasonable disagreement.[44] In short, disagreements among experts are a very complex problem. The prospect of unraveling disagreements and attaining an epistemically optimum belief or decision is still the subject of fierce controversy.[45]

Given that disagreements among experts are such a challenging problem, expecting that broad consensus could resolve them in an epistemically valuable manner is just as utopian as the belief that rivaling experts will feel spontaneously inclined to synchronize. The value of public debates and consensus in tackling the problem of expertism should not be sought in resolving disagreements between experts. In the epistemic division of labour, the epistemically most valuable balance of consensus and expertise, or consensus and experts, should be sought somewhere else.

5.5. *Division of epistemic labor: consensually trusting experts*

It is true that the mere possession of expertise doesn't make one impervious to value judgments. However, it is equally true that experts are, by definition, comparatively more successful in overcoming and

---

42 John Hawthorne and Amia Srinivasan. 2012. 'Disagreement Without Transparency: Some Bleak Thoughts', in Christensen David and Jennifer Lackey (eds.), *The Epistemology of Disagreement* (Oxford: Oxford University Press), pp. 9–30.

43 Feldman, 2006., 2007.

44 Elga, 2007.; Goldman 2010b., Sosa, 2010.; Peter, 2013a., 2013b.

45 For more, see Richard Feldman and Ted A. Warfield (eds.). 2010. *Disagreement* (Oxford: Oxford University Press); Christensen, David, and Jeniffer Lackey. (eds). 2012. *The Epistemology of Disagreement* (Oxford: Oxford University Press).

recognizing the prejudices, ideologies and interests of themselves and others, which then enables them to resolve problems. Experts don't only possess more (highly specialized) information, but are also better at structuring and contextualising that information. They are also better acquainted with appropriate methods of conducting research, articulating arguments, resolving difficulties and confronting alternative concepts. These abilities make them comparatively more capable of moderating the influx of their background values into the problem solving process. This suggests that experts, in comparison to non-experts, still deserve to be ascribed a special epistemic status. Despite the dissimilarities between the fields of science and decision-making context, the epistemic virtues of experts seem equally applicable in both areas. The epistemic responsibility and epistemic conscientiousness of experts (curiosity, caution, sensitivity to evidential weight) are equally pertinent in all domains of epistemic agency. An expert is an expert simply because he practices epistemic virtues better than others.

Despite Kitcher's justified scepticism towards the myth of value-neutral expertise, it is undisputed that experts are, regardless of their constraints, still comparatively the best guides to truth, or at least to avoiding false and detrimental solutions. It is important to emphasize that their special epistemic status does not automatically entail nor guarantee a special political or ethical social status. However, the fact that they have no automatic special political or ethical status is no cause for suspecting the validity of the epistemic one.

There is further rationale behind the experts' special epistemic status. Non-experts are – due to the existing (sub-ideal) epistemic circumstances – *epistemically dependent* on experts. Without the research and testimonies of experts on different topics, non-experts would have hardly any knowledge and their capacity to deal with diverse ordinary problems would be incomparably poorer and less efficient. Furthermore, the special status of experts stems from the fact that non-experts are unable to credibly evaluate the content expressed in the attitudes and decisions of experts. The reality of the epistemic dependence of non-experts on experts is correlated with the fact that non-experts simply lack the knowledge and evidence necessary to meaningfully assess the content of expert testimonies. In other words, experts have a special epistemic status because non-experts are so dependent on experts that they are obliged to trust them because they possess the status of an expert. It is obvious that this account of their special epistemic status can sound rather bad from the perspective of ethical/political equality. However, as I have already emphasized, their objectively existing special epistemic status in no way implies a special ethical or political status. I therefore hold that this is the exact reason why we must precisely define the status of experts, should we aim to finally overcome the constant fear that recognizing their special epistemic status necessarily brings about a special political status irreconcilable with a genuinely democratic system.

Let's summarize, there are three reasons why we attribute a special epistemic status to experts: (1) experts are superior in solving problems and forming true/correct beliefs (2) non-experts are epistemically dependent on experts in solving their own problems and forming true/correct beliefs and (3) non-experts lack the necessary evidence for credibly appraising expert judgments. It is important to immediately point out that recognizing the special epistemic status of experts does not imply that they should be automatically ascribed a *fundamental epistemic authority* which would justify an authoritarian epistemic status and uncritical feelings of blind trust. The decision to ascribe such authority to experts, which also justifies delegating them the entirety of epistemic labour, is not even epistemically justified, regardless of their special epistemic status.

In order to be epistemically responsible and rational, any trust – including that of non-experts in experts – must be based on appropriate evidence and reasoning. Deference to the epistemic authority of experts must not jeopardize the epistemic autonomy of any particular epistemic agent or his epistemically responsible behaviour. As blind and uncritical reliance on any decision, judgement or testimony simply cannot be considered rational, a belief based on such immediate deference can neither be epistemically justified.[46] Each epistemic agent must begin with an epistemically conscientious confidence in their own abilities and then develop the appropriate epistemic reasons behind accepting, rejecting or refraining from a judgment about someone's testimony. This must pertain to all credibility judgements, including those of expert testimonies. Consequently, authoritarian expertism, which presumes that the special epistemic status of experts automatically entails their fundamental epistemic authority, presupposes blind trust in others and denies the epistemic autonomy of an individual. Just like authoritarianism cannot provide political legitimacy, it can

46 Kieth Leher. 2006. 'Trust and Trustworthiness', in Lackey Jennifer and Ernest Sosa (eds.), *The Epistemology of Testimony* (Oxford, Oxford University Press), pp. 393–411; Lackey, 2006.; Prijić–Samaržija, 2011.

neither provide the epistemic – but now for epistemic reasons. Experts, much like everyone else, can only be ascribed *derived* epistemic authority. This means that their testimonies and attitudes, in order to be epistemically justified, must undergo a certain assessment by non-experts. Consequently, the special epistemic status of experts is not constituted by the means of an unilateral epistemic relationship in which experts impose paternalist judgments on non-experts, but through the specific qualities of evidence and assessments: we must have a certain evidential basis for trusting the testimonies and judgments of experts (given our dependence and lack of expertise), although it is not and cannot be the same as the one used when attributing trust to other non-experts.[47]

Although they are unable to evaluate the content of expert testimonies, non-experts are able to assess the overall credibility of experts, expert teams and institutions: our experience allows us to conclude whether an expert or his team successfully solve problems, and determine whether they are too slow or too expensive. We witness whether the proposed solutions reflect their limited value schemes (determined by their position of power, authority, ideology, etc.) and whether they are willing to acknowledge the standpoints of alternative approaches and non-experts. Non-experts can also assess whether their scientific research and procedures are epistemically responsible (respectful of other professionals who participate in the debate, adequately transparent) and ethically responsible (dedicated to the goal of the common good for all people). Moreover, we choose to trust experts on the basis of these relatively reliable social practices of assessing the credibility of certain groups of experts. Although we generally trust scientific institutions, we also prefer the institutions with exemplary results, ethics, transparency and similar virtues. This social practice of entrusting experts stems from a consensus-based assessment of credibility conducted by unrelated individuals and groups with different background beliefs. Even though we have acknowledged the vulnerability of experts to different value biases and the corrosion of scientific authority that sometimes arises from abuses of power, there is an evident spontaneous consensus on the special epistemic status of experts in general (as well as specific scientific groups and institutions) that experts are more capable at problem-solving than others, and that some of them are even more capable than other experts.

47 Prijić–Samaržija, 2011.

Consequently, public debates and consensus do not come into play when disagreements between experts are to be resolved, but when choosing trustworthy experts who deserve to be ascribed the status of epistemic authorities. Not all experts are epistemic authorities in the mere virtue of their reputation. All citizens as free, equal and epistemically autonomous participants in public debates should actively decide which experts, teams and institutions deserve special epistemic authority. Habermas' conclusion on the importance of institutionally governed public debates in which non-experts discuss experts thus becomes very relevant: different institutions need to encourage and educate non-professionals to actively and knowledgeably participate in such public debates. Once this epistemic job of consensually ascribing trust has been completed, experts are the ones who have to resolve problems because they are far more successful in it and will thus produce a better epistemic outcome for everyone. This does not mean non-experts should be excluded as soon as they have opted for the most credible experts: they need to continuously overlook their efficiency and repeatedly ascribe them trust. In exceptional situations of heightened suspicion towards the credibility of a previously chosen expert team or towards certain proposed solutions that could greatly affect everyone's lives, it is always possible to introduce an immediate debate or conciliation by the means of referendum.

Either way, epistemic authority is acquired in a similar representative manner as the acquisition of political authority. Non-experts ascribe trust to experts who will solve their problems on their behalf, as long as they cannot successfully solve them themselves. More importantly, they need to have sufficient evidence that those experts truly possess superior problem-solving capacity. A previously achieved consensus on trusting experts is epistemically crucial for successfully solving problems because it guarantees the selection of truly capable experts who will thus make decisions of the best available epistemic quality. This is precisely the epistemic value of consensus – ensuring epistemically most valuable decisions. My proposal is a certain amalgam of Rawls' and Habermas' proposals: it is a consensus that precedes the decision-making process (rather than a consensus that generates decisions), but which utilizes a public debate and conciliation of all interested participants to insure the epistemic quality of beliefs and decisions (rather than being just an initial decision-making requirement).

It is obvious that the selection of expert 'representatives' cannot be carried out in the political manner of elections and mandates. However, the basic principle is the same: epistemic and political autonomy are the starting points which, through public debates and consensus, generate trust in political and epistemic authorities. Consensus, a method that has undeniable democratic legitimacy, lies at the base of trusting experts and is thus an essential factor in ensuring the epistemic quality of decisions.

5.5.1. *Democratic and epistemic challenges of the consenusally derived authority of experts*

Although this proposal seems to fulfil the democratic requirements of public debates and consensus while optimally satisfying epistemic values, it is vulnerable to two directions of further objections: the first is epistemic because it may seem that the proposed option isn't the one which ensures the highest possible epistemic quality – it could offer more!; the other is political because it may seem that it still unnecessarily sacrifices democratic values to the epistemic.

First, it can be argued that a non-expert is simply insufficiently knowledgeable to assess who really is an expert and that a consensus on the superior credibility of certain experts is subject to the familiar problems of the uninformed majority and epistemic conservatism (just like any other consensus). This objection is partially justified because it is truly possible that consensual accounts of credibility will not detect the best experts, but, for instance, inferior experts more skilled at self-promotion. Nevertheless, it is important to emphasize that non-experts are still far more capable of detecting epistemic authorities who will make decisions in their place than of autonomously making informed decisions. Laymen possess more abundant evidence for evaluating successful experts than for solving problems or resolving conflicts among experts. Unlike the dubious involvement of non-experts in problem-solving processes, a non-expert can be considered *competent* to evaluate whom they should bestow trust. The evidence necessary for assessing the credibility of an informant is not the same as the evidential basis for evaluating the content of his proposition.[48] A non-expert has sufficient evidence for appraising the epistemic and moral character of an expert: while the first concerns general facts related to the reliability and sincerity of an individual, the other requires more sophisticated knowledge about the relevant field of expertise.

48 John Hardwig. 1991. 'The Role of Trust in Knowledge', *Journal of Philosophy*, 88: 693–708.

Possible insistence, by veritists, for example , on increasing epistemic quality by disputing the benefits of consensus in any decision-making process, including the process of detecting epistemic authorities, is not a proposal I could deem justified. At this point it would actually diminish the epistemic quality of the final decision because the consensual selection of experts greatly benefits from epistemic diversity and a broad evidential base. The democratic procedure of a public debate doesn't only ensure an expression of general will, but also confronts epistemically different individuals who bring diverse knowledge and experiences into the discussion.[49] Processes of making decisions in public debates address two principal goals: (1) they protect democratic values by encouraging the participation of all interested parties and, even more importantly, (2) introduce pluralism and value diversity, thus improving the final outcome by neutralizing the preferential 'situatedness' of the citizens who participate in selecting credible experts. A greater number of participants in debates about trustworthy experts, all of whom bring in their personal systems of values, certainly provide epistemic benefits. We have already stressed that deliberative democracy isn't epistemically valuable only because it facilitates the dissemination of different information and evidence, but also because it introduces different perspectives that involve different inputs: values, evidence, methods of processing information and weights attributed to evidence. Although emphasising the epistemic fertility of various perspectives cannot suffice when tackling truly complex problems (because participants who deliberate about sophisticated problems lack the necessary evidence, skills and relevant knowledge), it is certainly very influential when assessing the credibility of an informant or an expert because it concerns readily available records that can be credibly utilized by non-experts.

The second kind of objection may come from more radical egalitarians or authors who feel that my proposal drains the importance of consensus by implicitly sacrificing democratic values and demoting the importance of participation to the mere selection of experts. It could also be argued that the democratic act of consensus is reduced to a method of attaining an epistemically valuable decision. This criticism of epistemic instrumentalization of democratic procedures for epistemic purposes could only be persuasive if the alternative –

49 Elizabeth Anderson. 2006. 'The Epistemology of Democracy', *Episteme*, 3(1-2): 8–22.

utter denial of the special epistemic status of experts – didn't entail the political instrumentalization of epistemic values by reducing them to fair procedures. Namely, this objection leads us to an unresolvable position that makes the prospect of harmonization seem hopeless. The goal is not to denounce this or that type of instrumentalization, but to optimally harmonize epistemic and ethical/political values. I cannot agree that this is an instrumentalization that sacrifices ethical/political virtues. Should we recall Habermas' consensualist principle that justification stems from the interpersonal legitimacy of acceptance, we seem to have preserved the essential ideal of consensus. This proposal relies on epistemically autonomous individuals who conscientiously, responsibly and consensually decide on credible experts/epistemic authorities whom they will entrust due to the credence that their decisions will be better than the ones they could make on their own. Decisions made by epistemic authorities will then be considered justified in the virtue of their expertise, but also because there is a consensus (based on plurality and other democratic values) about their credibility. The final decision will, in this respect, have both the legitimacy of interpersonal consensus and the benefits of expertise. I do not think that this is a reduction of democratic justification to the epistemic, nor vice versa.

5.6. *Conclusion*

Consensualism is characterized by the stance that conciliation is a necessary precondition of any correct decision and that establishing consensus in public discussions among interested citizens is the best way of harmonizing epistemic values and the values of deliberative democracy. Different forms of consensualism share several common premises: (i) the epistemic justification and epistemic quality of decisions include the value of truth or their capacity to successfully resolve the problems of all interested parties (thus achieving the common good); (ii) the epistemic and democratic justifications of decisions/beliefs /judgments overlap in objectives as they both strive towards the common good by resolving the problems of all citizens (iii) a consensus generated within a public debate is the optimal way of making decisions which cater to the stated epistemic and democratic goal, (iv) privileged treatment of experts contradicts the rationale of consensus and is therefore a democratically and epistemically unacceptable method of making decisions.

Consensualism differs from proceduralism because it acknowledges the independent epistemic value of the epistemic result, either in the form of the epistemic value of truth/correctness or its problem solving capacity. In this sense, consensualism is a genuine attempt to devise a hybrid perspective that strives to harmonize epistemic and ethical/political values. While proceduralists reduce or sacrifice epistemic virtues to the ethical and political by refusing to acknowledge the existence of the epistemic value of decisions independent from the fair procedure, consensualists clearly postulate the importance of the epistemic virtues of truth, correctness and problem-solving capacity. Nevertheless, they have still retained the proceduralists' declarative and permanent fear that any introduction of experts, as a possible epistemic requirement, necessarily undermines not only the consensus itself, but also the democratic aim. That is precisely why consensualists fully sought the epistemic quality of decisions in the qualities of public debates, exchanges of reasons and civic conciliations. However, we have seen that such consensus cannot suffice to guarantee the desired epistemic quality of decisions. Any consensus attained in decision-making processes within our sub-ideal epistemic reality, which is far from the ideal of rational consensus in ideal conversational circumstances, simply cannot automatically generate epistemic quality by the virtue of a fair method. The methods of consensus and public debate inherent to deliberative democracy simply cannot justify epistemic optimism, and instead facilitate the emergence of unacceptable vices such as epistemic conservatism, narrowness and conventionality that can not generate epistemically valuable decisions.

Although the standpoint of consensualism is distinguished in opposition to expertism, we have seen that the only acceptable form of consensualism is the one which somehow distances itself from its more 'vulgar' version. While vulgar consensualism can result in the tyranny of ignorance, limited consensualism subtly introduces expertise by bringing in either experts or institutions. The democratic division of epistemic labour which allocates certain aspects of decision-making to either citizens or experts – thus including both consensus and expertise – has emerged as an extremely interesting option. A compromise between consensualism and expertism manifested itself in a certain 'enhanced' consensualism that includes the criterion of expertise, or 'enhanced' expertism that acknowledges the qualities of consensus.

I conclude that the initial version of consensualism revealed itself as an unacceptable hybrid position. Although the final role of consensus in democratic decision-making processes must not be denied, the exact formula of the desirable balance of expertise and consensus remains an important issue. This discussion about consensus has allowed us to eliminate the stance that experts possess a fundamental epistemic authority which implies blind trust or uncritical deference. Experts can only be ascribed a derived epistemic authority which stems from a (continuous) consensus about their credibility and reliability in solving problems or generating epistemically valuable decisions.

6.
RELIABILIY DEMOCRACY AND THE ROLE OF EXPERTS IN A DEMOCRATIC SOCIETY

6.1. *Reliability democracy and veritism*

The concept of *reliability democracy* was introduced by Alvin Goldman in order to distinguish it from the consensualist approach: he holds that those who focus on consensus as the objective of good deliberation could not label their stance as *epistemic* and contrasts them with those who plead for reliable, i.e., truth-conductive democratic procedures or decision-making methods. He calls this a *reliabilist approach to democracy* and classifies the proponents of such a justification of democracy as *reliability democrats*. While rational public deliberation isn't in itself sufficient to yield epistemically desirable doxastic outputs, it might be possible to add specific constrains to the standards of public deliberation so that – if a group satisfied those constraints in addition to the initial criteria – public deliberation could increase the group's reliability. Should we aim to epistemically defend democracy on the basis of its ability to generate correct political decisions, it would be helpful to demonstrate (i) how specific features of (deliberative) democracy contribute to the best decision and (ii) why such features are comparatively epistemically more valuable than available alternatives. Goldman offers an analysis of the Condorcet Jury Theorem as a paradigmatic democratic majoritarian decision-making method in order to illustrate his account of reliable decision-making processes.

I will proceed by presenting the position of reliability democracy as a derivative of Goldman's veritism. Namely, Goldman is a reliabilist in individual epistemology and a veritist in social epistemology. Reliability democracy is a stance generated by the addition of veritist criteria to a specific topic of social epistemology – the justification of democracy. Goldman's version of reliability democracy is a counter-position to proceduralism: as a fundamentally epistemological position, it focuses exclusively on the epistemological properties of social practices and institutions, while somewhat overlooking the significance of the ethical/political. It would be inappropriate to claim that Goldman considers the ethical and political justification of democracy unimportant, but it certainly isn't the focal point of his interest – nor is the harmonization of the epistemic and the ethical/political.

This is the exact reason why proceduralists objected that standard approaches to the epistemic justification of democracy, the best example of which is veritism, instrumentalize democratic procedures for epistemic purposes. However, it would be both rash and incorrect to conclude that this was indeed what veritism had intended (like proceduralism genuinely sought to reduce epistemic virtues to the ethical and political). Goldman's goal is to demonstrate the importance and methodology of analysing the social desirability of institutions from an epistemic perspective. However, when contextualized within our discussion about harmonizing epistemic and ethical/political virtues, Goldman's focus on epistemic assessments seems to entail a certain epistemic instrumentalism and a possible proclivity for elitism.

A far more fruitful stance for the purposes of our discussion is the position of Thomas Christiano, which he – being a philosopher of politics – didn't identify as reliability democracy, but which it definitely is. It's important because he seeks the possibility of achieving the desired epistemic goal in the reliable truth-sensitive mechanisms of deliberative democracy, while aiming to maximally preserve ethical and political values. I especially agree with Christiano's emphasis on the importance of appropriately dividing epistemic labour between citizens and experts. He himself offers a suggestion of a possible division of labour respectful of the assumption that the epistemic justification of democracy is just as important as the political or, in simpler terms, respectful of the thesis that democracy should have the epistemic property of generating epistemically high-quality decisions or solutions to problems. Although I principally agree with his version of reliability democracy, which doesn't sacrifice the democratic nor the epistemic desiderata, I will propose a certain addition that might imbue his solution with additional epistemic and political responsibility.

6.1.1. *Veritism as social reliabilism*

As the undisputable father of social epistemology[1], Goldman set the foundations of the discipline by making a key distinction between three approaches to assessing the epistemic desirability of social groups, practices and institutions: consensualism, expertism and veritism. Theories of justification in a social context were conceived as certain correlates of theories of justification from individual epistemology: coherentism, foundationalism and reliabilism[2]. Consensualism is an approach that evaluates social practices or institutions in terms of whether they are the product of conciliation and the extent to which they manage to further generate and promote it. Like coherentism, which only considers beliefs justified if they are internally justified, i.e., (somehow) coherent with other already existing beliefs, consensualism justifies those social entities and practices that have or generate the consensual support of existing stakeholders in social processes. Let's note that consensualist justification is also internal because it entirely stems from coherence with the existing stances of citizens. For example, according to the consensualist criterion, a desirable school curriculum would optimally reconcile the disparate views of all interested parties - teachers, parents, scientists, political options, religious standpoints and others. Expertism, on the contrary, justifies those social practices or institutions that accept and promote the attitudes of experts. Like foundationalism, which deems a certain group of beliefs fundamental in the sense that other beliefs are justified as long as they can be derived from the fundamental, expertism declares expert stances as fundamental, so other beliefs are only justified insofar as they reflect the beliefs of experts. Recalling the previous example of the school curriculum, a justified program would have to reflect and continuously promote the views of experts/scientists.

Finally, veritism assesses social practices or institutions on the basis of their reliability, their capacity to continuously generate true beliefs. Its social correlate is reliabilism, a theory of justification which justifies those beliefs that are generated by reliable processes or methods that guarantee the attainment of true beliefs. According to veritism, a school curriculum is justified if it generally generates true beliefs or foundations for the further production of truth. Coherentism

---

1 Goldman, 1987.

2 For more, see Prijic-Samarzija, 2005.

and consensualism seek justification in the internal coherence of beliefs, expertism and foundationalism in their association with the fundamental beliefs that are most likely to be true, and veritism and reliablism divulge it from reliable methods of forming beliefs.

Since we have already thoroughly discussed the positions of consensualism and veritism, we will now more closely outline Goldman's veritist attitude[3]. It is crucial to understand the veritist criteria for determining whether certain social practices, groups or institutions practice reliable methods. More specifically, we have to demonstrate when a certain practice generates true beliefs. While consensualism and expertism apply easily comprehensible methods of diagnosing social desirability, it is somewhat unclear how we should estimate the veritist capacities of practices and institutions, and how we should recognize the continuous reliability of a social entity. Veritist assessments utilize five criteria: (i) *reliability* or the ratio of generated true and false beliefs (ii) *power* or total productivity in producing beliefs; (iii) *fecundity* or the capacity of a social practice or institution to solve the problems of interested citizens; (iv) *speed* or the time needed to achieve the most important goals; (v) *efficacy* or the cost of achieving goals. In short, an epistemically justified institution will, for example, generate more true beliefs than falsities in the context of relevant productivity (so that we wouldn't be talking about a single true belief), make those beliefs effective in solving the significant problems of those concerned in the shortest possible time for the lowest possible price. Using Goldman's more specific example, a cultural institution that only educates a limited elite wouldn't satisfy the veritist criteria, regardless of its good veritist results and the welfare of that small elite. Such practices of cultural institutions are insufficiently fruitful and their final social effectiveness reveals them to be both too expensive and overly time-consuming. More specifically, Goldman would disregard a school curriculum that fails to generate true beliefs and doesn't appropriately cater to those who demand better education as undesirable even if it was based on a consensual attitude and the reconciliation of all relevant participants. A school curriculum that is suggested by experts, but which fails to address the issue of better education in highly particular circumstances, proves to be financially unsound or cannot be implemented in due time, would be regarded as equally undesirable.

---

3 For more, see in Goldman, 1987., 1991., 1992., 1999., 2014.

It is clear that Goldman simply supplemented the reliabilist criteria from individual epistemology (reliability and power) with social ones (fecundity, speed and efficacy). The epistemic value of a social practice or institution isn't only measured in terms of truth (recalling the example of a cultural institution), but also by the beneficial influence of true beliefs on citizens and society.

I personally think that this is one of the most creative contributions to social epistemology that doesn't only excellently identify potential approaches to the epistemic evaluation of social practices and institutions, but also demonstrates the fruitfulness of extending the already developed views of individual epistemology onto the social. In his later works, Goldman mostly develops and elaborates the position of veritism as a social reliabilism, continuously emphasizing that social practices and entities need to be evaluated in terms of their contribution to generating knowledge or true, justified beliefs. According to Goldman, social entities such as science, law, media, educational practices and institutions are as epistemically desirable as they develop reliable procedures or methods of generating true beliefs. Goldman meticulously elaborated Anglo–Saxon jurisdictional procedures, analysing whether the concrete procedures of advocacy, the jury system and judicial powers have the potential of reliably producing true beliefs. Despite objections regarding the alleged myth of objective and neutral science postulated by postmodernists, social constructivists and others, Goldman convincingly proves that science is still, in comparison with any alternative system of generating beliefs and solving problems, the one with the most reliable methods and procedures (experiments, publications, reviews, conceptual and critical analyses and arguments) of generating truth-conductive beliefs and theories. In other words, Goldman holds that truth is a value that couldn't possibly cause harm to society/citizens and democracy.

Goldman had never systematically analysed the relationship between veritism, consensualism and expertism, nor any of my further implications: for instance, the special role of experts in discussions can be a reliable procedure of generating true beliefs in a social world, just like certain forms of rational consensus that encourage epistemic diversity among participants can contribute to the truth. He has, however, emphasized that the essential veritist concept of truth can provide both consensualism and expertism with epistemic validity – the epistemic content of these positions depends on their involvement with the value of truth. This strong claim that assessments of social practices and entities must be pertinent to the traditional epistemic value of truth tactically opposed tendencies (dominant in traditional philosophy of politics, but also in constructivism and postmodernism) to negate this epistemic component in favour of the ethical and political. However, had we decided to identify epistemic quality with truth, the capacity of social practices and institutions to produce epistemically valuable beliefs would be excluded from any further analysis, and assessments of social desirability would be entirely reduced to political and ethical judgments. As was often exemplified by proceduralists, this reduction is a response to the challenging task of detecting what is true when it comes to social issues. Either way, Goldman honestly considers veritism, rather than consensualism or expertism, the optimum analytical platform for discerning epistemically desirable social practices: epistemic quality can only be guaranteed by truth-conductive and reliable procedures, rather than inferred from the mere facts of consensus or expertise. The mere possession of consensual or the stance of an expert stance does not guarantee truth. Methods of involving experts or attaining consensus can only be acceptable if they are proven capable of contributing to the best possible decisions. In other words, they must be comparatively epistemically more valuable than their alternatives by possessing specific epistemic properties most appropriate for the pursuit of truth.

Our earlier discussion has already made it evident that I'm inclined to fully agree with Goldman's conclusion that both the stances of experts (just because of their declarative expertise) and consensus (just because it was generated by conciliation) would be emptied of their epistemic qualities once they disregarded the epistemic virtues of truth, truth-conductivness, problem-solving and correctness. However, it should be noted that Goldman's concept of reliable and truth-conductive procedures would similarly lose much of its content without rival justificatory strategies: discursive conciliations and confidence in experts are the most promising existing candidates for the status of reliable procedures that generate epistemically valuable beliefs.

6.1.2. *Social reliability of the democratic methods of majority voting and deliberation*

Regarding the epistemic justification of democracy, Goldman puts emphasis on assessing whether the paradigmatically democratic procedure of majority rule is genuinely a reliable method of ensuring epistemically valuable decisions. French Enlightenment figure Marquise de Condorcet argued that majority rule only increases the probability of a true decision in cases of binary voting (yes/no). Furthermore, his Condorcet Jury Theorem says that if each individual voter in a group is likely not to hold a true opinion in a binary dilemma, the resulting majority judgment would have significantly more chances to be true than any individual attitude. As the size of the voting body increases, the likelihood of the majority being right rapidly approaches the value of 1.0. A similar accolade to the epistemic power of information pooling was articulated as 'the wisdom of crowds'. It is best illustrated by a little experiment in rural England, where 800 people were invited to estimate the weight of a displayed ox. Despite the fact that most participants seriously erred in their individual judgments, the resulting average estimate was almost completely accurate.

Nonetheless, Goldman proves that majority rule is not an unconditionally reliable and truth-conductive method, but only conditionally. Firstly, the group tends to be right only if each individual voter has the probability of 0.52 of being correct. But there is no *a priori* guarantee that each voter will have such a likelihood to be right. Should there be a probability that each individual voter will be wrong, we would be hard-pressed to unconditionally expect a true outcome. Secondly, CJT requires voters to form their opinions completely independently of each other, where the condition of independence is difficult to satisfy. In short, Goldman attempts to show that this method – just like any other manifestation of the paradigmatically democratic practice of majority rule – is not an (unconditionally) reliable way of attaining true/correct or otherwise epistemically valuable decisions.

Goldman is equally critical of deliberation as a method that, according to many proponents of deliberative democracy, should precede voting in order to epistemically improve the voters' stances. According to Goldman, deliberation doesn't entail a single property that objectively guarantees the epistemic quality of decisions. His rationale builds on the core stance that actual circumstances of forming beliefs and making decisions are a sub-ideal epistemic environment which cannot autonomously produce truth from a free flow of ideas by the means of some 'invisible hand'. [4] We have repeatedly outlined empirical

---

4 Goldman, 1991a., 1999. See also Alvin I. Goldman and James C. Cox. 1996. 'Speech, Truth, and the Free Market for Ideas', *Legal Theory,* 2: 1–32; Alvin I. Goldman and Moshe Shaked. 1991. 'An Economic Model of Scientific Activity and Truth Acquisition', *Philosophical Studies*, 63: 31–55.

evidence in favour of some kind of deliberative pessimism – the realization that people who participate in discussions are inadequately informed, capacitated and motivated to make epistemically valuable decisions. It has also been shown that knowledge and the capacity to acquire correct beliefs are inversely proportional to self-confidence and the openness towards questioning one's own views in order to embrace new, different and sophisticated data. In addition, debaters are more likely to hold on to their existing prejudices, assumptions and personal interests than to reflect upon epistemic responsibility and the common good.

In other words, it seems that democratic methods in themselves – as methods which respect participation, inclusiveness and fairness – are not reliable processes that automatically ensure desirable epistemic quality. In order to fulfill the desired epistemic goal, these methods must posses additional attributes that improve their capacity to generate epistemically valuable beliefs and decisions. Goldman's veritism may seem to imply a certain pessimism regarding the epistemic justification of democracy and the sheer possibility of harmonizing epistemic and political/ethical values. Although this may sound unfavourable for democratic decision-making procedures, it would be rash to conclude that it is entirely impossible to epistemically justify democracy. Goldman's principal intention is to underline the importance of developing reliable or more reliable democratic processes that will improve the likelihood of attaining epistemically valuable decisions. There is no need to perceive Goldman's standpoint – or any other point that gives primacy to the epistemic quality of decisions – as a threat to democratic values. Instead, they are a plea for epistemically justified democratic decision-making methods. For instance, Goldman notes that epistemically diverse groups of voters gather wider evidential pools and thus reliably augment the likelihood of attaining true decisions. Moreover, he refers to a study that portrays successful problem-solving as a function of methodological diversity rather than the individual abilities of participants[5]. Aware of the prospect of hybrid assessments, Goldman and Blanchard postulate the promising potential of social moral epistemology to appraise the morality of social practices somehow related to the production of knowledge, truth

5 Lu Hong and Scott Page. 2004. 'Groups of Diverse Problem Solvers Can Outperform Groups of High-Ability Problem Solvers', *Proceedings of the National Academy of Sciences of the United States*, 101(46): 16385–16389.

or justification[6]. However, Goldman refrains from a more detailed pursuit of this discussion about hybrid virtues and remains focused on purely epistemic inquiries.

6.2. *Division of labour and reliable democratic mechanisms*

The standpoint of reliability democracy teaches us that social epistemology or, more precisely, its assessment of the epistemic properties of democracy oriented towards postulating criteria for social decision-making methods aims to improve this system by encouraging rational, justified, reliable and truth-oriented processes. In other words, proponents of reliability democracy assume the stance that the qualities of democratic systems shouldn't only be defended in terms of equal rights, but also in the context of their ability to generate epistemically valuable political decisions. Goldman writes:

> "Writers who emphasize the way that genuine democracy makes use of 'situated knowledge' to improve the community's overall knowledge-ability make roughly this kind of social-epistemological contribution to democratic theory."[7]

This comment is obviously aimed at those philosophers of politics whose focus on political justification results in continuous negligence towards the epistemic.

Thomas Christiano is certainly one of the authors whom Goldman would describe as a valuable contributor to social epistemology: Christiano is a political philosopher who, without declaratively engaging in social epistemology as such, provided an important social-epistemological contribution to democratic theory. Christiano elaborates the methodology of making epistemically optimal decisions in a deliberative democracy.[8] Having diagnosed the core problem of democracy as the question of integrating the plausible idea that some people are more knowledgeable about certain issues than others with the democratic ideals and principles of equality and freedom, he inquires whether we can successfully harmonize epistemic and political goals. This early diagnosis already discloses his stance that any justification of democracy must include both civic consensus and the role of experts. Reliability democracy, and especially

6 Goldman and Blanchard, 2015.
7 Goldman, 2010a., p. 25.
8 Christiano, 2008., 2012.

Christiano's excellent version of it, should therefore not be misjudged as a position that challenges the aforementioned proposals. It simply insists on the attitude that final decisions must possess epistemic value that is determined in terms of truth and seeks this goal in reliable democratic methods, which are unmistakeably epistemically more effective than their alternatives. Such methods will then, in one way or another, present the inclusion of a rational consensus and the role of experts as a fundamental advancement of existing democratic methods.

***

We will easily contextualize his stance once we have classified possible approaches to harmonizing epistemic and political goals into three main groups. The first approach to this issue is *traditional*, a standpoint that strictly separates epistemological and political values and goals. Consequently, traditionalists sternly reject not only the necessity, but also the sheer possibility of harmonizing political and epistemic justifications of democracy. These political philosophers share a prevalent and widespread credence in the primacy of the political justification of democracy: they mainly approach discussions about democratic with the aim of preserving the values of equality and freedom or resolving political issues, and pay little attention to the epistemic quality of decisions.[9] The aim of deliberation is not to generate (more) informed or epistemically better decisions, but to approach the intrinsic ideal of political equality. Deliberation has instrumental value in resolving conflicts and disagreements and is a method that allows disagreeing parties to resolve their dissent by the means of public, rational and impartial discourse. Instead of being perceived as an epistemic process that pursues epistemic values, public discussion is depicted as a strictly political process oriented towards the desired political result; exchanges of reasons are a means of rapidly conciling different stances, rather than producing epistemically valuable decisions.[10]

The second *reductionist* approach stems from constructivist tendencies to reduce epistemic goals and values to the political and ethical. This approach is best characterized by the position of (pure) epistemic proceduralism.[11] As evident from its very name, epistemic proceduralism accentuates the importance of epistemically justifying

---

9 Rawls, 1971., 1993., 1997.; Gaus, 1997., 2009.

10 Manin, 1987.; Sustain 1993., 2006.; Michelman, 1989.; Benhabib 1996.; Fishkin, 1992.

11 Estlund, 1997., 2008.; Peter, 2008., 2012.

democracy and argues that a fair democratic procedure is in itself sufficient to guarantee epistemically valuable decisions. In spite of its efforts to appear focused on the epistemic justification of democracy and potentially hybrid in its orientation, this approach is essentially reductionist as it infers the epistemic quality of decisions from fair political procedures and fails to acknowledge independent epistemic value independent from the democratic procedure. Even when they recognize the procedure-independent epistemic value of truth and the possibility that the final result of a democratic discussion may not be of highest possible epistemic quality because of an imperfect procedure, proceduralists defend the primacy of decisions made in fair procedures over alternative solutions of higher epistemic quality.

Finally, only the third *hybrid perspective* genuinely strives to appropriatelly unite epistemic desiderata with the democratic ideals of equality and freedom. This approach proposes the division of epistemic labour between experts and citizens in decision-making processes and is the only one that can be considered truly hybrid in attempting to harmonize epistemic and political values. As we have seen, this approach includes certain aspects of both *consensualism* and *expertism* because it bases the division of labour on harmonizing civic stances in relation to those of experts. Christiano's attitude towards the division of epistemic labour reveals him as a true reliability democrat. Unlike Kitcher's emphasis[12] on the role of experts in ensuring an epistemically valuable consensus, he proposes democratic truth-sensitive mechanisms – reliable methods and procedures that divide epistemic labour between citizens and experts in order to produce correct, truth-conductive and true beliefs/decisions.[13] Thomas Christiano evidently favours the idea of harmonizing epistemic and political justification by dividing epistemic labour between citizens and experts.

> "The purpose of democratic deliberation is epistemic and practical, it is to uncover facts about interests and equality and how best to pursue them for the purpose of making good collective decisions. (...) The process of deliberation requires a division of labour (...). But the division of labour has traditionally been a problem for democracy and a problem for an egalitarian society. (...) The question is how can we enjoy the advantages of the division of labour and politics while treating each other as equals?"[14]

12 Kitcher, 2011a.
13 Christiano, 2012.
14 Christiano, 2012., p. 27–28.

Christiano's proposal to divide epistemic labour between experts and citizens remains recognizes the problems commonly generated by epistocratic approaches. What is more, he personally criticizes the privileged treatment of experts in decision-making processes due to the impossibility of consensually discerning the truly most compentent experts. He accentuates the distinction between technical and moral competences. The concept of democracy/equality is not an intuitively plausible method of truth searching in science – a field that prioritizes the stances of the most educated. On the other side, he notes, no distribution of social power based on ranking moral competence could satisfy the public because of the controversies surrounding the possible ranking methods. There is no test (substantial or procedural) that could adequately assess moral competence. This does not mean that Christiano presupposes that all individuals are equally competent, that we ought to think of each other as equally competent, or even that our competencies are incommensurable. He simply understands that people will probably deviate in their assessments of other people's competences. Each person has the right to conclude that another person is more competent than herself and/or others, and to think of that person as a certain advisor or leader with regard to moral subjects. Christiano's main point is that, even if we assume that there is genuine expertise in moral issues and politics and that there are relevant inequalities in moral competences, no expertise could be generally acceptable in a way that would allow us to simply delegate the entire decision-making process to experts:

> "(...) a scheme that gives greater political power to the well-educated must inevitably appear to many to give their interests greater weight than the others. This conclusion and the principles of equality and weak publicity together imply that such a distribution of power would be unjust."[15]

Christiano thus strives to define an option that would approach experts with seriousness without succumbing to usual epistocratic blunders: he claims that we cannot defend a democratic deliberation in which ordinary citizens continously ignore relevant scientific knowledge whilst deliberating on issues that clearly require such information. In other words, he calls for an epistemic division of labour that respects truth-sensitive democratic decision making procedures. A rejection of

15 Christiano, 2008., p. 121.

epistocracy doesn't automatically entail a comprehensive refusal to include experts in the division of epistemic labour. Since experts can improve the epistemic quality of decisions, epistemic justification of democracy must not ignore the advantages of their contribution.

6.2.1. *Role of experts in reliable democratic mechanisms*

Christiano holds that any democratic decision-making process needs to be truth-sensitive. Given that truth-insensitivity can be identified as one of the chief challenges of democratic deliberation, we must inquire how to unite specialized scientific knowledge with democratic deliberation with the goal of reaping its evidently positive influence on good decision-making.

According to Christiano, any discussion about the democratic division of labour ought to begin by defining the role of citizens. Citizens are the driving element of society because (i) they choose the aims of society, (ii) they are the sources of different and competing research programs in various expert domains and (iii) they assess and evaluate whether socially defined goals have been appropriately met. Expertise is not as relevant in deciding on social goals as it in developing legislation and policies. Christiano stresses that the Downsian model of division of labour between citizens and politicians (experts) is a vastly oversimplified picture.[16] A good division of labour needs to include the process of differentiated deliberation between various levels of experts: deliberation among interest group associations, political parties, political staffers, newspapers, media, universities (experts in economics, sociology, law, political science, and the natural science) think tanks, parts of the administration, web logs and other institutions and groupings characteristic of democratic societies. These various experts use their particular expertise to determine how to implement the aims decided on by citizens. Expertise plays a dual role in democratic deliberation: on one hand, there are highly sophisticated deliberations among experts regarding the best theories for crafting policies; on the other hand, expertise acts as a certain external filter of deliberations among other parts of the division of labour – such as politicians and ordinary citizens.

There are four main democratic mechanisms within the deliberative process that ensure that (i) experts devotedly pursue the

16 Downs, 1957.

aims of citizens (*principal agent problem*) and that (ii) decisions are of the highest attainable quality (*problem of truth-sensitivity*). These four principles – solidarity, overlapping understanding, competition, sanctions – guarantee truth-sensitivity and simultaneously defend civic interests.

Solidarity is a mechanism by which two persons may be motivated to support each other's aims because of the similarity of their backgrounds and like-mindedness. People are like-minded when they share political and moral aims and have some broadly common sense of how to achieve these aims. When citizens share this like-mindedness with experts they can trust that the experts will pursue these common aims despite the fact that their opportunities and capacities for understanding and monitoring the experts are relatively limited. *Overlapping understanding* refers to the state of affairs in which two or more people share some expertise and do not share other expertise. This overlapping intelligibility allows citizens to partially appreciate the displayed rationale despite being unable to fully understand the experts' theories. The fact that there are many persons who understand different parts of the rationale makes it possible to monitor the theorizing and honesty of experts. *Competition* between experts sustains the quality of the decision-making process at the highest level. Each set of overlapping experts ensures that members who support their own viewpoint/party and those who support others genuinely act in accordance with the best available theories. Different expert approaches to political viewpoints, conceptions of aims and political parties or fractions ensure that they will regard the evidence, reasoning and arguments that opposing experts would not take into account. Finally, the system imposes a variety of *sanctions* upon those who fail to pursue the aims in a faithful and competent manner. The system includes networks of scientists who monitor the efficacy of policies in attaining goals. Given that a context immediately recognizes incompetence, errors and unfaithfulness, substandard experts would be denied their trust-worthiness, perceived competence, political support, political and administrative positions, etc.[17]

It is crucial to repeat that Christiano – despite recognizing the role of experts – doesn't support a certain form of expertism. He seeks the core of epistemic justification in reliable democratic mechanisms that insure the production of truth-sensitive decisions by engaging experts:

---

17 Christiano, 2012., pp. 37–42.

> "When the mechanisms I described are working well, the external connection between the social science and the policy-maker can be a reliable one for producing reasonably good decisions."[18]

He is a reliability democrat *par excellence* in Goldman's sense because he precisely detects this 'additional constraint on the standards of public deliberation' which appropriately satisfies the epistemic rationale of truth conduciveness. Possible additions to public debates that need to be introduced and cultivated are, for example, networks of experts with different backgrounds and from various institutions that monitor the implementation of policies they hadn't made themselves; the imperative to publicly present policies and their outcomes in order to enable civic reviews and criticism – thus encouraging the commitment of scientists who wish to be rewarded instead of criticized; competitive teams of experts who propose different policies in order to make other teams more motivated to improve them; mechanisms of educating or informing non-experts to make them more capable of evaluating experts or achieving overlapping understanding. These and similar procedures have the quality of being truth-conductive: experts are given a key place in decision-making so as to ensure the production of epistemically top quality decisions. Procedures are deliberately designed to preserve the qualities of democracy and enable the achievement of ethical/political goals, while improving epistemic quality.

6.2.2. *Role of citizens in reliable democratic mechanisms: external and internal epistemic justification*

We must note that Christiano doesn't expect citizens and politicians to completely comprehend specific expertise or complex scientific theories in order to consider a decision-making process epistemically or democratically justified. This implies that citizens and politicians can choose which theory to act upon or which decision to accept without possessing all available evidence or fully understanding the underlying rationale. The crucial precondition of truth-sensitive decisions is a set of reliable democratic mechanisms that citizens and politicians can rely on. In this respect, the belief, judgment or decision attained by the most reliable procedures is epistemically *external* to citizens. Reliability democracy at large, and Christiano as its current representative, promote external epistemic justification: a decision

18 Christiano, 2012., p. 44.

remains epistemically justified as long as it is produced by a truth–sensitive mechanism, even if citizens and politicians are not fully aware of the reasons which make that decision epistemically justified or true. Citizens and politicians who favour one policy over another cannot comprehensively defend it against their adversaries in the policy-making world as their confidence stems from the fact that a certain community of experts claims something and that there are reliable mechanisms that prevent them from abusing their expert status.

Epistemically, the problem of deference to experts boils down to the objection that we cannot be justified/responsible in accepting expert stances if we cannot understand them, grasp them or credibly assess their correctness: I cannot be epistemically justified nor responsible in saying that a certain decision doesn't strike me as understandable or at all true while simultaneously agreeing to accept it as true – even under the assumption that this is truth-conductive. Furthermore, deference implies an imperative of blind trust and essentially disconnects citizens from the decision-making process by invoking an undesirable element of epistocracy: the mere fact that democratic mechanisms are truth-sensitive (much like the fact that experts allegedly know better) cannot suffice to justify the coercion of citizens to obey. It seems that the externalism of reliability democracy can imply epistemically unjustified deference (which underwent substantial proceduralist critiques) or a blind confidence in decisions we do not understand, as well as a democratically unjustified imperative to obey a decision or solution that is not, in the relevant sense, ours.

Christiano's promising proposal to divide epistemic labour between citizens and experts on the basis of clearly defined roles and reliable or truth-sensitive democratic mechanisms can be adapted to dodge the critique of deference almost inherent to debates about epistocracy. We have repeatedly shown that citizens and politicians simply lack the necessary expertise to appraise the content of experts' beliefs, judgement and decisions.[19] Even scientists do not have enough evidence to understand or assess the reports of other specialists in their field.[20] We are all, more or less, in the position of a non-expert who does not have (or even cannot ever attain) a sufficient level of expertise or experience to understand and evaluate all decisions made

19 Richard Foley. 1994. 'Egoism in Epistemology', in Schmitt, Frederick F. (ed.), *Socializing Epistemology: The Social Dimensions of Knowledge* (Lanham, Md: Rowman and Littlefield), pp. 53–73.

20 Hardwig, 1991.

by all experts. However, this does not automatically mean that (i) our reliance and trust are necessarily blind or even gullible, nor that (ii) we are forcefully coerced into deferring to experts or reliable mechanisms.

The inevitability of our reliance on experts stems from an important epistemic need derived from epistemic dependence and our lack of expertise. However, we should demand that citizens and politicians have relevant epistemic access to decisions. They have to participate in the decision-making procedure in an epistemically active and responsible way: their confidence in experts and reliable democratic procedures needs to be based on an awareness of their epistemically dependant position and, consequently, on an epistemically conscientious rationale behind relying on experts and democratic mechanisms that ensure the truth-sensitivity of decisions. In brief, the stern externalism assumed in reliability democracy should be substituted with a more epistemically and democratically justified internalist approach: citizens have to rely on experts and truth-sensitive procedures on the basis of reasons, evidence or because they ackowledge the reliability of decision-making processes. A result of deliberation is not epistemically and democratically justified in virtue of the fact that it is based on a reliable mechanism which delegates a special role to experts, but because citizens assess or understand that the expert decision is, for some reason, acceptable. For example, the inclusion of credible experts who generate policies in a competitive and diverse scientific knowledge environment and subject them to several serious reviews (the external condition) is unacceptable unless citizens are provided adequate evidence to know that these conditions are met (the internal condition).

There are reasons to assume that Christiano supports a similar view:

> "The policy-maker's decision is not completely unjustified because they have reason to think that the theory on which they are operating is well thought of in the expert community. The endorsement of a number of experts gives them confidence that the theory is a good one though they do not see the reasons directly. (…) The policy-makers act on the basis of information shortcuts when they take the assent of experts as defining the boundaries of acceptable science. (...) But that reliability, I contend, cannot be established without the phenomena of solidarity, overlapping understanding, sanctions, and competition being present at least to some significant degree."[21]

21 Christiano, 2012., pp. 45–46.

So, in contrast to the reliabilist concept of externalism which considers decisions epistemically and democratically justified as long as there are reliable democratic mechanisms that produce truth-sensitive decisions, I would like to emphasise the necessity of more participation or an ameliorated epistemic and democratic access of citizens and policy makers to decisions. More precisely, while the responsibility of a reliability democrat lies in ensuring a reliable democratic procedure, the internalist approach I am proposing stresses that it is necessary for citizens and policy-makers to understand why it is rational to bestow reliance and trust to expertise and reliable democratic procedures. Even if citizens and policy-makers cannot have comprehensive understanding or possess all the evidence needed to appraise the entirety of expert stances, their reliance or trust would be epistemically justified as long as they have enough evidence about the reliability of procedures through which experts make their decisions. For instance, that could consist of evidence about the experts' moral and epistemic characters (or the reputation of their institutions) or evidence about whether the relevant contextual (conversational) circumstances prevent deception, lying and incompetence or support trustworthiness. Citizens and policy-makers could also demand proof that Christiano's truth-sensitive mechanisms – such as solidarity, overlapping understanding, competition and sanctions – are present and responsibly implemented. More precisely, a good democratic division of epistemic labour needs to encourage more epistemic agency in citizens: they should have an active role in assessing which particular experts deserve trust and whether reliable mechanisms truly ensure the experts' trustworthiness.

It is true that the final epistemic quality of a decision depends on overall expertise and the reliability of procedures rather than on whether citizens or policy-makers possess the relevant evidence. However, the internalist approach assumes that the epistemic justification of deliberative democracy doesn't only espouse epistemically valuable decisions, but also concerns itself with the epistemic autonomy of citizens and their active epistemic participation/responsibility in accepting decisions. As we have previously elaborated, internalists wouldn't describe the special epistemic status of experts as a fundamental authority that implies deference or blind trust, but only as derived authority. Unlike fundamental authority, there is nothing undemocratic and epistemically unjustified in derived authority because citizens trust experts on the basis of a (consensually articulated) conscientious stance that it is more rational to trust these particular experts than to make decisions on their own. Moreover, the derived authority of experts only differs from the derived authority of non-experts to a degree that preserves the democratic egalitarian rationale. It seems that this additional requirement of internal access may render Christiano's reliability democracy more resistant to objections regarding epistemic authoritarianism and anti-egalitarianism, and even more impervious to criticisms of reliability epistocracy.

***

As we have seen, experts deserve to be given an important role in decision-making processes within deliberative democracy. Acknowledging the contribution of experts is not anti-democratic and is in no way synonymous with a defence of epistocracy. We have proved that neither the epistemic goal of truth nor the introduction of experts entail the alleged instrumentalization of democracy for epistemic purposes.

Our ongoing discussion about the epistemic justification of deliberative democracy has outlined several key conditions that should be incorporated into democratic procedures in order to ameliorate their reliability: (i) education – public discussions and exchanges of reasons should be based on educational and informative content that improves the participants' ability of conscientiously deliberate about various topics (ii) diversity – public debates should include citizens and experts with different perspectives who come from different communities and institutions, thus expanding the available pool of evidence (iii) non-egoism (inclusiveness, fairness, pluralism)–participants in public debate, both citizens and experts, must be aware of the cognitive constraints imposed by their presuppositions, worldviews and value systems, come to terms with their capacity to understand certain topics and maintain a disposition of openness towards different perspectives (iv) institutional organization –public discussions and decision-making processes must be initiated, monitored and guided by relevant institutional procedures that guarantee adherence to prerequisites (i) – (iii).

I have attempted to show that apprehension towards experts is both non-democratic as it neglects the potential of democracy to be an epistemically justified system and unfounded because there are obvious truth-sensitive mechanisms capable of controlling their influence. We have seen that the choice to include experts as epistemic authorities who are deserving of trust does not interfere with the epistemic autonomy of individuals and rational epistemic egalitarianism. This thesis will be further elaborated on the basis of evident discursive inconsistencies: given that ascribing trust to political authorities is not held questionable from the perspective of political autonomy, there is no reason to denounce the same trust as anti-democratic in the case of epistemic authority.

6.3. *Epistemic authority and epistemic autonomy*

We have repeatedly emphasized that objections to the concept of epistemic authorities in democracy can be classified as those which challenge the *democratic* or political justification of their special status in decision-making processes and those which question the *epistemic* justification or the actual epistemic advantages of their unique role in making decisions. Our initial assumption was that the epistemic quality of decisions, as an integral aspect of epistemic justification, should not be a threat to democracy and that the political/ethical and epistemic justifications of democracy should be harmonized. However, this attempt to introduce the epistemic quality of decision-making as a criterion of justification generated a fear of epistocracy – especially among debaters who come from philosophy of politics – which led to an unjustified denunciation of the role of expertise in democratic decision-making. Thus far, I have attempted to point out several facts. Firstly, if we want to responsibly discuss the epistemic quality of decisions, we must confront the continuously emerging issue of the status of experts and inquire whether democracy really can afford to relinquish people who ameliorate decision-making procedures. Secondly, the problem of experts cannot be resolved by brashly denying the very existence of experts in political affairs or by immediatelly reducing any recognition of expertise as a precarious apology of epistocracy. It is true that experts are constrained by their subjective perspectives and that the domain of political decision-making is unique in character, but it cannot be claimed that this neutralizes their expertise or that all people are equally expert in politics. Anyone who genuinely strives to justify democracy in both epistemical and political/ethical terms must acknowledge the advantages of dividing epistemic labour. A proper harmonization of virtues *must* be possible because its alternative will always prove in some way deficient: the system will either be epistemically ineffective and irresponsible or politically unjust. We have demostrated the possibility of developing reliable mechanisms of democratically involving experts, on the one hand, and reliable mechanisms of epistemically guiding deliberation, on the other.

Finally, we must resolve the claim that reliance on experts somehow disputes our epistemic autonomy and that the mere fact of deference to authorities entails something immensely hamful to us and our intellectual capabilities – something that almost jeopardizes the ethical/political dimension of our involvement in the intellectual life of democracy. Let us continue by subjecting the aforementioned challenge to the status of experts to more detailed scrutiny.

6.3.1. *Rational and egoistic epistemic autonomy*

Epistemic autonomy has been touted as the highest epistemic value in the works of Plato, Descartes, Locke and Kant.[22] Moreover, these philosophical greats unanimously supported the stance that truth necessitates an epistemically autonomous agent who is independent of authorities and thus capable of free reflection. We can never consider others as trustworthy as we perceive ourselves because of the constant prospect of mistakes caused by deception, intentional or unintentional lies, incompetence, their passions or interests and even blatant malice or capriciousness. Epistemic self-sufficiency assumes the position of our so-called privileged access to our mental states and gives primacy to the first person perspective: everyone should rely primarily on their own cognitive abilities and conclusions to later evaluate and eventually adopt the attitudes of others from that perspective. An intellectually autonomous person has no need for authorities because there is no rationally grounded argument for relying on the authorities of others, according to Elisabeth Fricker.[23] While she is definitely able to accept the attitudes of others, she is free not to – irrespective of the objective epistemic quality of those attitudes.

---

22 Plato, 1997.; Locke, 1690/1975. See also, Descartes, Rene. *The Philosophical Writings of Descartes*, vol.1, ed. and trans. by Cottingham John, R. Stoothoff and D. Murdoch (New York: Cambridge University Press, 1967/1985); Immanuel Kant. *Groundwork of the Methaphysics of Morals*, ed. and trans. by Gregor Mary (New York: Cambridge University Press, 1785/1997).

23 Elizabeth Fricker. 2006. 'Testimony and Epistemic Autonomy', in Lackey Jennifer and Ernest Sosa (eds.), *The Epistemology of Testimony* (Oxford: Oxford University Press), pp. 225–250.

On the other hand, we recognize the existence of epistemic authorities, experts whose beliefs we consider epistemically justified and whom we perceive as trustworthy. An epistemic authority is a person whom other people, following a conscientious appraisal, select as a guide to truth under the assumption that it is better to accept their attitude than to defend their own.[24] Note that the definition of an epistemic authority is not identical to the definition of an expert: the status of an epistemic authority stems from their relationship with another person who assumes that their superior expertise puts them in the position of an authority. Epistemic autonomy and reliance on epistemic authorities are not incompatible unless epistemic autonomy is interpreted as a radical epistemic egoism. Linda Zagzebski, for instance, defends the justifiedness of trusting epistemic authorities by rejecting such an interpretation of epistemic autonomy: "The most extreme form of epistemic self-reliance is one in which someone refuses to take the fact that someone has a given belief as a reason to believe it herself."[25] She claims that everyone agrees that certain people are more intelligent and educated than others or at least have better access to particular fields of information but that some still do not consider that a sufficient reason to acknowledge their epistemic authority in those domains. This kind of epistemic egalitarianism seems unjustified and irrational. In other words, it seems epistemically unfounded to deny that other people have good reasons to trust themselves in the manner I trust myself. Likewise, it seems epistemically justified to accept the attitude of another person should the circumstances encourage us to believe that it is more justified to rely on another than on oneself. Such trust in epistemic authorities is a necessary aspect of rationally understood epistemic autonomy because it stems from respect for epistemic authorities based on our readiness to rationally accept the attitudes of other persons whose expertise about a given subject we had – by means of intellectual conscientious assessment – perceived as more relevant than our own:

> "The authority of another person's belief for me is justified by my conscientious judgement that I am more likely to form a belief that survives my conscientious self-reflection if I believe what the authority believes than if I try to figure out what to believe myself."[26]

---

24 Zagzebski, 2012., 52.
25 Zagzebski, 2012., 52.
26 Zagzebski, 2012., p. 111.

Rational epistemic autonomy does not clash with trusting epistemic authorities. On the contrary, blindly rejecting expert attitudes in the virtue of epistemic egalitarianism can be an act of epistemic irresponsibility and radical dogmatism.

It is interesting that political philosophers, and they aren't alone, generally accept political authorities and the trust they are given. The tradition of modern liberalism infers political authority from our own authority over ourselves and the consequent autonomy to freely bestow our trust to political authorities. Such trust in political authorities is not considered a sacrifice of personal autonomy. The same stance should be assumed in discussing epistemic autonomy and epistemic authority. Epistemic autonomy, rationally understood, gives citizens the right and the obligation to accept the attitude of an epistemic authority on the basis of reasons independent from the contents of the expert's utterance. Citizens can also accept a stance different from their own should a conscientious appraisal lead them to the conclusion that it is better trust to the expert than themselves.[27] Epistemic authority, as we have previously emphasized, is not a *fundamental epistemic authority* that threatens epistemic autonomy, but a derived epistemic authority which constitutes a substantial aspect of rational epistemic autonomy.

6.4. *Peer disagreement: a conflict between the virtues of epistemic autonomy and trust in epistemic authorities*

A conscientious debate about the role of experts in democratic processes and the production of epistemically valuable decisions mustn't overlook the question of disagreement amongst experts who have proposed different solutions to a problem. Should we genuinely strive to defend the idea that experts or epistemic authorities ought to have a special place in decision-making processes, we are obliged to relieve the concern that disagreements can hinder the acquisition of good decisions. It should immediately be repeated that the mere fact that experts do not always agree in no way entails a relativization of their expertise or the unfounded conclusion that all disagreements arise from insurmountable differences in their subjective values, as suggested by some authors. However, our attempt to define reliable democratic methods of making quality decisions certainly requires

27 Zagzebski, 2012., pp. 106–113.

a model of resolving situations in which experts need to make a decision and disagree on how to solve the problem.

I see the situation of disagreement between experts as a certain conflict between the value of the expert's own epistemic autonomy and the value of trusting epistemic authorities. In simpler terms, a conflict between trusting your expertise and trustin the expertise of others. Every expert holds his epistemic self-sufficiency in high regard values and believes that his particular intellectual autonomy entails a certain responsibility for the reasons, evidence and arguments presented in his work. On the other hand, experts are the ones who most ardently emphasize the importance of expertise and reliance on experts. Moreover, trust among experts in times of heightened specialization, when there are no experts who can encompass vast areas of knowledge while maintaining consistent quality, is not just a choice, but a necessity.[28] Disagreements bring these two values into a state of conflict. We must inquire whether an expert in a situation of disagreement should believe in himself and persevere in his attitude, or, respecting his peer's expertise, decide to trust other epistemic authorities.

Within the domain of 'epistemology of disagreement', situations of disagreement are usually exemplifed by paradigmatic situations of disagreement between *experts*, situations in which equally informed and expert persons assume different attitudes about the same problem. And while philosophers who discuss peer disagreement usually find both the cause and the solution in their relationship to the available evidence and the justifiedness of the proposition which had stirred the disagreement, I am inclined to approach the problem from another perspective. I prefer the perspective of virtue epitemology that puts emphasis on the epistemic agent forced to resolve the conflict between the value of autonomy and the value of trusting epistemic authorities. I will proceed to briefly present the existing discussion and clarify what the conflict is actually about. In the end, I will try to argue in favour of *epistemic responsibility* or the attitude that disagreeing experts – just like anyone else – must adhere to epistemic virtues. In the case of democratic decision-making, we are speaking of adherence to hybrid virtues that harmonize ethical/political and epistemic virtues.

***

28 Hardwig, 1991.

As I have already mentioned, discussions of disagreement primarily pertain to disagreement between *peers*, where a peer is defined as a person with access to identical evidence (evidential peers), but also as a person comparable in terms of abilities and dispositions needed to correctly interpret that evidence (cognitive peers).[29] Disagreement is then defined as a situation in which peers do not agree in the sense that – on the basis of equal cognitive abilities and the same evidential grounds – one of them believes *p* while the other believes *not-p*. Philophers who discuss disagreement can be roughly classified into three groups with regard to the proposed solutions: the first group includes those who claim that it is best for experts, in the light of their disagreement and the fact that their stances bear equal weight, to suspend their attitudes; the second involves philosophers who argue that disagreements can be resolved by accepting that each side – since we are dealing with expert attitudes based on meticulous research – has the right to maintain its position; the third group consists of those who claim that disagreement is not a situation that needs to be resolved at all, but that experts can prudently remain in reasonable disagreement. I will now briefly outline each of these views and sketch out the undesirable epistemic and political consequences of each one of them.

If both disagreeing parties share the same evidence, the only reasonable conclusion is that only one party can be right; the wrong position should thus be revised or rejected in order to consenually accept its alternative. According to the *Equal Weight View*, two conflicted conclusions cannot possibly follow from the same evidence. However, although we have assumed that it is impossible for both parties (one claiming p and the other not-p) to be right on the basis of the same evidence, it still isn't known which side is in the wrong. In that circumstances it is best to relinquish both positions and suspend the conclusion until another occassion. Namely, neither side has any reason to believe that the peer whom they have disagreed with has made a mistake (precisely because they had access to the same evidence) one the one hand, but there is no reason to give up their own attitude on the other. Suspension thus emerges as the only solution to a disagreement between two sides who acknowledge the equal epistemic authority of the other.[30] It is important to note that this position presupposes the

29 Christensen and Lackey, 2012.

30 For more, see Feldman and Warfield, 2010.; Christensen, 2007.; Elga, 2007.; Feldman, 2007.

uniqueness thesis, according to which only one solution (and definitely not two clashing conclusions) can be justified by *unique* or identical evidential grounds. Peers who have access to the same evidence cannot be justified in supporting different attitudes.

This approach, often referred to as the *conciliatory view*, is valuable because it presumes respect for the epistemic authority of another person as well as for one's own. However, such a model of resolving disagreements inevitably leads to skepticism, especially in areas susceptible to frequent disagreements such as decision-making processes in society. If experts suspended their attitudes every time they disagreed, many problems would have to remain unresolved and decisions would be made seldom and with difficulty. Knowing that institutional and social functioning is abundant with disagreement this cannot be an advisable social practice. Although it adheres to the ethical and political values of inclusiveness and respect and despite its non-egoistic approach to epistemic autonomy, this inefficency renders it incapable of meeting the criteria of the hybrid approach.

Advocates of the second approach, the *Steadfast View*, evade the skeptical consequences of the previous approach by rejecting the thesis that unique evidence must justify only one solution. They instead accept the weaker *Permissiveness Thesis*, according to which the entirety of evidence can justify more than one point of view, so individuals are justified in prioritizing their own. In other words, it is justified to reject or ignore evidence that we have found ourselves in a situation of disagreement (*higher order evidence*) and to insist that the initial evidence which supports our original stance (*first order evidence*) justifies our decision to maintain it. The fact that a peer disagrees with us is thus irrelevant as long as we have confirmed that our stance is firmly grounded in evidence. Consequently, as the mere fact of disagreement requires a certain resolution (rather than the suspension of any decision), it seems rational for each party to respond by sticking to their initial position. Although this is not actually a matter of resolving disagreements, but merely of resolving the dilemma between maintaining one's own attitude or accepting that of another, proponents argue that abandoning one's own *evidence-based* standpoint in favour of a stance which we can only assume is equally grounded purely because of the existence of disagreement is in fact – irrational. What is more, radical advocates of this position – the Extra Weight View – actually find it rational to attribute more weight to one's own position simply because it is reasonable to have more confidence in one's own standpoint than in an (incompatible) another.[31] They claim that it is almost impossible to reject one's own standpoint only because it clashes with that of our peer, just like it is impossible to believe that our initial belief is not rational because others disagree with us.[32] An approach which automatically attibutes extra weight to our beliefs simply because they are ours clearly presupposes the first person perspective, but it also prioritizes the value of epistemic autonomy over the value of respecting the epistemic authority of others. Even the mildest version of this stance which postulates evidence about disagreement as an addendum to existing records – the *Total Evidence View* – argues that the mere fact of disagreement doesn't suffice to make someone reasonably renounce their original point of view.[33]

This stance successfully evades any objections about scepticism because it clearly postulates the correctness of one's own attitude over those of others. However, the weaknesses of this approach lie in its mistrust of other epistemic authorities and a specific justification of dogmatism evident in the epistemically egoistic rejection of all attitudes that are not ours or disagree with ours. Although it's common among experts, the dogmatism generated by this position could never be an epistemically justified social practice or contribute to the production of quality decisions. The fact that we can discern several good epistemic reasons in favour of this position doesn't render it capable of resolving the conflict between epistemic autonomy and epistemic authority.

Finally, the *Opacity View* is the third approach to resolving disagreements. This attitude declaratively rejects the concept of completely unique and overlapping evidence inherent to the very definition of peer disagreement.[34] Ernest Sosa argues that such overlap

---

31 Wedgwood, 2010.

32 Peter van Inwagen. 2010. 'We're right: they're wrong', in Feldman Richard and Ted A. Warfield (eds.), *Disagreement* (Oxford: Oxford University Press), pp. 10-28.

33 Thomas Kelly. 2005. 'The Epistemic Significance of Disagreement', in Gendler Tamar and John Hawthorne (eds.), *Oxford Studies in Epistemology*, vol. 1 (Oxford: Oxford University Press), pp. 167–196; Thomas Kelly. 2010. 'Peer Disagreement and Higher-Order Evidence', in Feldman Richard and Ted A. Warfield (eds.), *Disagreement* (Oxford: Oxford University Press), pp. 183–217.

34 Goldman, 2010b; Sosa 2010.; Peter, 2013a., 2013b., 2016. See also Earl Conee. 2010. 'Rational Disagreement Defended', in Feldman, Richard and Ted A. Warfield (eds.), *Disagreement* (Oxford: Oxford University Press), pp. 69–90.

is impossible for two reasons: (i) the entirety of evidence that someone possesses is too sophisticated and complex to be fully available to an epistemic agent while forming their stance (ii) we form our beliefs over long periods of time and don't only base them on concrete available evidence, but acknowledge various subtle influences from sources such as socialization, environmental impacts and like[35]. In other words, since peers cannot grasp the entire concrete evidential base due to the various complex influences underlying their attitudes, it is almost unbelievable that anyone even assumed that disagreeing peers could share overlapping evidence. Goldman makes a similar claim that the concept of overlapping evidential grounds is untenable because peers use different systems of epistemic norms to justify their beliefs.[36] Either way, this stance is characterized by the claim that inevitable differences in available evidence make disagreements something to be expected, which justifies the decision to remain in reasonable disagreement. The specific nature of evidence and the processes of forming and justifying our beliefs makes it impossible for disagreeing parties to claim that they had used the same or unique evidential material. This makes it rather difficult to expect that the parties will manage to resolve their disagreement by subjecting the evidence to more detailed scrutiny. In other words, disagreement is a natural consequence of different underlying beliefs and epistemic norms for evaluating one's beliefs, so there is nothing irrational in remaining in disagreement. Both disagreeing parties can rationally remain in disagreement even after an extensive and open discussion.

We have to admit that this stance dodges both scepticism and dogmatism: it avoids scepticism or the alleged 'spinelessness' by claiming that disagreeing parties are justified in maintaining their own position even if they highly respect the authority of their peer. It also avoids dogmatism or 'egoistic stubbornness' because the choice to stick to one's own attitude is not a consequence of ignoring the authority of our peer, but of our innate inability to relinquish a standpoint justified by our specific evidence. It is crucial to note that the Opacity View accepts the thesis that different conclusions cannot follow from unique evidential grounds (the uniqueness thesis) and dismisses the possibility that different attitudes can be based on the same evidence (the permissiveness thesis): its final conclusion is that unique evidential grounds are simply impossible to achieve.

---

35 Sosa, 2010., p. 290.
36 Goldman, 2010b.

Advocates emphasize the fact that this position circumvents both insecurity and fearfulness on the one hand and rigidity and stubbornness on the other, in order to promote tolerance towards different views and a desirable pluralism.[37] Nonetheless, this stance isn't devoid of its epistemic shortcomings. It implies a certain relativism or the attitude that different perspectives cannot be meaningfully compared nor normatively evaluated because their different (opaque) background beliefs and systems of norms can make them equally justified. This position thus perceives all incompatible views by disagreeing experts equally justified in the virtue of their different (unavailable or opaque) underlying evidential pathways and epistemic norms. As such, it obviously cannot be applied in social situations which require agency. This approach is somewhat odd in addressing the problem of disagreement by denying the very problem of disagreement. Their central claim is that this isn't really a matter of disagreement, but of an inevitable pluralism of standpoints. While the pluralism of standpoints and the concept of reasonable disagreement can initially seem like the right candidate for a socially desirable and politically correct approach, this attitude is untenable because it ultimately generates a defeatist stance about the redundancy of insisting on true solutions – rendering it ineffective in solving problems and making decisions.

6.5. *Disagreement and real-world epistemology*

As we have seen, all three positions reduce the controversy of disagreement to the question of how closely expert attitudes should be tied to available evidence (first and second order). Disagreements are consequently resolved by either suspending both attitudes or by maintaining the initial conflicted stances. First of all, it is relevant to note that the possibility of conciliation or the choice to accept the position of our peer is not even offered as a rational option. Secondly, this epistemic debate, in spite of its high sophistication and the usage of relevant and grounded arguments, actually didn't offer a single solution to real circumstances of peer disagreement. None of the three approaches manages to resolve disagreement: the first approach simply returns to the stage before the disagreement was established and the other two choose to remain in disagreement. Third, not only does none one of these approaches offer a solution to specific situations which

---

37 Peter, 2013a, 2013b., 2016.

require a decision or a reconciliation, but they do not even register it as an important problem that needs to be taken into account.

The fact remains that traditional epistemology rarely referred to the practical problems of real life. Here it is clearly evident that disagreement is discussed in the context of utterly idealized circumstances, in which epistemic agents are imagined as persons of almost unlimited logical abilities who are unburdened by concrete real-world situations. We have already pointed out that standard analytic epistemology entirely abstained from problematizing actual epistemic situations and that some epistemologists even argued that dealing with real epistemic issues isn't real epistemology.[38] However, disagreement is not just a theoretically interesting problem, but an important practical question of social epistemology and justification of democracy. Its appraisal and subsequent resolution in real social circumstances must take into account various different social or situational constraints of the disagreeing parties. With all due respect for the legitimacy of a purely epistemological perspective, applied epistemology approaches the controversy of disagreement as an epistemological problem connected with the agency of the epistemic agent. I have myself vocally opted for an approach in which the epistemic quality of a belief implies a certain efficiency in forming beliefs and making decisions that successfully resolve problems. Moreover, the particular problem of peer disagreement confronts us with an even more ambitious task: disagreements must be resolved so that the final decision is both epistemically optimal and politically/ethically correct. Our efforts to tackle this issue can benefit from undertaking a perspective that regards a wider picture than the one which only considers whether propositions are grounded on evidence. Instead of the traditional propositional approach, we can assume the framework of virtue epistemology and focus on an epistemic agent who has found himself in a real situation of disagreeing with his peer – a situation that needs to be resolved and which is characterized by the dilemma between trusting oneself and trusting other experts. However, before trying to imagine ourselves in the position of an epistemic subject who seeks to resolve the disagreement, it is important to understand the 'social situatedness' of disagreement.

38 Alston, 2005.

6.5.1. *Ideal theories and real-world epistemology: non-unitary character of epistemic situations*

These solutions to the problem of disagreement stem from ideal epistemological theories about the constituents of a justified or rational belief and thus abstract from concrete circumstances, obviously presuming that the application of idealized theoretical principles – regardless of which one – must be equally and invariably justified in all circumstances. Actual social circumstances in which peers disagree are evidently left entirely overlooked. It is true that Sosa and Goldman have shown that experts' beliefs and judgments are very specifically contextually and socially situated, as well as inevitably moulded by subtle and previously adopted conceptual and theoretical frameworks which experts interpret on the basis of personal epistemic norms. However, this account fails to comprehensively exhaust the social situatedness of disagreement.

The fact remains that real instances of disagreement confront us with a concrete (evidential and cognitive) peer. An epistemic agent who finds himself in a situation of disagreement with a person whom he recognizes as an expert and an epistemic authority doesn't only reconsider the (more or less accessible) evidence, but the entire context of disagreement. The agent evaluates the other expert on the basis of their peer relationship, his epistemic and moral character (trustworthiness, credibility and sincerity), as well as upon the particularities of the issue at hand, which includes their intentions, presuppositions and specific institutional backgrounds.

Although we are speaking about evidential and cognitive peers, there can never be a complete overlap in available evidence or specific expert profiles. Another person may be more or less knowledgeable than me in certain domains, and especially regarding highly specific issues; my peer may have special theoretical interests, intentions, experiences, professional histories and theoretical constraints when arguing in favour of an attitude that clashes with mine – he may be more or less susceptible to various underlying stereotypes and prejudices, and like. The epistemic character of an expert, which plays an important role in assessing their credibility and epistemic authority, cannot be derived from merely reconsidering available evidence. Experts may have additional practical intentions to defend their theories in order to achieve, preserve or reclaim their reputation, secure professional or financial gains and avoid the indignity of having their position 'defeated' in a disagreement. We might also be dealing with banal capriciousness, cowardice, status anxieties and other professional or less professional egoistic motives that hinder or increase the reliability of an expert. The moral character of the expert, much like the epistemic, is relevant when calculating the credibility of an epistemic authority. The epistemic and moral characters of an expert are differently manifested in different situations. For example, assessments of someone's authority cannot overlook the number of other experts who share their position in circumstances of disagreement. While the sheer number of experts on one side doesn't necessarily guarantee the quality of that position or automatically increase the reliability of that expert in a disagreement, it is certainly not an entirely irrelevant factor for evaluating his credibility.[39] These and numerous additional reasons can affect our assessment of an expert's credibility despite the fact that he is an evidential and cognitive peer. Such situational and relational elements should not be ignored when resolving disagreement.

We must note that situational and non-epistemic factors still cannot prevail: should our peer hold an epistemically valuable position, the sheer fact that he is a capricious person in search of fame cannot justify our decision to insist on the initial attitude. What is more, the competitive moral character of a peer who strives to be better than others can actually motivate his rival to conduct thorough research. It is obviously most desirable to resolve disagreements by assessing the content of beliefs and the presented arguments. However, we can easily imagine – and justify – an expert's choice to maintain his position despite being unable to find evidence against a peer's belief only because the peer's overwhelming ambition to succeed renders the reliability and objectivity of his research somewhat questionable. In an opposite example, an expert is justified in questioning his own ability to correctly interpret evidence because he might be influenced by his desire to quickly resolve the problem. In brief, it seems that our assessments of a peer's authority in relation to our own involve a certain kind of calibration.[40] Although we begin by assessing the subject of disagreement or the available evidence (direct calibration), we also acknowledge the surrounding situational and relational factors

39 Jeniffer Lackey. 2012. 'A Tentative Defense of the (Almost) Equal Weight View', in Christensen David and Jeniffer Lackey (eds.), *The Epistemology of Disagreement* (Oxford: Oxford University Press), pp. 98–118.

40 Kitcher, 1993.

(indirect calibration). It is important to note that calibrations can never produce overlapping evidence about both experts and their opposing attitudes: this makes disagreements unlikely to be left unresolved since peers are inclined to opt for a single expert with more epistemic authority.

Unlike the ideal-theoretical approach of standard analytic philosophy, the perspective of social epistemology is 'real-world' inasmuch as it takes into account the complex nature of real epistemic disagreements and the necessity of their resolution. Real-world epistemology perceives the subtleties of real situations commonly neglected by ideal theories that begin and end in abstract principles. Since no disagreement is identical to another due to a myriad of features that characterize a specific epistemic situation, it's surprising that proponents of the aforementioned solutions to disagreement downright eliminated the prospect that our understanding of the other's perspective could encourage us to reconsider our attitude or prioritize the authority and evidence of another expert – or *vice-versa*.[41] No View, regardless of how consistent it may be, can guarantee a good solution in circumstances that are sub-ideal or that involve experts whose evidence is affected by interests, accepted theories, social perspectives, political assumptions, and the like. For example, the dogmatic attitude that we have the right to insist on our starting position can be clever advice when disagreeing with experts who harshly impose their interests, beliefs and decisions or who ignore the prejudices and stereotypes underlying their positions. On the other hand, it is entirely unacceptable when dealing with reputable experts known for offering successful and innovative solutions that were initially criticized. Likewise, maintaining a reasonable disagreement can be a solution in the abstract domain of philosophical discussions, but not in urgent situations of climate intervention, judicial decision-making, economic rescues and bankruptcies. Since epistemic situations of disagreement vary in urgency, they require different criteria of situational assessments. When making decisions that affect most citizens – for example, deliberating whether to withdraw suspicious agricultural products from the market – criteria of epistemic assessments must be high and the smallest situational factor relevant to the disagreeing parties

41 In elaborating their account of rational consensus, Lehrer and Wagner put emphasis on repeatedly evaluating a peer's credibility with the goal of gradually approach and accepting their viewpoint. See Lehrer and Wagner, 1981.

must be taken into account.[42] On the other hand, issues of epistemic internalism and externalism can contend with a lower standard of assessment because philosophical discussions benefit from continuous disagreements. Decisions about policies that affect our everyday lives within a democratic society is often more reminiscent of 'agricultural' than philosophical discussions.

To conclude, every situation of disagreement is comprised of a special and complex set of features alongside the mere facts of conflicted judgments and their (somewhat) overlapping underlying evidence. Calculations about untangling disagreements must acknowledge many situational, contextual and local variables which render the invariant and robust application of ideal theories – inadequate. Despite their theoretical relevance, ideal and abstract theories cannot suffice in real circumstances that require efficient decision-making. We instead require real-world epistemology, an approach that enables us to assess the subtleties inherent to the actual epistemic circumstances of making beliefs/decisions/judgments. An approach conscious of the non-idealized or realistic character of disagreement doesn't limit itself to abstract propositions, but also acknowledges the subject who reflects upon the features of the situation in which he acts.[43] However, it should be emphasized that this approach – although it insists on efficiency and the real character of epistemic situations – doesn't discard rational discussions about evidence nor the aforementioned arguments, but strives to complement them.

42 For detailed discussions regarding the contextual assessment of epistemic criteria, see Stewart Cohen. 1986. 'Knowledge and Context', *Journal of Philosophy,* 83: 574-583; Stewart Cohen. 1988. 'How to be Fallibilist', *Philosophical Perspectives,* 2: 91-123; Stewart Cohen. 1998. 'Contextualist Solutions to Epistemological Problems', *Australasian Journal of Philosophy,* 76: 289-306; Stewart Cohen. 1999. 'Contextualism, Scepticism and the Structure of Reasons', *Philosophical Perspectives,* 13: 57-89; Williams, 2001a. and Michael Williams. 2001b, 'Contextualism, Externalism and Epistemic Standards', *Philosophical Studies,* 1: 1-23.

43 A similar approach to the dichotomy between ideal and real-world philosophical theories can be found in Jonathan Wolff, 2015a. 'Testing, Treating and Trusting', in Cohen, Glen I., N. Daniels and N. Eyal (eds.), *Identified Versus Statistical Lives* (New York: Oxford University Press), pp 213–218, and Wolff, 2015c.

6.5.2. *Disagreement and epistemic responsibility: belief and acceptance*

It is surprising that none of the aforementioned views even considers the possibility of trusting another expert in a situation of disagreement. Some meek level of respect towards the other expert can perhaps be found in the position which considers his opinion as valuable as our own, thus arguing for a state of reasonable disagreement or the decision to take a step back. However, all three views assume the position of the epistemic autonomy of experts which denies the 'rational requirement' to confide in epistemic authorities. Interestingly, this epistemological attitude almost implies that any consensus in a situation of peer disagreement is epistemically irrational and thus epistemically unacceptable.

In opposition to this stance, I don't think we should presuppose the reign of epistemic autonomy (nor of trust in epistemic authorities). It is far more rational to approach a particular disagreement by seriously and conscientiously wondering who is more deserving of confidence and, despite the initial credence in our own attitude, reflecting on which stance is more likely to survive future challenges, less susceptible to risks and more efficient in terms of cost and time. We need to carefully reflect upon the dissonance between *trusting ourselves* and *trusting others* by wondering what would be correct from the perspective of some future self-reflection. Would we be more satisfied with our current attitude or a different one?[44] It is important to note that any current reflection about the future always starts with confidence in our own abilities: we inevitably, necessarily and almost primordially start from ourselves; self-confidence is both rational and justified because we have better access to our own beliefs (no matter how imperfect) than to anyone else's. However, this does not mean that we must end every disagreement by insisting on our own position. We are equally likely to conclude, in the light of disagreement, that it is better to trust the epistemic authority whom we had disagreed with or to suspend our own attitude. A situation of disagreement is a situation of conscientiously and responsibly appraising our own attitude and that of the other. We need to realize that specific situations may require a solution that we hadn't expected – the mere fact of disagreement doesn't automatically imply a suspension nor a retention of our initial belief.

44 Zagzebski, 2012., p. 214.

The position I propose rests on three assumptions: (i) the assumption that disagreements are the complex result of substantive evidence and specific relational and situational features; (ii) the assumption that the dissonance inherent to disagreements cannot be considered a desirable solution – not because of the alleged impossibility of rational disagreement, but because we are naturally inclined to resolve disagreements and divulge a good solution[45]; (iii) the assumption of self-confidence which respects the ideal of epistemic autonomy without encouraging the epistemic egoism inherent to attitudes that defend the priority of one's own attitude or the rationality of disagreement.

Consequently, I reject the assumption that we are always (for one reason or another) justified in maintaining our own stance (or in the worst case suspending it) and never rational in accepting the other's. On the contrary, the distrust of others expressed in the disbelief that they may have equally good reasons behind their beliefs – or better reasons – implies a certain intellectual arrogance and irresponsibility, or even irrationality. It implies the unlikelihood of our mistake, the impossibility that we are the ones vulnerable to situational pressures – and it definitely rejects the notion that we might make more mistakes than others. In the end, I am aware that the absence of conciliation in the previous proposals probably stems from the assumption that each expert has already done everything in his power and that he virtually cannot side with the opposing attitude. However, this assumption is yet another artificial and idealized construction of disagreement – we are unlikely to – despite the initial conviction in our own stance – entirely dismiss the possiblity of mistakes, revision and event the greater credibility of the other expert. There are no definite beliefs and judgments that couldn't be changed in a situation of disagreement precisely due to the fact of disagreement. The thesis that experts can abstract from the social situatedness of their beliefs and the subjectivity of assessing their own supporting evidence is blatantly idealistic. Real situations and epistemic contexts always leave room for revisions. In other words, I argue that we can be equally rational in accepting the attitudes of others and maintaining our own, thus showing respect for the ideal of trusting the expertise of others. Knowing this, the proposed options ought to acknowledge the possibility of accepting the greater

45 Zagzebski claims that we naturally strive to resolve dissonances, which would immediately make it rational to try and settle disagreements. See Zagzebski, 2012.

credibility of another expert regarding the issue at hand and choosing to side with his stance. Or accepting some consensual solution. In the 'agricultural' scenario, this could even include the consensual decision to withdraw the product from the market until more detailed research has been conducted.

Of course, the proposed approach also allows us to maintain our initial position. It would be irrational to require that we always give up our own attitude, regardless of whether conscientious scrutiny had convinced us that it is indeed rational. Likewise, we might simply be unable to relinquish a standpoint we consider rational despite knowing that it would be epistemically responsible to suspend it or even accept the attitude of another expert. We cannot stop believing in our initial position although we, for example, believe that the person we have disagreed with outshines us in terms of credibility.[46] This stance obviously presumes that our beliefs are external to our control and a necessary consequence of (interpreting) the available evidence. We can not believe something only because we want to believe it, because we highly respect our peers or because the context requires us to give up our attitude. However, even if our beliefs truly didn't depend on our choices, the act of accepting another person's attitude is an epistemic decision within our control. Hence, the *context of believing* and the *context of doing* determine our futher conduct: if the situation requires immediate action, it is neither irrational nor impossible to accept a stance that we find hard to believe. Should the context of believing and doing not require a decision, it is possible to wait for further evidence that may prove decisive. It is therefore realistic to presume a conflict between the values of trusting yourself and trusting another expert which cannot always be immediately resolved. The distinction between belief and acceptance, where accepting another's stance is an epistemic decision fully under our reflexive control, enables us to resolve the most difficult of disagreements.

Once again, the only tenable recommendation is to act in accordance with the epistemic virtue of responsibility that excludes the radical intepretation of epistemic autonomy and implies a conscientious epistemic agent trying his best to form the best possible belief in the given circumstances. Should the context demand immediate agency,

---

46 Catherine Z. Elgin. 2010. 'Persistent Disagreement', in Feldman Richard and Ted A. Warfield (eds.), *Disagreement* (Oxford: Oxford University Press), pp. 53–68.

the option of acceptance enables us to resolve the disagreement. Disagreements between experts can be resolved by opting for only one of the stances. There is no paramount obstacle for experts to resolve their disagreements in situations which require urgent action.

In conclusion, regardless of the complex nature of resolving disagreements, disonnances between experts are not a reason to deprive them of their special role in the processes of forming beliefs/judgments/ decisions and solving problems within the system of deliberative democracy. They cannot be a sufficient reason because the complexity of resolving disagreements isn't exhausted in conflicts among experts – similar challenges arise in all instances of peer disagreement. The dilemma inherent to all cases of disagreement is the simple choice between trusting oneself or deferring to another person.

6.5.3. *Rational epistemic autonomy and the derived epistemic authority of experts*

Despite insisting on the feasibility and importance of resolving disagreements between experts by making a decision and opposing the proposals articulated within epistemology of disagreement, I once again find it important to note that my defense of trusting epistemic authorities does not imply a rejection of epistemic autonomy. As we have repeatedly emphasized, the role of epistemic authority and our relation to epistemic authorities is derived from our own authority. This means that my proposed relationship with epistemic authorities isn't susceptible to the sacrifice of intellectual autonomy inherent to numerous approaches that defend confidence in epistemic authorities. The thesis that epistemically justified trust must be derived implies that there can be no fundamental authorities. Unlike certain philosophers who argue that other people generally deserve to be ascribed fundamental authority in testimonial situations[47], I claim that not even experts deserve such a status. Each person, and every expert, is only rational in trusting another person or expert on the basis of a conscientious and epistemically responsible assessment of their beliefs, their characters and the situation in which the belief is defended.[48]

---

47 For instance, see Coady, 1992.; Foley,1994. See also Tyler Burge. 1993. 'Content Preservation', *Philosophical Review*, 102: 457–488.

48 Prijic-Samarzija, 2007.

These preconditions of trusting others can generally be applied when solving disagreements among experts. Although we evaluate experts much like anyone else, we must not ignore the fact of their expertise. Epistemic autonomy does not entail defiance to authorities, but rather a conscientious appraisal of authorities as persons whose initial credibility is comparatively higher than that of non-experts; this certainly implies the likelihood that a layman will be better off by accepting the attitude of an expert than relying on his own.[49] In brief, my stance on the dilemma between epistemic autonomy and trust in epistemic authorities is a certain compromise between epistemic egoism and a defense of the fundamental authority of experts. Ascribing experts fundamental authority doesn't only clash with the virtue of intellectual autonomy, but generates the additional problem of disagreement. If peers automatically ascribed each other fundamental authority, disagreements would culminate in an absurd situation where everyone would accept the position of the other. If they insisted on egoistic epistemic autonomy, they would never give up their own position. This stance on rational epistemic autonomy and the derived authority of experts provides us with the flexibility needed for a real-world approach. Likewise, it is also justified from an ethical/political perspective. Everyone is epistemic autonomous and no one

49 Issues of epistemic autonomy and derived authority become inevitably more complex when considering a realistic situation in which a disagreement is left unresolved and a non-expert must choose which of the two conflicted experts he should trust. The issue of non-experts having to recognize and trust experts was first desribed by Plato in his early dialogue *Charmides* (Plato, 170d-e). Although there is a distinct social environment in favour of relying on experts – both in theory and in practice – we are certainly justified in wondering whether non-experts can possess sufficient evidence to responsibly ascribe trust to experts on the basis of their own epistemic autonomy. Following a lengthy, detailed and highly sophisticated discussion, Goldman concluded that there was no reliable algorithm that could aid laymen in making the right choice between two conflicting expert standpoints. However, there is no reason to be skeptical towards the prospect of recognizing and trusting a single expert in a situation of disagreement. Everyone can always utilize numerous methods of evaluating and confirming the claims of conflicting experts. These methods mostly pertain to inquiries about the experts' prior successfullness, which implies the importance of providing additional information, education and different external inputs from meta-experts who can aid laymen in understanding both the content of disagreement and the credibility of experts. Alvin I. Goldman. 2001. 'Experts: Which Ones Should You Trust?', *Philosophy and Phenomenological Research*, 63: 85–109.

has fundamental authority: all citizens are equal in being trusted on the basis of conscientious assessments of their stances, their characters and the particularities of the given context.

***

We can conclude our final discussion on experts with three theses: (i) it cannot be argued that there are no experts in the domain of politics; (ii) disagreements between experts are not an obstacle to ascribing them trust; (iii) ascribing trust to experts and epistemic authorities does not jeopardize our epistemic or political autonomy any more than deciding to trust political authorities.

An epistemic authority or an expert is someone whom other people are inclined to trust, conscientiously believing that it is wiser to accept the opinion of that expert than to maintain their own. Decisions to trust experts stem the fact that experts simply possess a greater range of true information/beliefs about the issue at hand and are more skilled in successfully using those information/beliefs in making decisions and acquiring, questioning, and increasing the amount of information/beliefs about new issues in the given domain.[50] There is no valid argument against the presence of experts in the domain of politics.[51] Although it is true that experts who share the same domain often disagree, this doesn't allow us to automatically deduce that they cannot solve problems or reach a consensual agreement about the right decision. There is no overruling reason why experts couldn't autonomously resolve disagreements in a manner that is both epistemically and ethically/politically justified. However, we can not ensure epistemic and ethical/political justification by insisting that experts exist and are capable of making decisions which are comparatively better than those made by non-experts: for their role to be justified, it is necessary that laymen recognize them as epistemic authorities and ascribe them their trust in a justified manner. We have shown that non-experts can do so in a manner that doesn't jeopardize their (rationally understood) epistemic nor their political autonomy. Let us conclude that the continuous apprehension towards the status of experts, the possibility of resolving disagreements and the prospect of

50 Goldman, 2001.

51 We are obviously not trying to argue that politicians – as people whose political functions stem from their allegiance to certain parties – are the experts. It has been shown that politicans and citizens share the same relationship to experts and face the same problems when deciding whether to trust them as epistemic authorities.

recognizing experts or attributing them epistemically responsible trust is neither epistemologically nor politically justified.

At the very end, I would like to emphasize that the solutions I have offered reflect my previously discussed desire to preserve a hybrid perspective: our debate about the justification of deliberative democracy must be equally sensitive to epistemic and ethical/political virtues. Our procedures for ensuring the epistemic quality of decisions must include experts/professionals while fully preserving the democratic rationale. The dilemma between democracy and truth is an illusory problem. We can simultaneously ensure both by assuming the hybrid model of evaluating democracy (democratic institutions and belief/judgment/decision-making processes) provided by extended real-world social epistemology and by relinquishing the traditional approach that strictly divides justification between ethics and philosophy of politics on the one hand and epistemology on the other.

6.6. *Conclusion*

The last option in our discussion about the epistemic justification of democracy is reliability democracy, the stance that institutions, social practices and systems are justified if they involve reliable procedures, methods or mechanisms which produce epistemically valuable beliefs and decisions. Reliability democracy is the stance that deliberative democracy, in order to be epistemically justified, must generate beliefs, judgments and decisions that are true, truth-sensitive or truth-conductive.

Advocates of this approach argue that no inherent feature of democratic decision-making methods – regardless of whether we're speaking about majority vote or democratic deliberation – automatically guarantees the epistemic quality of beliefs and decisions. Should they aim to deserve their epistemic justifiedness, democratic procedures must include additional mechanisms for ensuring truthfulness. In other words, neither the mere fact of consensus nor the sheer inclusion of experts can guarantee epistemic quality. We need to develop reliable democratic mechanisms or truth-sensitive procedures. It has been shown that these reliable procedures presuppose the division of epistemic labour between citizens and experts: experts just as the establishment of a rational consensus are an indispensable component of epistemically justified reliable democratic procedures. We have proceeded to prove that the introduction of experts ensures higher epistemic quality without automatically entailing epistocracy, in spite of numerous previous suspicions. This ensures a hybrid perspective: we have managed to epistemically justify democracy while fully preserving its ethical/political justification.

Objections against the inclusion of experts generally attained their persuasiveness by defending the ideals of epistemic autonomy and epistemic egalitarianism. We have seen, however, that they often resorted to an unjustified defence of egoistic epistemic autonomy which clashes with the rational assumption of trusting epistemic authorities following epistemically responsible assessments. It should be emphasized that my proposal is equally apprehensive of the egoistic interpretation of epistemic autonomy and the concept of the fundamental authority of experts, which presupposes a blind trust and uncritical deferrence to experts. Experts can only be attributed (epistemically and ethically/politically justified) derived epistemic authority: we are only justified in trusting experts following an epistemically autonomous conclusion that they are more deserving of trust than we are. To make this possible, we were obliged to prove that disagreements among experts, despite the suspicion prevalent within the epistemology of disagreement, do not hinder their status of epistemic authorities who are the best guides to true or truth-conductive beliefs and decisions.

I conclude with the stance that the dilemma between democracy and truth is – a false dilemma. Truth and experts are not a threat to democracy. It is entirely possible to simultaneously secure both and thus resolve the conflict between epistemic and ethical/political virtues. This false impression that a conflict actually exists can be largely blamed on the traditional approach: while original discussions about the justification of democracy within philosophy of politics were blind to central epistemic values, epistemology neglected the fruitfulness of appraising social entities and practices from an epistemic perspective. Our solution assumes the hybrid approach to evaluating democracy (democratic institutions and belief/judgment/decision-making practices) provided by extended real-world social epistemology. This approach is unique in simultaneously evaluating social entities and practices from both perspectives. Values can be balanced and harmonized in a manner that does not entail the reduction or instrumentalization of one virtue in favour of the other or a merely hypothetical respect towards the other discipline. We must always remain aware of the situational and contextual nature of hybrid evaluations, as well as the inadequacy of ideal-theoretical approaches which neglect the non-unitary character of real-world situations and the usage of contextually sensitive epistemic standards.

BIBLIOGRAPHY

Adler, Jonathan. 2002. *Belief's Own Ethics* (Cambridge, MA: A Bradford Book, MIT Press)

Ahlstrom-Vij, Kristoffer. 2012. 'Why Deliberative Democracy is (Still) Untenable?',
Public Affairs Quarterly, 26(3): 199–220

—— 2013a. 'In Defense of Veritistic Value Monism', *Pacific Philosophical Quarterly*, 94(1): 19–40

—— 2013b. 'Why We Cannot Rely on Ourselves for Epistemic Improvement', *Philosophical Issues* (a supplement to *Noûs*), 23: 276–296

—— 2013c. *Epistemic Paternalism: A Defence* (Basingstoke, UK: Palgrave Macmillan)

Alcoff, Linda. M. 2010. 'Epistemic Identities', *Episteme*, 7(2): 128–137

Alston, William. 1988. 'The Deontological conception of epistemic justification', *Philosophical Perspectives*, 2:257–299

—— 2005. *Beyond 'Justification': Dimensions of Epistemic Evaluation* (Ithaca: Cornell Universiti Press)

Anderson, Elizabeth. 2006. 'The Epistemology of Democracy', *Episteme*, 3(1-2): 8–22

—— 2012. 'Epistemic Justice as a Virtue of Social Institutions', *Social Epistemology*, 26(2): 163–173

—— 2014. 'The Social Epistemology of Morality: Learning from the Forgotten History of the Abolition of Slavery', in Brady, Michael and Miranda Fricker (eds.), *The Epistemic Life of Groups: Essays in the Epistemology of Collectives* (Oxford: Oxford University Press), pp. 75–94

Annis, David. B. 1978. 'A Contextualist Theory of Epistemic Justification', *American Philosophical Quarterly*, 15(3): 213–219

Arendt, Hannah. 1958. *The Human Condition* (Chicago: University of Chicago Press)

—— 1973. *On Revolution* (Harmondsworth: Pelican Books)

Aristotle. *Nicomachean Ethics*, 2nd edn, trans. by Terence Irwin (Indianapolis: Hackett Publishing Co., 1999)

Arnim, Hans F. A. von (ed.). *Stoicorum Veterum Fragmenta*, 4 vols (Leipzig: Teubner, 1903-1924)

Arrow, Kenneth J. 1963. *Social Choice and Individual Values*, sec. ed. (New York: Wiley)

Arrow, Kenneth J., A. K. Sen, and K. Suzumura (eds.). 2002. *Handbook of*

Social Choice and Welfare, vol.1 (Amsterdam: North-Holland)
—— (eds.). 2011. *Handbook of Social Choice and Welfare*, vol. 2 (Amsterdam: North-Holland)
Audi, Robert. 2004. 'The A priori Authority of Testimony', *Philosophical Issues*, 14 (1): 18–34
Baccarini, Elvio and Viktor Ivanković. 2015. 'Mill's Case for Plural Voting and the Need for Balanced Public Decisions', *Prolegomena* 14(2): 137–156
Barnes, Barry, and David Bloor. 1982. 'Relativism, Rationalism, and the Sociology of Knowledge', in Hollis Martin and Steven Lukes (eds.), *Rationality and Relativism* (Cambridge, MA: MIT Press), pp. 21–44
Bessette, Joseph M. 1980. 'Deliberative Democracy: The Majority Principle in Republican Government', in Goldwin, R. A. and W. A. Schambra (eds.), *How Democratic Is the Constitution?* (Washington: American Eterprise Institute), pp. 102–116
Benhabib, Seyla. 1996. *Democracy and Difference* (Princeton: Princeton University Press)
Bohman, James. 1996. *Public Deliberation: Pluralism, Complexity, and Democracy* (Cambridge, MA: MIT Press)
—— 2006. 'Deliberative Democracy and the Epistemic Benefits of Diversity', *Episteme*, 3(3): 175–191
Bohman, James., and William Rehg. (eds.). 1997. *Deliberative Democracy: Essays on Reason and Politics* (Cambridge, MA: The MIT Press)
BonJour, Laurence. 1985. *The Structure of Empirical Knowledge* (Cambridge, MA: Harvard University Press)
Brady, Michael. S. and Duncan H. Pritchard (eds.). 2003. *Moral and Epistemic Virtues* (Oxford: Blackwell)
Brady, Michael and Miranda Fricker. (eds.). 2016. *The Epistemic Life of Groups: Essays in the Epistemology of Collectives* (Oxford: Oxford University Press)
Bratman, Michael. 1993. 'Shared Intention', *Ethics*, 104: 97–113
Burge, Tyler. 1993. 'Content Preservation', *Philosophical Review*, 102: 457–488
Burton, Robert A. 2013. *A Skeptic's Guide to the Mind: What Neuroscience Can and Cannot Tell Us About Ourselves* (New York: St. Martin's Press)
Carpini, Michael, X. Deli and S. Keeter, S. 1996. *What Americans Know about Politics and Why It Matters* (New Haven, CT: Yale University Press)
Christensen, David. 2007. 'Epistemology of Disagreement: The Good News', *Philosophical Review,* 116:187–217
—— 2012. 'Epistemic Modesty Defended', in Christensen, David and Jeniffer Lackey (eds.), *The Epistemology of Disagreement* (Oxford: Oxford University Press), pp. 1–23
Christensen, David and Jeniffer Lackey. (eds). 2012. *The Epistemology of Disagreement*, (Oxford: Oxford University Press)
Christiano, Thomas. 1996. *The Rule of the Many: Fundamental Issues in Democratic Theory* (Boulder, CO: Westview Press)

—— 2008. *The Constitution of Equality* (Oxford: Oxford University Press)
—— 2012. 'Rational Deliberation between Experts and Citizens', in Mansbridge
Jane and John Parkinson (eds.), *The Deliberative System* (Cambridge, MA: Cambridge University Press), pp- 27–51
Coady, Cecil A. J., 1992. *Testimony* (Oxford: Oxford University Press)
Code, Lorraine. 1987. *Epistemic Responsibility* (Hanover: University Press of New England and Brown)
—— 1995. *Rhetorical Spaces – essays on gendered locations* (London/NY: Routledge)
—— 2006. *Ecological Thinking: The Politics of Epistemic Location* (Oxford: Oxford University Press)
—— 2010. 'Testimony, Advocacy, Ignorance: Thinking Ecologically about Social Knowledge', in Haddock, Adrian, A. Millar and D. Pritchard (eds.), *Social Epistemology* (Oxford: Oxford University Press), pp. 29–50
Cohen, Joshua. 1986. 'An Epistemic Conception of Democracy', *Ethics,* 97: 26–38
Cohen, Stewart. 1986. 'Knowledge and Context', *Journal of Philosophy,* 83: 574–583
—— 1988. 'How to be Fallibilist', *Philosophical Perspectives,* 2: 91–123
—— 1998. 'Contextualist Solutions to Epistemological Problems', *Australasian Journal of Philosophy,* 76: 289–306
—— 1999. 'Contextualism, Scepticism and the Structure of Reasons', *Philosophical Perspectives,* 13: 57–89
—— 2012. 'A Tentative Defense of the (Almost) Equal Weight View', in
Christensen, David and Jeniffer Lackey (eds.), *The Epistemology of Disagreement* (Oxford: Oxford University Press), pp. 98–118
Conee, Earl. 2010. 'Rational Disagreement Defended', in Feldman, Richard and Ted A. Warfield (eds.), *Disagreement* (Oxford: Oxford University Press), pp. 69–90
Craig, Edward. 1990. *Knowledge and the State of Nature* (Oxford: Oxford University Press)
David, Marian. 2001. 'Truth as the Epistemic Goal', in Steup, Matthias (ed.), *Knowledge, Truth, and Duty* (Oxford: Oxford University Press), pp. 151-169
Dancy, Jonathan. 2004. *Ethics without Prnciples* (Oxford: Claredon Press)
Derrida, Jacques. 1976. *On Grammatology* (Baltimore, MD: John Hopkins University)
Descartes, Rene. *The Philosophical Writings of Descartes*, vol.1, ed. and trans. by Cottingham John, R. Stoothoff and D. Murdoch (New York: Cambridge University Press, 1967/1985)
Downs, Anthony. 1957. *An Economic Theory of Democracy* (New York: Harper)
Dewey, John. 1976. 'Creative Democracy: The Task Before Us', in Boydston, Jo A. (ed.), *John Dewey, The Later Works, 1925 – 1953.* (Carbondale and
Edwardsville: Southern Illinois University Press), pp. 224–230
Elga, Adam. 2007. 'Reflection and Disagreement', *Noûs,* 41: 478–502

——2010. 'How to Disagree about how to Disagree' in Feldman, Richard and Ted A. Warfield (eds.), *Disagreement* (Oxford: Oxford University Press), pp. 175–186

Elgin, Catherine Z. 2010. 'Persistent Disagreement', in Feldman, Richard and Ted A. Warfield (eds.), *Disagreement* (Oxford: Oxford University Press), pp. 53–68

Elster, Jon. 1983. *Sour Grapes* (Cambridge: Cambridge University Press)

——2002. 'The Market and the Forum: Three Varieties of Political Theory', in Christiano Thomas (ed.), *Philosophy and Democracy* (Oxford: Oxford University Press)

Estlund, David. 1997. 'Beyond Fairness and Deliberation: The Epistemic Dimension of Democratic Authority', in Bohman, James and William Rehg (eds.), *Deliberative Democracy: Essays on Reason and Politics* (Cambridge, MA: The MIT Press), pp. 173–204

—— 2003. 'Why Not Epistocracy?', in Reshotko, Naomi (ed.), *Desire, Identity and Existence: Essays in honor of T. M. Penne* (Kelowna, BC: Academic. Printing and Publishing) pp. 53–69

—— 2008a. 'Epistemic Proceduralism and Democratic Authority', in Geenens, Raf and Ronald Tinnevelt (eds.), *Does Truth Matter? Democracy and Public Space* (Springer: Dordrecht), pp. 15–27

—— 2008b. *Democratic Authority* (Princeton: Princeton Univeristy Press) Fantl, Jeremy and Matt McGrath. 2002. 'Evidence, Pragmatics and Justification', *The Philosophical Review*, 111: 67–94

Feinberg, Joel. 1989. 'Autonomy', in Christman John (ed.), *The Inner Citadel* (New York: Oxford University Press), pp. 27–53

Feldman, Richard. 2006. 'Epistemological puzzles about disagreement', in Hetherington Stephen (ed.), *Epistemology Futures* (Oxford: Oxford University Press), pp. 216–236

——2007. 'Reasonable Religious Disagreements', in Antony, Louise (ed.), *Philosophers Without Gods: Meditations on Atheism and the Secular* (Oxford: Oxford University Press), pp. 194–214

Feldman, Richard and Ted A. Warfield (eds.). 2010. *Disagreement* (Oxford: Oxford University Press)

Fishkin, James. 1992. *The Dialogue of Justice: Toward a Self-Reflective Society* (New Haven: Yale University Press)

Foley, Richard. 1994. 'Egoism in Epistemology', in Schmitt, Frederick F. (ed.), *Socializing Epistemology: The Social Dimensions of Knowledge* (Lanham, Md: Rowman and Littlefield), pp. 53–73

Foucault, Michel. 1975/1977. *Discipline and Punish*, trans. by Alan Sheridan (New York: Pantheon)

——1961/2006. *History of Madness*, ed. by J. Khalfa and J. Murphy, trans. by Jean Khalfa (New York: Routledge)

——1980. *Power/Knowlwdge: Selected Interviews and Other Writings 1972-1977*, ed. by Colin Gordon (New York: Pantheon)

——1991. *Discourse and Truth: The Problematizations of Parrhesia*, ed. by Joseph Pearson (Evanston: Northwestern University Press)

Fricker, Elizabeth. 1987. 'The Epistemology of Testimony', *Aristotelian Society Supplementary* 61: 57–83
—— 1994. 'Against Gullibility', in Matilal Bimal K. and Arindam Chakrabarti (eds.),
Knowing from Words (Dordrecht: Kluwer Academic Publishers), pp. 125–161
—— 2006. 'Testimony and Epistemic Autonomy', in Lackey, Jennifer and Ernest Sosa (eds.), *The Epistemology of Testimony* (Oxford: Oxford University Press), pp. 225–250
Fricker, Miranda. 1998. 'Rational authority and social power: Towards a truly social epistemology', *Proceedings of the Aristotelian Society,* 98(2): 159–177
—— 2006. 'Powerlessness and Social Interpretation', *Episteme,* 3(1-2): 96-108
—— 2007. *Epistemic Injustice* (Oxford: Oxford University Press)
—— 2010. 'Can There Be Institutional Virtues?', in Gendler, Tamar S. and John Hawthorne (eds.), *Oxford Studies in Epistemology,* 3: 235-252
—— 2012. 'Group Testimony: The Making of a Good Informant', *Philosophy and Phenomenological Research*, 84: 249–276
—— 2013. 'Epistemic justice as a condition of political freedom', *Synthese,* 190(7): 1317-1332
Fuller, Steve. 1988. *Social Epistemology* (Bloomington, IN: Indiana University Press)
Gaus, Gerald. 1996. *Justificatory Liberalism: An Essay on Epistemology and Political Theory* (Oxford: Oxford Universty Press)
—— 1997. 'Reason, Justification and Consensus: Why Democracy Can't Have It All', in Bohman, James and William Rehg (eds.), *Deliberative Democracy: Essays on Reason and Politics* (Cambridge, MA: The MIT Press), pp. 205–242
—— 2012. *The Order of Public Reason: A Theory of Freedom and Morality in a Diverse and Bounded World* (Cambridge, MA: Cambridge University Press)
Gigone, Daniel and Reid Hastie. 1993. 'The common knowledge effect: Information sharing and group judgment', *Journal of Personality and Social Psychology,* 65: 959–974
Gilbert, Margaret. 1989. *On Social Facts* (New York. Routledge)
—— 2004. 'Collective epistemology', *Episteme,* 1(2): 95-107
Gilbert, Margaret and Daniel Pilchman. 2014. 'Belief, Acceptance and What Happens in Groups: Some Methodological Considerations', in Lackey, Jennifer (ed.), *Essays in Collective Epistemology* (Oxford: Oxford University Press), pp. 189–212
Goldman, Alvin I. 1979. 'What Is Justified Belief?', in Pappas, George (ed.), *Knowledge and Justification* (Dordrecht: Reidel), pp. 1–25
—— 1986. *Epistemology and Cognition* (Cambridge, MA: Harvard University Press)
—— 1987. 'Foundations of Social Epistemics', *Synthese*, 73(1): 109–144
—— 1991a. 'Epistemic Paternalism: Communication Control in Law and Society', *Journal of Philosophy,* 88: 113–131
—— 1994. 'Argumentation and Social Epistemology', *Journal of Philosophy*, 91: 27–49

—— 1992. *Liaisons: Philosophy Meets the Cognitive and Social Sciences*, (Cambridge, MA: Cambridge University Press)
—— 1999. *Knowledge in a Social World* (Oxford: Oxford University Press)
—— 2001. 'Experts: Which Ones Should You Trust?', *Philosophy and Phenomenological Research*, 63: 85–109
—— 2004. 'The Need for Social Epistemology', in Leiter, Brian (ed.), *The Future for Philosophy* (Oxford: Oxford University Press), pp. 187–207
—— 2010a. 'Why Social Epistemology is Real Epistemology?', in Haddock, Adrian, A. Millar and D. Pritchard (eds.), *Social Epistemology* (Oxford: Oxford University Press), pp. 1–29
—— 2010b. 'Epistemic Relativism and Reasonable Disagreement', in Feldman, Richard and Ted A. Warfield (eds.), *Disagreement* (Oxford: Oxford University Press), pp. 187–215
—— 2014. 'Social Process Reliabilism: Solving Justification Problems in Collective Epistemology', in Lackey, Jennifer (ed.), *Essays in Collective Epistemology* (Oxford: Oxford University Press), pp. 11–41
Goldman, Alvin I. and Thomas Blanchard. 2015. 'Social Epistemology', in *Stanford Encyclopedia of Philosophy* <https://plato.stanford.edu/entries/epistemology-social/> [accesed 19 June 2017]
Goldman, Alvin I. and James C. Cox. 1996. 'Speech, Truth, and the Free Market for Ideas', *Legal Theory,* 2: 1–32
Goldman, Alvin I. and Moshe Shaked. 1991. 'An Economic Model of Scientific Activity and Truth Acquisition', *Philosophical Studies*, 63: 31–55
Goldman, Alvin I. and Dennis Whitcomb (eds.). 2011. *Social Epistemology: Essential Readings* (New York: Oxford University Press)
Goodin, Robert E. 2003. *Reflective Democracy* (Oxford: Oxford University Press)
—— 2006. 'The Benefits of Multiple Biased Observers', *Episteme*, 3(3): 166–174
Greco, John. 1999. 'Agent Reliabilism', in Tomberlin, James (ed.), *Philosophical*
Perspectives (Atascadero, Calif.: Ridgeview Publishing Co.), pp. 273–296
—— 2000. 'Two Kinds of Intellectual Virtue', *Philosophy and Phenomenological Research,* 60: 179–184
—— 2002. 'Virtues in Epistemology', in Moser Paul (ed.), *Oxford Handbook of Epistemology* (New York: Oxford University Press), pp. 287–315 Greco, John, J. Turri and M. Alfano. 2011. 'Virtue Epistemology', <http://plato.stanford.edu/entries/epistemology-virtue/> [accesed 19 June 2017]
Habermas, Jürgen. 1971/2001. *On the Pragmatics of Social Interaction*, trans. by Fultner, Barabara, (Cambridge, MA: The MIT Press)
—— 1987. *Theory of Communicative Action* (Boston: Beacon)
—— 1990. *Moral Consciousness and Communicative Action*, trans. by C. Lenhardt, and S. W. Nicholson (Cambridge, MA: The MIT Press)
—— 1996. *Between Facts and Norms: Contributions to a Discourse Theory of Law and Democracy*, trans. by Rehg William (Cambridge, MA: The MIT Press)
—— 1998. *Inclusion of the Other: Studies in Political Theory*, ed. by Cronin,

C., and P. De Greiff (Cambridge, MA: The MIT Press)
—— 2003. *Truth and Justification*, trans. by Barbara Fultner (Cambridge, MA: The MIT Press)
—— 2008. *Between Naturalism and Religion*, trans. by Ciaran Cronin (Cambridge: Polity)
Haddock, Adrian, A. Millar and D. Pritchard (eds.). 2009 *Epistemic Value* (Oxford: Oxford University Press)
—— (eds.). 2010. *Social Epistemology* (Oxford: Oxford University Press)
Hankinson–Nelson, Lynn. 1990. *Who Knows: From Quine to Feminist Empiricism* (Philadelphia: Temple University Press)
Hardin, Richard. 2002. 'Street-Level Epistemology and Political Participation', *Journal of Political Philosophy*, 10: 212–229.
Hardwig, John. 1991. 'The Role of Trust in Knowledge', *Journal of Philosophy,* 88: 693–708
Harrington, James. *The Commonwealth of Oceana and A System of Politics* (Cambridge: Cambridge University Press, 1656/1992)
Hawthorne, John and Amia Srinivasan. 2012. 'Disagreement Without Transparency: Some Bleak Thoughts', in Christensen, David and Jennifer Lackey (eds.), *The Epistemology of Disagreement* (Oxford: Oxford University Press), pp. 9–30
Hobbes, Thomas. *Leviathan* (Harmondsworth, UK: Penguin Books, 1651/1968)
Horkheimer, Max, and Theodor W. Adorno. 1978. *Dialectic of Enlightenment*, (New York, Seabury)
Hong, Lu and Scott Page. 2004. 'Groups of Diverse Problem Solvers Can Outperform Groups of High-Ability Problem Solvers', *Proceedings of the National Academy of Sciences of the United States*, 101(46): 16385–16389
Hume, David. *An Enquiry Concerning the Human Understanding and Concerning the Principles of Morals*, ed. by Selby–Bigge, Lewis A., sec. edn. (Oxford: Clarendon Press, 1748/1902)
—— *A Treatise of Human Nature*, ed. by Selby-Bigge, Lewis A. and P.H. Nidditch (Oxford: Oxford University Press, 1739/1978)
Inwagen, Peter van. 2010. 'We're right: they're wrong', in Feldman, Richard and Ted A. Warfield (eds.), *Disagreement* (Oxford: Oxford University Press), pp. 10-28
Kant, Immanuel. *Groundwork of the Methaphysics of Morals*, ed. and trans. by Gregor Mary (New York: Cambridge University Press, 1785/1997)
Kelly, Thomas. 2005. 'The Epistemic Significance of Disagreement', in Gendler, Tamar and John Hawthorne (eds.), *Oxford Studies in Epistemology*, vol. 1 (Oxford: Oxford University Press), pp. 167–196
—— 2010. 'Peer Disagreement and Higher-Order Evidence', in Feldman, Richard and Ted A. Warfield (eds.), *Disagreement* (Oxford: Oxford University Press), pp. 183–217
Kitcher, Philip. 1990. 'The Division of Cognitive Labor', *Journal of Philosophy*, 87: 5–22
—— 2001. *Science, truth, and democracy* (Oxford and New York: Oxford

University Press)
—— 2011a. *Science in a Democratic Society* (Amherst, NY: Prometheus Books)
—— 2011b. *The Ethical Project* (Cambridge, MA: Harvard University Press)
Kornhauser, A. Lewis and Lawrence G. Sager. 1986. "Unpacking the Court", *Yale Law Journal*, 96: 82–117
—— 2004. 'The Many as One: Integrity and Group Choice in Paradoxical Cases', *Philosophy and Public Affairs*, 32: 249–276
Kruger, Justin and David Dunning. 1999. 'Unskilled and Unaware of It: How Difficulties in Recognizing One's Own Incompetence Lead to Inflates Self-Assessments', *Journal of Personality and Social Psychology*, 77(6): 1121–1134
Kuhn, Thomas. 1962. *The Structure of Scientific Revolutions* (Chicago: University of Chicago Press)
Kvanvig, L. Jonathan. 1992. *The Intellectual Virtues and the Life of the Mind: On the Place of the Virtues in Contemporary Epistemology* (Savage, Maryland: Rowman and Littlefield)
—— 2003. *The Value of Knowledge and the Pursuit of Understanding* (Cambridge, MA: Cambridge University Press)
—— 2005. 'Truth and the Epistemic Goal', in Steup, Matthias and Ernest Sosa (eds.), *Contemporary Debates in Epistemology* (Malden, MA: Blackwell Publishing), pp. 285–295
—— 2010. 'Virtue Epistemology', in Pritchard Duncan and Sven Bernecker (eds.), *Routledge Companion to Epistemology* (New York: Routledge), pp. 199–207
Lackey, Jennifer and Ernest Sosa. (eds.). 2006. *The Epistemology of Testimony* (Oxford: Oxford University Press)
—— 2008. *Learning from Words: Testimony as a Source of Knowledge* (Oxford: Oxford University Press)
—— 2012. 'Disagreement and Belief Dependence: Why Numbers Matter', in Christensen, David and Jennifer Lackey (eds.), *The Epistemology of Disagreement* (Oxford: Oxford University Press), pp. 243–268
—— (ed.). 2014. *Essays in Collective Epistemology* (Oxford University Press)
Lahroodi, Reza. 2007. 'Collective epistemic virtues', *Social Epistemology*, 21: 281–297
Latour, Bruno and Steve Woolgar. 1986. *Laboratory Life: The Construction of Scientific Facts* (Princeton: Princeton University Press)
Latour, Bruno. 1987. *Science in Action* (Cambridge, MA: Harvard University Press)
Laudan, Larry. 2006. *Truth, Error, and Criminal Law: An Essay in Legal Epistemology* (New York: Cambridge University Press)
Lehrer, Kieth and Carl Wagner. 1981. *Rational Consensus in Science and Society* (Dordrecht, Reidel)
Lehrer, K. 1990. *Theory of Knowledge* (Boulder, Westview)
—— 2006. 'Trust and Trustworthiness', in Lackey, Jennifer and Ernest Sosa (eds.), *The Epistemology of Testimony* (Oxford, Oxford University Press),

pp. 393–411

List, Christian and Robert E. Goodin. 2001. 'Epistemc Democracy: Generalizing the Condorcet Jury Theorem', *The Journal of Political Philosohy*, 9(3): 277–306

List, Christian and Philip Pettit. 2002. 'Aggregating Sets of Judgments: An Impossibility Result', *Synthese*, 140: 207–235

—— 2011. *Group Agency: The Possibility, Design, and Status of Corporate Agents* (Oxford: Oxford University Press)

Locke, John. *An Essay Concerning Human Understanding*, ed. by Nidditch, Peter H. (Oxford: Oxford University Press, 1690/1975)

—— *Second Treatise on Civil Government* (Indianapolis, IN: Hackett, 1690/1980)

Longino, Helen. 2002. *The Fate of knowledge* (Princeton: Princeton University Press)

Lyotard, Jean-François. 1984. *The Post-Modern Condition* (Minneapolis: University of Minnesota Press)

Manin, Bernard. 1987. 'On Legitimacy and Deliberation', *Political Theory,* 15: 338–368

McCarthy, Thomas. 1998. 'Legitimacy and diversity: Dialectical reflections on analytical distinctions', in Rosenfeld, Michael and Andrew Arato (eds.), *Habermas on Law and Democracy* (Berkeley: University of California Press), pp. 115–153

Michelman, Frank. 1989. 'Conceptions of Democracy in American Constitutional Argument: The Case of Pornography Regulation', *Tennessee Law Review,* 56(2): 291–319

Mill, John Stuart. *On Liberty,* (New York: Oxford University Press, 1859/1960)

—— *Considerations on Representative Government* (Buffalo, NY: Prometheus Books, 1861/1991)

Miščević, Nenad. 2011. 'After Foucault – Social Epistemology facing new and old knowledges', <http://www.transeuropeennes.eu/en/articles/282> [accesed 19 June 2017]

Montmarquet, James. 1992. 'Epistemic Virtue', in Dancy, Jonathan and Ernest Sosa (eds.), *A Companion of Epistemology* (Oxford: Blackwell), pp. 158-177

—— 1993. *Epistemic Virtue and Doxastic Responsibility* (Savage, Maryland: Rowman and Littlefield)

Moran, Richard. 2006. 'Getting Told and Being Believed', in Lackey, Jennifer and Ernest Sosa (eds.), *The Epistemology of Testimony* (Oxford: Oxford University Press), pp. 272–306

Pappas, George. 2000. 'Epistemic Deference', *Acta Analytica*, 15(24): 113–26

Parry, Richard. 2014. "Episteme and Techne", in *Stanford Encyclopedia of Philosophy* <https://plato.stanford.edu/entries/episteme-techne/> [accesed 19 June 2017]

Peter, Fabienne. 2008. *Democratic Legitimacy* (New York: Routledge)

—— 2013a. 'The Procedural Epistemic Value of Deliberation', *Synthese*, 190(7): 1253–1266

—— 2013b. 'Epistemic Foundations of Political Liberalism', *Journal of Moral Philosophy,* 10(5): 598–620
—— 2016. 'The Epistemic Circumstances of Democracy', in Fricker, Miranda and Michael Brady (eds.), *The Epistemic Life of Groups* (Oxford: Oxford University Press), pp. 133–149
Pettit, Philip. 1982. 'Habermas on Truth and Justice', in Parkinson, G. H. R. (ed.), *Marx and Marxism,* Royal Institute of Philosophical Supplements (Cambridge: Cambridge University Press), pp. 207–228
—— 2003. 'Groups with Minds of Their Own', in Schmitt, Frederick (ed.) *Socializing Metaphysics* (Lanham, MD: Rowman and Littlefield), pp. 167–193
—— 2014. 'How to Tell if a Group Is an Agent', in Lackey, Jennifer (ed.), *Essays in Collective Epistemology* (Oxford: Oxford University Press), pp. 97–121
Pettit, Philip and David Schweikard. 2006. 'Joint Actions and Group Agents', *Philosophy of the Social Sciences*, 36(1): 18-39
Plato. *The Republic* (Harmondsworth, UK: Penguin Books, 1974)
—— *Complete Works*, ed. by John M. Cooper (Indianapolis: Hackett Publishing Co., 1997)
Plutarch. *Moralia*, trans. by W.C. Helmbold, Loeb Classical Library, vol. 6 and vol. 8, part 2 (Cambridge: Harvard University Press, 1993)
Popper, Karl. 1962. *Conjectures and Refutations: The Growth of Scientific Knowlwdge* (New York, Basic Books)
Prichard, Duncan. 2004. 'The Epistemology of Testimony', *Philosophical Issues*, 14: 326–348
Prijić–Samaržija, Snježana. 2005. *Društvo i spoznaja* (Zagreb: Kruzak)
—— 2007. 'Trust and Contextualism', *Acta Analytica*, 22(2): 125–38
—— 2011. 'Trusting Experts: Trust, Testimony and Evidence', *Acta Histriae,* 19 (1–2): 249-262
—— 2014a. 'Epistemičko opravdanje demokracije: epistemička vrijednost proceduralne pravičnosti', *Prolegomena*, 13(2): 373-392
—— 2014b. "Hybrid Virtues", *Etica e Politica / Ethics and Politics*, 16/2: 1167–1180
—— 2016a. 'The Division of Epistemic Labour in Democracy', *Anali Hrvatskog politološkog društva: Thomas Christiano's political theory: an exchange*, 12: 67–81
—— 2016b. 'Socijalna i epistemička (ne)pravda', in Prijić-Samaržija, Snježana, L. Malatesti and E. Baccarini (eds.), *Moralni, politički i epistemološki odgovori na društvene devijacije* (Rijeka, HR: Faculty of Humanities and Social Sciences, University of Rijeka), pp. 37–50
—— 2017. 'The Role of Experts in a Democratic Decision-making Process', *Etica & Politica / Ethics & Politics,* 19/2: 229–246
Prijic–Samarzija, Snježana and Petar Bojanić. 2014. 'Social Epistemology Between Revisionism and Expansionism', *European Journal for Analytic Philosophy*, 10(2): 31– 48
Prijić–Samaržija, Snježana and Nebojša Zelič. 2009. 'Overlapping consensus: normative understanding and doxastic voluntarism', *Croatian Journal of*

Philosophy, 9(25): 101–115
Reid, Thomas. *Essay on the Intellectual Powers of Man*, in Beanblossom, Ronald and Keith Lehrer (eds). *Thomas Reid's Inquiry and Essays* (Indianapolis, Hacket, 1983)
Rawls, John. 1971, *Theory of Justice* (Cambridge, MA: Harvard University Press)
—— 1993. *Political Liberalism* (New York: Columbia University Press)
—— 1997. 'The Idea of Public Reason, Postscript', in Bohman, James and William
Rehg (eds.), *Deliberative Democracy: Essays on Reason and Politics*, (Cambridge, MA: The MIT Press), pp. 93–144
Riggs, Wayne. 2002. 'Reliability and the Value of Knowledge', *Philosophy and Phenomenological Research*, 64: 79–96
—— 2003. 'Understanding 'Virtue' and the Virtue of Understanding', in DePaul, Michael and Linda Zagzebski (eds.), *Intellectual Virtue: Perspectives from Ethics and Epistemology* (Oxford: Oxford University Press), pp. 203–226
—— 2006. 'The Value Turn in Epistemology', in Hendricks, Vincent and Duncan Pritchard (eds.), *New Waves in Epistemology* (Aldershot: Ashgate), pp. 300–323
Roberts, Robert and Jay Wood. 2007. *Intellectual Virtues: An Essay in Regulative Epistemology* (Oxford: Oxford University Press)
Rorty, Richard. 1979. *Philosophy and the Mirror of Nature* (Princeton: Princeton University Press)
Rosenfeld Michael and Andrew Arato. (eds.), 1998. *Habermas on Law and Democracy* (Berkeley: University of California Press)
Rousseau, Jean-Jacques. *The Social Contract* (New York: Pocket Books, 1762/1967)
—— *Emile,* trans. by Allan Bloom (New York: Basic Books, 1763/1979)
Schmitt, Frederick. 1994. *Socializing Epistemology* (Lanham, MD: Rowman & Littlefield)
Schumpeter, A. Joseph. *Capitalism, Socialism and Democracy,* New York: Harper, 1942/1976)
Searle, R. John. 1995. *The Construction of Social Reality* (New York: Free Press)
——2010. *Making the Social World* (Oxford: Oxford University Press)
Sesardić, Neven. 2005. *Making Sense of Heritability* (Cambridge, MA: Cambridge University Press)
—— 2012. *Iz desne perspective* (Zagreb, HR: Večernji list)
Shapin, Steven. 1975. 'Phrenological Knowledge and the Social Structure of Early Nineteenth-Century Edinburgh', *Annals of Science*, 32: 219–243
Shapin, Steven and Simon Schaffer. 1985. *Leviathan and the Air-Pump,* Princeton (New Jersey: Princeton Univrsity Press)
—— 1994. *A Social History of Truth* (Chicago: University of Chicago Press)
Solomon, Miriam. 2006. 'Norms of epistemic diversity', *Episteme*, 3(1-2): 23–36
Sosa, Ernest. 1980. 'The Raft and the Pyramid: Coherence versus Foundations

in the Theory of Knowledge', *Midwest Studies in Philosophy*, 5: 3–25
—— 1991. *Knowledge in Perspective: Selected Essays in Epistemology* (London: Cambridge University Press)
—— 2007. *A Virtue Epistemology* (Oxford: Oxford University Press)
—— 2010. 'The Epistemology of Disagreement', in Haddock, Adrian, A. Millar and D. Pritchard (eds.), *Social Epistemology* (Oxford: Oxford University Press), pp. 278–297
—— 2015., *Judgment and Agency* (Oxford: Oxford University Press)
Stanly, Jason. 2005. *Knowledge and Practical Interests* (Oxford and New York: Clarendon Press)
Strevens, Michael. 2003. 'The Role of the Priority Rule in Science', *Journal of Philosophy*, 100(2): 55–79
Sunstein, Cass. 1993. *The Idea of Democracy* (Cambridge: Cambridge University Press)
—— 2006. 'Two Conceptions of Procedural Fairness: Social Research', *An International Quarterly,* 73(2): 619–646
Tollefsen, Deborah P. 2002. 'Challenging epistemic individualism', *Protosociology*, 16: 86–117
—— 2015. 'Rewiew: Essays in Collective Epistemology by Jennifer Lackey (ed.)',<http://ndpr.nd.edu/news/essays-in-collective-epistemology> [accesed 19 June 2017]
Tuomela, Raimo. 2004. 'Group knowledge analyzed', *Episteme,* 1(2): 109–127
Warnke, Georgia. 1999. '*Legitimate Differences*' (Berkeley: University of California Press)
Weber, Max. 1964. *The Theory of Social and Economic Organization* (Basingstoke: Macmillan)
Wedgwood, Ralph. 2010. 'The Moral Evil Demons', in Feldman, Richard and Ted A.
Warfield (eds.), *Disagreement* (Oxford: Oxford University Press), pp. 216–246
Weisberg, Michael and Ryan Muldoon. 2009. 'Epistemic Landscapes and the Division of Cognitive Labor', *Philosophy of Science*, 76(2): 225–252
Williams, Michael. 2001a. *Problems of Knowledge* (Oxford: Oxford University Press)
—— 2001b. 'Contextualism, Externalism and Epistemic Standards', *Philosophical Studies,* 1: 1-23
Wittgenstein, Ludwig. 1969. *On Certainty*, ed. by Anscombe, G. E. M. and G. H. von Wright (Oxford: Basil Blackwell)
Wright, Crispin. 2007. 'The Perils of Dogmatism', in Nuccetelli, Susana and Gary Seay, (eds.), *Themes from G.E. Moore* (Oxford: Oxford University Press), pp. 25–48
—— 2009. 'Fear of Relativism', *Philosophucal Studies*, 141: 379–390
Wright, Sarah. 2014. 'The Stoic Epistemic Virtues of Groups', in Lackey, Jennifer (ed.), *Essays in Collective Epistemology* (Oxford University Press), pp. 122–141
Wolff, Jonathan. 2014. 'Social Equality and Social Inequality', in Fourie, Carina, F. Schuppert and I. Wallimann-Helmer (eds.), *Social Equality:*

Essays on What It Means to be Equals (New York: Oxford University Press)
—— 2015a. 'Testing, Treating and Trusting', in Cohen, Glen I., N. Daniels and N. Eyal (eds.), *Identified Versus Statistical Lives* (New York: Oxford University Press), pp 213–218
—— 2015b. 'Equality as A Basic Demand of Justice', in Cohen, Joshua, G. Rosen, A. Byrne and S. Shiffrin, (eds.), *The Norton Introduction to Philosophy*, (New York: Norton), pp. 1047–1055
—— 2015c. 'Political Philosophy and the Real World of the Welfare State', *Journal of Applied Philosophy* 32(4): 360–272
Zagzebski, Linda. 1996. *Virtues of the Mind: An Inquiry into the Nature of Virtue and the Ethical Foundations of Knowledge* (Cambridge, MA: Cambridge University Press)
—— 1998. 'Virtue Epistemology', in Craig, Edward (ed.), *Encyclopedia of Philosophy*, (London: Routledge), pp. 617–621
—— 2003. 'The Search for the Source of Epistemic Good', *Metaphilosophy*, 34: 12–28
—— 2012. *Epistemic Authority: A Theory of Trust, Authority, and Autonomy of Belief* (Oxford: Oxford University Press)
Zollman, Kevin. 2007. 'The Communication Structure of Epistemic Communities', *Philosophy of Science*, 74(5): 574–587
—— 2010. 'The Epistemic Benefit of Transient Diversity, *Erkenntnis*, 72(1): 17–35

INDEX

R

S

MIMESIS GROUP
www.mimesis-group.com

MIMESIS INTERNATIONAL
www.mimesisinternational.com
info@mimesisinternational.com

MIMESIS EDIZIONI
www.mimesisedizioni.it
mimesis@mimesisedizioni.it

ÉDITIONS MIMÉSIS
www.editionsmimesis.fr
info@editionsmimesis.fr

MIMESIS COMMUNICATION
www.mim-c.net

MIMESIS EU
www.mim-eu.com

Printed by Agrisys Holding SA – July 2018